AF600715

"I AM"

Monotheism and the Philosophy of the Bible

MARK GLOUBERMAN

"I AM"

Monotheism and the Philosophy of the Bible

UNIVERSITY OF TORONTO PRESS
Toronto Buffalo London

© University of Toronto Press 2019
Toronto Buffalo London
utorontopress.com

ISBN 978-1-4875-0340-6

Library and Archives Canada Cataloguing in Publication

Glouberman, M., author
"I AM" : monotheism and the philosophy of the Bible/Mark Glouberman.

Includes bibliographical references and index.
ISBN 978-1-4875-0340-6 (cloth)

1. Monotheism – Biblical teaching. 2. Bible – Philosophy. I. Title.

BS544.G66 2019 231 C2018-902825-4

This book has been published with the help of a grant from the Federation for the Humanities and Social Sciences, through the Awards to Scholarly Publications Program, using funds provided by the Social Sciences and Humanities Research Council of Canada.

University of Toronto Press acknowledges the financial assistance to its publishing program of the Canada Council for the Arts and the Ontario Arts Council, an agency of the Government of Ontario.

Canada Council for the Arts Conseil des Arts du Canada

Funded by the Government of Canada Financé par le gouvernement du Canada

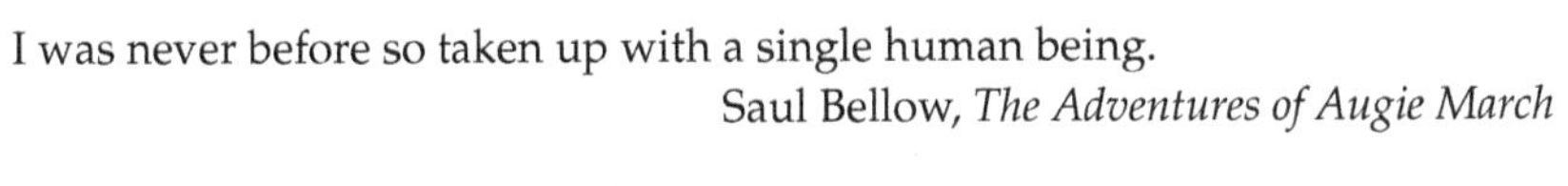

I was never before so taken up with a single human being.

Saul Bellow, *The Adventures of Augie March*

Contents

Preface

The [Hebrew] Bible is a work of philosophy. Abraham is a professor – the first professor of biblical philosophy. Chapter 21 of the Book of Genesis reports the inaugural lecture in the subject. "Abraham planted a tamarisk tree in Beer-Sheba, and called there on the name of the Lord" (33).

Among the trees of knowledge in the philosophical garden, Abraham's tamarisk is an exotic. *Bibleism* (as I'll call the Bible's philosophical position) has at its heart a principle (*the principle of particularity*, I'll call it) that isn't part of philosophy as it took shape in Greece.

Abraham is a philosopher. His philosophy isn't of the Greek variety. Here, in both senses of the term, are a few *implications* of the two propositions.

Abraham's being a philosopher implies that *any belief system whose validity is predicated on the Bible's status as Holy Writ is predicated on a mistake.* Whatever authority the Bible's pronouncements have is not had because of a special source; from which it follows that what is pronounced cannot be questioned, much less dismissed out of hand, on the grounds that there's no such source.

A second implication of the philosophical character of Abraham's activity is that *the core propositions of Bibleism are not advanced in a parochial or sectarian spirit.* The Bible's criticism of men and women who resist what Abraham professes comes therefore to this: they stand to the reality that the Bible deals with in a comparable condition to the condition, in regard to numbers, of unbelievers that 2 + 2 = 4.

If Bibleism is, as I argue in these pages that is, a contender for rational adherence, it can be inferred from its non-Greek character that *mainstream philosophers are excluded from part of the truth.* Oblivious (or neglectful) of the principle of particularity, they are at least one resource short. If so, *they* stand to reality in a comparable condition to the condition of the innumerates mentioned a moment ago.

Neither singly nor together do the two propositions imply that Abraham isn't imparting to men and to women God's plan for them. He could yet be doing so – in the rational mode of the philosopher. But this isn't what he is doing. That it isn't – that it couldn't be – follows from a substantive feature of his position. The deity on whom Abraham calls in Beer-Sheba is *a personification of the mentioned principle. People* have plans; *principles* don't. (Honesty, the best policy, doesn't have a policy.) What, then, is Abraham doing? Like Plato in regard to the Forms, he is identifying the principle and defending it.

"I am the Lord your God …; you shall have no other gods before me" (Exodus 20:2–3). This, the commandment of commandments, promulgates the principle. Since the Bible-based belief system, the system standardly labelled "monotheism," has no historical antecedent, the claim of novelty built into the formulation isn't window dressing.

The quoted words also trumpet the principle's importance. In what does *that* consist? The substantive disagreement between the supporters of God and those whom the Bible represents as ignorant (or rejective) of him is anthropological, not theological. At issue is the nature of men and women – unquestionably a matter of importance; indeed of as much importance to unbelievers, ancient or modern, as to believers.

In expounding Bibleism this book therefore expounds a view of what men and women are, a view to which intellectual activity of the Greek-based type is, according to the Bibleists, unequal. In advocating for what the Bible teaches, the book defends the view, at the same time defending the Hebrew style of intellection through which it is exposed. The recovery of the Bible's philosophy will make clear that at stake in our attitude towards what by tradition Moses indited is something closer to you and to me than an obscure being to whom we stand in an obscure relationship. If the Bibleists are right, at stake is, as Moses tells the children of Israel, something "very near to you" (Deuteronomy 30:14). At stake is the capacity of each of us meaningfully to say "I am."

It's in Beer-Sheba that Abraham, the first professor of biblical philosophy, first announces his project. The first academic post that *I* held was, as it happens, in Beer-Sheba. It happens, also, that I was the first in the Department of Philosophy at Beer-Sheba's newly founded University of the Negev to reach the professorial rungs on the ladder of rank. I was, then, the first in modern Beer-Sheba to bear the title "professor of philosophy." Given what I'm here professing, some irony flows from this snippet of personal history. For if back then the idea of the illustrious co-urbanite's precedence in the discipline had crossed my mind, I would have wondered whether I wasn't getting too much sun. Singing from the same hymnal as the members of the institution's Department of Jewish Thought, I took the Bible to be presenting in Abraham a prophet acting on a higher call, and I took the truth-content of the call to be indissociable from its time and from its place and from the nation of which Abraham is the founding father.

This book is the product, then, of four substantial shifts in my perception of *the* book: from seeing the Bible as anchoring an account of the world in a transcendent being, to seeing it as exploring the structure of things entirely in down-to-earth terms; from seeing the biblical message as culture-specific, to seeing the Bible as, at least in intention, comprising truths of unrestricted generality; from regarding the project of delineating the structure as an amalgam of the political, the sociological, and the psychological, to seeing it as philosophical; from seeing the project, *qua* philosophical, as amenable to execution in Greek, to viewing it as needing some Hebrew. Since most students of the Bible are located on the before-side of the before-and-after grid that structures this personal description, my conversion might be of more than autobiographical note.

Some of the material produced in the course of the activity whose end result is this book has appeared in print. Thanks go to the officials of *Dialogue: Canadian Philosophical Review*, *The Heythrop Journal*, *Iyyun: The Jerusalem Philosophical Quarterly*, *New Blackfriars*, *Philosophy and Theology*, and *Sophia* for permitting me to draw on the publications.

For support that facilitated the research I am indebted to Kwantlen Polytechnic University's Office of Research and Scholarship.

The duty to do so doesn't diminish my pleasure in saluting the friends and the colleagues who lent me a hand: Bill Barthelemy, Steven Burns, Roger Ebertz, Len Husband, Jonathan Katz, Shalom Lappin, Yuval Lurie, Eva Shorr, Chaim Tannenbaum.

May I take the opportunity to mention three teachers whom I had the good fortune of encountering along the way? Rabbi Moshe Feder taught me in my primary and secondary school days. From André Gombay I learned as an undergraduate. G.J. Warnock guided my early graduate studies. It pleases me to think that they, each of whom combined in his person a quiet grace and civility, would have enjoyed one another's company.

The book is dedicated to the memory of Eytan, my brother, and to the memory of Steven, my nephew.

"I AM"

Monotheism and the Philosophy of the Bible

Introduction
The Canaanite Camel

When Philo philosophizes on the Bible,[1] Plato is his guide. It's from Aristotle that Maimonides gets the resources for articulating the metaphysics of Holy Writ. Kant's ideas inform Hermann Cohen's reflections on what the tradition represents as the revelations of Abraham and of Moses. Emmanuel Levinas's dealings as a philosopher with the charter document of Judaism are shaped by Husserl and Heidegger. J.B. Soloveitchik (to name a thinker of our time situated deep within the milieu of devout observance) appeals to Kierkegaard to clarify the Torah's message.

Philo, Maimonides, and the others (the list goes on) have it back to front. Philo should be criticizing the Academy in the Bible's terms. Maimonides should be quoting Abraham to teach Aristotle, the master of those who know, philosophy that *he* doesn't know. Königsberg should be hearing the word out of Beer-Sheba from Cohen, and Copenhagen, from Soloveitchik. *Should* in each case, for the Bible, which Philo, Maimonides, and the others talk about when they are at home and when they are away, which they inscribe upon their doorposts and their gates, and in which they educate their children, is a work of philosophy.

Why do the philosopher-interpreters of the Bible make Abraham speak their Greek when they ought to instruct the canonical figures in his Hebrew? Such is the difference between the Bible's philosophical character and the philosophical character of recognized works of philosophy that thinkers schooled in the classics are programmed to mistake Abraham's offering.

The following factor of intellectual history magnifies the programming's effect on the moderns among the Bible's philosophically minded interpreters. Probably, it influences you, the reader, too.

After the Enlightenment, reflective belief in God couldn't return to what prior to then it had been. Cohen, Martin Buber, Levinas, and so on, heirs of the critique of naive religiosity that the Enlightenment philosophers mounted, reconstruct the biblical deity's significance with this in mind. But since God's self-identification, "I AM WHO I AM" (Exodus 3:14), is a *direct* expression of the Bible's philosophical principle, Bibleism gets lost in the veiling of God's presence. May it not be inferred that the thinkers in our midst who liken inheritors of the Enlightenment to self-blindfolders have got it right? It may not. According to those who do the likening, the self-identification, "אהיה אשר אהיה," is God's calling card.

A trio of propositions is present here. One: The Bible's *philosophical* terms are Greek to Western philosophical thinkers. Two: The Bible's philosophy isn't subject to Enlightenment strictures. Three: In reconstructing the religious content of chapter-and-verse, the modern defenders of the Bible toss out its philosophy.

How does the Bible's religious content link to its philosophy? The biblical character named "God" is a device to get the principle of particularity across.[2] Theologians mistake the wrapping for the gift.

As to the fashioners' use of such wrapping: the gaudiness falls into place if the Bible is viewed in its context. Deities and their doings figure prominently in the position against which the Bible is set. In Beer-Sheba, Abraham is addressing the local tribesmen. For his message to penetrate, he has to mute their Laocoöns. What better tactic than to construct a Canaanite Camel?

To judge from the narrative, the tactic didn't succeed. There were, it seems, no takers.[3] Worse yet, the tactic backfired. The Cohens, to whose forebears Abraham next presented the gift, were confused by the Camel. God they identified as the ground of the truth of the Bible's principle, rather than as its ship for crossing the desert of disbelief.

It would be astonishing if Jewish thinkers of a philosophical cast of mind were not responsive to the Bible's philosophical content. Responsive they are, usually in the area of ethics. Thus Buber's I–Thou relationship. Thus Levinas's unqualified obligation to the other. So far, so good. But when the thinkers appeal to Greek-based resources to articulate the sense of the good and the right that their cultural experience inculcates, they violate the first commandment. "I am the Lord your God …; you shall have no other gods before [God]" (Exodus 20:2–3). "Do not," that is to say, "subordinate the principle which God represents to the principles represented by the gods." Nor does the disquiet sometimes voiced by the thinkers regarding the resources take us much farther. Who's to say that when the biblical basis is accurately set out, they, committed as they are to the philosophical truth, won't prefer what turns out to be the devil they know?

"I AM" builds on an earlier book of mine. In *The Raven, the Dove, and the Owl of Minerva: The Creation of Humankind in Athens and Jerusalem,* I show that the Bible's image of the sector of being comprising men and women accords better with what the mirror reflects than do the images that ancient Greece sculpts or paints or puts into words. Although the greater fidelity I put down at the time to the Bible's being outside the sphere of Greek-type philosophy, this I equated with the Bible's being outside the sphere of philosophy itself. "[O]pposition to the Bible from the side of philosophy," I wrote, "is due to an internal disciplinary bias."[4] In the course of further work on the book's theme, I came to see that a principle having all the hallmarks of principles that are accounted philosophical by the tradition of abstract reflection that traces back to Greece primes the beliefs about men and women whose internalization makes for membership in the culture of which the Bible is the founding document. Questions crowded in. Could the absence of the stop from the Greek organ of abstract reflection make it impossible for the instrument to sound the philosophical word out of Zion? Could the variety of of-all-and-for-all truth in which Athens trades inhabit a level so remote from the lived reality of men and women as to make them unrecognizable to themselves? If the pagan environment contributed to philosophy's DNA, might Commandment One's opposition to the "other gods" not enfold a critique of the Greek instrument itself? Did philosophy have to be ceded to Athens? The answers that emerged – positive to the first three questions, negative to the fourth – were such that pressure mounted to take the position regarding the Greek sources and the Bible that philosophers take when assessing different philosophical ensembles: at least one is truth-defective.

Usually, scholarly interpreters represent the Bible's attitude towards paganism as dismissive. Despite their accentuation of the negative – in context, the expected rhetorical tactic – the Bibleists are conciliatory. The connection between Bibleism and that which Bibleism's proponents excoriate is dialectical. The philosophical specifics of the Bible's message won't become clear unless it's appreciated that the messengers accept some elements of the pagan way.

Why is it that the scholars see antithesis where there is synthesis? An influential factor in the Jewish context – a factor that can serve as an emblem of the insufficiently historical thinking that affects the products of much intellectual engagement with the Bible – is *Talmud-centrism.*

The belief system labelled "Judaism" is based as much on the activity of the rabbis of the Talmud as on the Bible. True, interpretive elaboration begins immediately the Bible's core part is put together – in the decades following the destruction of Solomon's Temple in 586 BCE. But the rabbinic work that contributes so massively to Judaism's character derives from Pharisaic thought and practice of the late Second Temple period. It's not that the Torah and the Talmud are far apart in time. It's that the rabbis of the Talmud, occupied as they are with the lives of the descendants of the children of Israel in a world markedly different from the world of the thinkers directly behind the Bible, are not antiquarians. A telling vignette from the Talmud's Tractate Menachoth (29b) has Moses occupying a back-row seat in Rabbi Akiva's seminary when God vouchsafes him a glimpse of the talmudic sage and his disciples expounding the law. "Not being able to follow their arguments he was ill at ease."[5] One therefore cannot say "Amen" to Levinas's claim that "we must be extremely timid when interpreting biblical texts [where] the Talmud has already said something about them."[6]

Because of its different concerns, the Talmud obscures the formative context of the Bible – as therefore does Judaism. "I am the Lord your God" is seen as enjoining the men and women of the first millennium's Jewish community to abide by the practices and to live within the institutions of which the Mishnah speaks and on which the Talmud enlarges – not as advancing, against the pagans, the principle of particularity.

The chapters that follow will show that in professing themselves monotheists, adherents to the religious belief systems for which the Bible is scripture read *into* the text what they claim to read *out of* it. It will also be shown that by not questioning the association of monotheism with theology – which *they* regard as a science without a subject – secular critics perpetuate the misunderstanding.

Students of Western philosophy know that dissatisfaction with the position dominant at the time galvanized Kant into action. In titling his magnum opus "Critique of Pure Reason" rather than, say, "Experience and the Structure of Reality" Kant foregrounds the inseparability of the work's constructive part from the criticism that he levels in it against rationalism. In much the same manner, the philosophical thinking of *his* age plays into Abraham's enterprise.[7] The standard packaging of the biblical position as Abraham's acceptance of a *new* deity acknowledges the critical element. But for the purely verbal reason that "new" pairs so easily with "old," the contribution of what Abraham criticizes to what he defends gets minimized. "New" also however pairs with "other." In urging you to try something new, I might be pointing to a gap in your repertoire, not trying to get you to scrap what you already have. Just so, the "other gods" against which Commandment One of the Ten rails and to which the Shema Yisrael proscribes allegiance are, as we'll see, not entirely superseded in the new dispensation.

"Abraham accepts a new deity" leads students of the Bible astray in a second way. Here, the problem word is "deity." The religious belief systems that take Abraham's "God" referentially, hence as a possible object of worship, go considerably beyond Bibleism. Let me go slightly beyond "go considerably beyond."

Like Christianity, Judaism is an institutionalized expression of *a use to which the biblical materials are put*. Because Judaism is closer to the Bible's philosophical core than is Christianity, adherents to Judaism who protest the Christian appropriation of the Tanakh aren't just sore losers. But although they are right to reject the portrayal of the Tanakh as a *praeparatio evangelica*, they too are making use of the Bible; and, relevantly to my concerns, Bibleism in the use that they put it to is a shadow of its true self.[8]

These, then, are the present book's main findings. A position deserving of the name "philosophy" is present in the Bible, and is indeed its core. This position differs in character from the products of Greek-based philosophical thinking. Appeal to the Bible's philosophy, because it taps into the book's rationale, makes for better interpretation of the text than is furnished in the rabbinic frame. The Bible's philosophy is the trunk of a tree whose major limbs are the familiar branches of abstract reflection that comprise philosophy's subject matter: moral philosophy, epistemology, political philosophy, action theory, and so forth. In each of these areas, the Bible has something to offer.

This is a work in philosophy, one with an unexpected subject. A corollary of the main thesis is that the thinkers responsible for the Bible merit a place alongside Plato and Kant. The philosophy of the Bible – *Bibleism*, in my coinage – is, moreover, more than more of the same only better. It corrects a substantial failing of Greek-based philosophical thinking. Cheekily, this book, like the Bible itself, might therefore be characterized as an attempt to convert the philosophical infidels.[9]

The campaign mounted in these pages against the usual conception of philosophy is intertwined with the attack on the usual understanding of the Bible. But although my ideal reader will therefore have both Scripture and philosophy, let me allay the apprehensions of those with only one of the two. The textual materials that I call upon to establish the misunderstanding turn out to be among the best-known, and the technical resources to which I appeal in the course of the metaphilosophical critique turn out to be relatively easy going. If the book's thesis did not go against the idea of providence, I'd characterize the happy circumstance as providential.

As the Contents page indicates, the chapters of Part One present the basics, while those of Part Two apply Part One's findings in a variety of areas of philosophical activity. Let me put some flesh on these bare bones.

Chapter 1 introduces the book's issues. (1) The meaning of the thesis that the Bible is a philosophical text depends on what philosophy is understood to be. The nature of the reflective activity is explained. (2) The distinction between Greek-based philosophical thinking and the philosophical thinking of the Bible – the latter's being trans-Graecian, so to speak – is crucial to the book. To secure the distinction, I look at philosophy's origin. But in the course of retelling the oft-told tale, I do something new: I bring out the linkage between the style of thinking perfected by Plato and Aristotle and the pagan background out of which it developed. In effect, the philosophical principle that the Bible identifies is absent from Greek-based abstract thinking because of how that style of thinking was constituted, genetically speaking, and hence, as I'll show, is constituted, logically speaking. This is what gives metaphilosophical force to the biblical attack on idolatry. (3) The category of the general dominates Greek-based philosophy. By contrast, irreducible particularity is at the heart of Bibleism. Bibleism's philosophical distinctiveness consists in *liberating ontology from the metaphysics that dominates Greek philosophy*. The metaphysics / ontology distinction connects to a number of themes that dominate treatment of the Bible. (4) A crucial theme is the meaning and significance of monotheism, the Bible's basic ism. An upshot of the analysis is that the ism is not *au fond* theological. It belongs to philosophical anthropology. (5) The playing up of God in the Bible is the playing up of particularity. Observe that God, the (non-pagan) biblical deity, is instrumental in bringing into existence the first man (to whom each of us traces back, according to the Bible). Observe that in the pagan context, men and women are parts of the natural world. It may be inferred that according to the Bible's thinkers, each person has – contrary to what the pagan thinkers hold – a non-natural element in his or her make-up. What is this element? It's more *the sole*, so to speak – the separateness of the person from the system that is nature – than the soul. In this, each man and each woman is like the biblical deity, God, who is one by nature and who is separate from nature. (6) Another target of chapter 1 is the widely held position that Jewish thought is not philosophical. That position is held, I explain, because the holders understand philosophy in Greek terms. This goes for Leon Roth, whose defence of the view is my main exhibit. But it goes for Philo and for Maimonides too, who consult Plato and Aristotle when they philosophize on the Bible. (7) As for the few who treat the Bible philosophically and non-apologetically, they, it emerges, are out of touch with its philosophical content. It's only their general feel for the biblical outlook that keeps them from straying even farther.

In chapters 2, 3, and 4, I turn to the Bible itself. Chapter 2 reconstructs Abraham's philosophical contribution from materials in the narrative. Through his deeds as well as in his words, Abraham advances the new principle to a pagan world that has no knowledge of it.

There would be no Bible if not for the new principle. But with regard to the extra-personal realm, the principle doesn't apply. This is what I argue in chapter 3. Genesis 1's cosmogonic story isn't meant to depend on what most would understand to be the literal truth of the words with which it begins, "In the beginning God created the heavens and the earth." The cosmogonic story is in fact the pagan story cleansed of myth. The physical world is represented as unfolding from a condition of formlessness in accordance with the natural principles that govern space, time, and all that they contain. It follows that if worship is in point, the other gods may in regard to the extra-personal realm be worshipped.

Chapter 4 addresses the centre of the Bible's philosophy – its philosophical anthropology. In their dealings with human reality, the Bibleists, I show, religiously observe a distinction between plural and singular forms of pronouns and nouns. In Genesis 1 no singular form is used in referring to men and women; no plural form is used in Genesis 2. The distinction thusly marked is between the species, humankind, which is part of the natural order, and particular men and women, with whom God shares his one-ness and (hence) who are not entirely natural. By surveying translations, I illustrate how frequently the plural forms of Genesis 1 swamp the singular forms of Genesis 2. The imposition of uniformity, done so thoughtlessly, amounts to ignoring the distinction between Greek philosophy or metaphysics (Genesis 1) and Bibleism or ontology (Genesis 2). Nor does the problem here affect only translators. Those who operate in the Bible's original language also trample on the distinction.

Part Two uses the results of Part One in a number of central areas of philosophical activity, in each case illustrating, by reference to philosophical classics and contemporary philosophical discussion, how the Bible, through its distinctive philosophy, contributes to live debate.

PART ONE

Foundations

1
Philosophy: Pagan and Jewish

Not Just Tribal

In its beginning is a natural history. The story of the birth and of the career of a nation winds through it. Both in the form of a menu of do's and don'ts and also through the portrayal of characters in action, it serves up a guide to life, a guide that in its telling is stamped "APPROVED" from on high.

The Bible comprises these things and many more. First and foremost, however, the Bible is a philosophical document.

To say that the Bible is *first* a philosophical document is to say that its root inspiration is the same as that of acknowledged works of philosophy, "to understand how things in the broadest possible sense of the term hang together in the broadest possible sense of the term."[1] Given what philosophical activity consists in, it is to say, too, that this understanding is sought with the same faculties that are instrumental in getting us from home to work and back, in plotting the trajectories of comets, in extracting square roots, and the like. To say that the Bible is *foremost* a philosophical document is to say that teachings of the sort that are the stock in trade of philosophers constitute the core around which the various other things that it instructs about are arranged; or, if I may muddy the waters by adding complexity unavoidable in view of the Bible's own complexity, it is to say that when of the various other things this or that one resists being so arranged, the depth of the philosophy constitutes a ground for assigning it a lesser importance.

Since truths of philosophy do not divide Israelites from Moabites, the implication (with apologies to Ira Gershwin) is that it isn't just tribal what's writ in the Bible; and, further to the preceding qualification, that when what's writ is tribal, that, for the Bible, is trouble.

The Bible's philosophical core is compact. A few chapters of Genesis and ... mission accomplished. The core comprises an account of the nature of men and women as creatures on earth. "What is Man?" That is the question. Among creatures, we, men and women, are distinctively distinctive. That is the position. Compared to how any non-human creature differs from a person, one non-human creature differs from another as Edam does from Gouda. Presented in the form of a unique affinity between Adam and God, the distinctive distinctiveness is made sense of in terms of an anatomy of being of the sort that Aristotle's *Metaphysics* supplies.

The Bible's scheme is of the sort that Aristotle's *Metaphysics* supplies. A category of being is however recognized that isn't part of The Philosopher's net. According to the Bible, men and women, uniquely among creatures, are *particulars*.

I'm not the first without an apologetic motive to read the Bible philosophically. The most influential who do this miss the Bible's philosophical core. They philosophize in Greek. Metaphysics, from which the particular is absent, is taken by them to subsume ontology, to which it is basic.

Mightn't a Hellene have had an Abraham-type (philosophical) epiphany? Since Mesopotamia was also unreceptive to Abraham's message, describing the Greek environment as uncongenial is insufficient for the negative. The fact is, though, that the Greece of the day was even unfriendlier. After philosophy had taken shape, Greece's cultural élite were full of themselves. Philosophy proved so powerful an instrument that no less than Zeus's favourite, Athena, was associated cultically with it. *That* – the self-assurance – is what lengthened the odds against a Hellenic Abraham. What about hostility from the latest legatees of Hellas? Mainstream philosophers inherit the confidence. Being less than clear about the meaning of that which the devout within *their* culture guard so zealously, their Jerusalemite counterparts do little to counteract the attitude.

"Monotheism": The Original Sin

Subject to a bit of Socratic midwifery, even those whose knowledge of the Bible is patchy will deliver the idea that the Bible advocates for what the term "monotheism" connotes. There's even a good likelihood that they will be able to quote the liturgy about the ism from memory.

> Hear O Israel, the Lord is our God, the Lord is one. (Deuteronomy 6:4)[2]

> I am the Lord your God ...; you shall have no other gods before me. (Exodus 20:2–3, Deuteronomy 5:6–7)

It's as we expect, then, that in introducing the Bible to the broader readership, scholars focus on monotheism. "[T]he genesis of the biblical way is bound up with the beginnings of the monotheistic concept; both converge in the age, and ... the person, of Abraham."[3] Thus E.A. Speiser, in the Introduction to the Genesis instalment of the Anchor Bible Series. Again: "The history of the biblical process is ultimately the story of the monotheistic ideal in its gradual evolution."

Speiser's position wouldn't alarm the faithful. Witness the following lines from *To be a Jew*, a classic guide to Jewish life in which Rabbi Hayim Halevy Donin explains the "How?" of being a Jew by answering the "Why?" "In what was a radical departure from polytheism and idolatry, Abraham the Hebrew was the first to give effective expression to this monotheistic faith."[4]

Students of Speiser's scholarship will think that "monotheism" has a direct biblical counterpart. That a lettered person like Donin, who writes from a traditionalist perspective, offers not the briefest explanatory/justificatory footnote further disarms the critical faculty into accepting that the word, understood as it usually is, expresses a core biblical view.

The word "monotheism" is of Greek provenance. "Polytheism" is its natural lexical antonym. To see how poorly the Hellenic duo fit Hebrew teachings, ask whether Olympian religion would be monotheistic were Zeus alone on Olympus. Or whether it was monotheistic at the outset when Chaos reigned alone. If a pantheon of one deity is monotheistic, the answer in both cases has to be "yes." But anyone whose use of "monotheism" is attuned to the Bible would deny that Abraham's *aperçu* comes to this, that on high two's a crowd.[5] The "many gods" position couldn't have eventuated the "one god" position in a game of musical thrones. To have become biblical-type monotheists, the Greeks would have had to leave Olympus, as Abraham left Shinar. It would not have sufficed for them to reduce the number of *their* deities.

The Shema Yisrael,[6] the main affirmation of adherence to the Bible's teachings, asserts that God is one. The assertion encodes a philosophical proposition. If, as I contend, the Bible's character as philosophy isn't recognized, it follows that monotheism, the chief biblical ism, is misunderstood. To have made sense of what in the Bible "monotheism" labels, and hence to have made sense of the Bible itself, the Greek thinkers would have had to pick up some Hebrew.

The Shema encodes a philosophical proposition. The theological assertion "There is one and only one deity" is understood – *misunderstood* – to express the Bible's basic truth. The error here, to which the scholars give their blessing, is the original sin of Jewish self-understanding. As a consequence, the Bible isn't seen as the exposition of Bibleism, the non-Greek philosophical position. It's taken to be the origin of the religion called "Judaism" at whose centre is the worship of God.

It will be some time before the identity of the Bible's basic truth is revealed. Here is a paraphrase that serves at least to shift the emphasis from theology: "Hear O Israel, God is one. Because of that, God is the deity."

The View from the Bridge of Jewish Scholarship

The received position is that what is distinctively philosophical isn't biblical and that what is distinctively biblical isn't philosophical. Relevant entries in the *Encyclopedia Britannica* and on Wikipedia confirm "received." Let's look at a scholarly source whose position both popular compilations echo.

In the essay "Is there a Jewish Philosophy?," Leon Roth mounts a case for "No" to his title's question.[7] Roth aligns himself in this regard with Julius Guttmann's *Philosophies of Judaism: The History of Jewish Philosophy from Biblical Times to Franz Rosenzweig*:

> The Jewish people do not begin to philosophize because of an irresistible urge to do so. They received philosophy from outside sources, and the history of Jewish philosophy is a history of the successive absorption of foreign ideas which were then transformed and adapted according to specific Jewish points of view.[8]

Take for instance the greatest of the thinkers to whom the label "Jewish philosopher" gets applied. What does Roth find in Maimonides? Lots of philosophy. But

> the genuinely philosophical side … is derived from without, that is, from the non-Jewish culture of the … time. Maimonides … select[ed] … such ideas as would offer an account of Judaism which should be consonant with the spirit, or, if you like, the vocabulary, of the age.[9]

> [Maimonides's] originality consisted not in his philosophy, which was that of Aristotle ... but in what resulted when he applied his Aristotelianism to Judaism.[10]

Nor does Roth understand "philosophy" idiosyncratically. The conception with which he works is mainstream:

> Philosophy is not just the activity of weighing experiences, any experiences. The experiences it weighs are of a certain dimension and importance. They may be, for example, those ubiquitous elements which seem to appear in all, or almost all, the things with which we come into contact – space, time, form, matter, or more abstractly and more difficultly, causation. These are *fundamentals*, pervasive factors the removal or alteration of which would change the nature of things altogether.[11]

In saying that philosophy that doesn't get there from outside is not to be found within the Jewish frame, Roth is therefore saying that the most general claims within this frame fall short of identifying or expressing "pervasive factors &c." The philosophy of Judaism is philosophy in name only: "so-called philosoph[y]."

Roth sums it up thus (my emphasis):

> The philosophy of Judaism is the thinking and rethinking of *the fundamentals of Judaism.*

Meat, dairy products, vegetables, and grains are fundamental food groups. Bagels and latkes, mainstays of Jewish cuisine, aren't.

The Ultimate Basis

Roth's case for "No" depends, ultimately, on the nature of the book upon whose contents the Jewish philosophers whom he calls "so-called" philosophize. Here, *in my words,* is a distillation of Roth's quite representative thinking in regard to this book:

> The Bible, the deepest product of reflective thought in the Jewish frame, is occupied with the lives of the members of the Israelite community. In its chapters and its verses the foundations are laid for a distinctive way of life, several of whose footings are respect for learning, valorization of family, commitment to institutions for assisting the less fortunate without

> absolving them of the responsibility that they bear for their plight or lifting from the shoulders the obligation to work for its amelioration, discouragement of excess in the use of intoxicants. None of these is a general norm of attitude or pattern of conduct. Ways of life that are less cooperative are quite actual, as are more Dionysian modes of living and lifestyles in which studiousness is frowned upon as bookish passivity. Add that membership in the group goes hand in hand with a set of practices that are found nowhere else – sabbath observance, dietary laws, Temple ritual – and it's case closed.

Seeing the Jewish way whose rudiments the Bible advances as one of many, Roth concludes that Jewish thought, if it keeps to its own grounds, is parochial.[12]

The Case for "Yes": Preliminaries

Although forceful, the case for "No" to "Is there a Jewish philosophy?" isn't airtight. One weak spot concerns Roth's appeal to the practice of the various reflective thinkers in the Jewish context who think in philosophical terms. *From the fact that Maimonides and the others exit the Jewish frame for their philosophy, the most that can be inferred is that they see no philosophy in it.* A second weak spot has to do with Roth's understanding of the Bible. *From the fact that the Jewish way differs from other ways, one could conclude that the truths at its centre are culture-specific only if all philosophical positions are notational variants of one another.*

In one respect, my account misrepresents Maimonides. Although Aristotelian terms saturate his expositions, Maimonides held that a Jewish philosophy, which he asserts got lost during the Egyptian captivity, had at the inception of the biblical process been articulated.[13] After the liberation, Moses presents a guide for living that, while it accords with the philosophical principles, doesn't lay them out.

> Surely, this commandment that I am commanding you today is not too hard for you, nor is it too far away. It is not in heaven, that you should say, "Who will go up to heaven for us, and get it for us so that we may hear it and observe it?" Neither is it beyond the sea, that you should say, "Who will cross to the other side of the sea for us, and get it for us so that we may hear it and observe it?" No, the word is very near to you; it is in your mouth and in your heart for you to observe. (Deuteronomy 30:11–14)

Eight centuries before Maimonides, Augustine adumbrated a view of the same ilk. In *The City of God*, VIII.11, he suggests that Plato, whose philosophy *he* summons to the interpretation/defence of Scripture, was for a time enrolled at the feet of Jeremiah.[14]

The desire to keep his position tethered to the Bible motivates the Bishop's fantasy. But the substance of the fantasy attests to a belief that the Bible has philosophical content. More pertinently to present concerns, don't Maimonides's words also imply that foundational thinkers on the Jewish side oppose Roth's "No"?

Since the claim about a Mosaic philosophy is a flourish in the Maimonidean picture, Roth's non-mention of it does no harm to his case. But now that *I*'ve mentioned it, shouldn't I go easier on the son of Maimon? Two points of difference absolve me of heartlessness. One: The philosophy is not lost. Maimonides himself had it in plain sight, although he, Maimonides, did not know that that is what he was looking at. Two: The Bible's philosophy has Greek reflections only *per accidens*.

Maimonides regards Aristotle's thought as approximating the Bible's (lost) philosophy. That is the same compliment Augustine pays Plato. The problem runs deeper than the Academy and the Lyceum. Greek philosophy is the problem. Although the poet wasn't thinking of the ancient mariner whom the tradition calls "the first philosopher," Coleridge puts it prettily: "Water, water, everywhere, / Nor any drop to drink."

I mentioned Moses at Sinai. This part of the Bible's story contains the essence of the Bible's philosophy. Moses asks God:

> If I come to the Israelites and say to them, "The God of your ancestors has sent me to you," and they ask me, "What is his name?" what shall I say to them? (Exodus 3:13)

God's answer (14) is the quintessence.

> God said to Moses, "I AM WHO I AM." He said further, "Thus you shall say to the Israelites, I AM has sent me to you."

In giving the name, God is asserting a philosophical principle, the distinguishing principle of biblical thought.

The implication is plain: in "appl[ying] his Aristotelianism to Judaism," Maimonides changes the subject. Since the character called "God" is the carrier of the principle, Maimonides is in violation of the Shema.[15]

Roth, following the second Moses rather than going back to the first one, perpetuates the mistake.

During the discussion in "Is there a Jewish philosophy?," Roth addresses the Christian case.

> In the twenties or early thirties there was a grand debate on the phrase ["Christian philosophy"]. Many different views were expressed, from that of the extreme religionists that there is no genuine philosophy which is not Christian to that of the extreme secularists that philosophy and Christianity have no connection with one another whatsoever. The honours of the debate went to the secularists; but the religionists made the excellent point that religion poses certain fundamental problems which all philosophies must attempt to meet.[16]

Roth is foursquare with the secularists. Yet may it not be that some of the problems that religions pose are posed from the religious quarter not because they have irreducibly religious content but for the non-theological reason that the secular are insensible to them? Couldn't some of the problems that the figure of God is appealed to to solve be of this class? If so, the figure of God in the treatment of these problems would convey something of significance to all – something philosophical. Here, again, is Roth's thumbnail of philosophy:

> The experiences [that philosophy] weighs are of a certain dimension and importance. They may be, for example, those ubiquitous elements which seem to appear in all, or almost all, the things with which we come into contact – space, time, form, matter, or more abstractly and more difficultly, causation. These are *fundamentals*, pervasive factors the removal or alteration of which would change the nature of things altogether.

The reader will expect me to say that for the God-fearing, God's removal *would* change things altogether. Say it I do. True, in my saying of it the devout will find only a pale facsimile of the deity in whom their hopes for felicity and salvation repose. But their disappointment on this score is neither here nor there so far as the relevant takeaway is concerned, namely that the items on Roth's list bespeak the style of interest in the world definitive of natural science. Distinctively human aspects are add-ons: consciousness, emotional ties, suffering, destiny, mortality, morality. If the religious focus on these, and if the secular look elsewhere, that would, if anything, identify a blind spot in secularism.

Roth's confidence that of the fundamentals of Judaism none is "a factor the removal or alteration of which &c." is as high as this statement of his is rhetorical: "Buddhists or Taoists could be forgiven if they were sceptical about [the claims of Bible-citing philosophers]."[17] But in the absence of *genuine* alternatives to the Bible-based form of life, an inference from the distinctiveness thereof to the Bible's sectarian character doesn't go through. The Bible-based form of life could look sectarian only because it is presented overdressed – a clothed body in an anatomy class. If this ism (Buddhism, say) or that (Taoism) comes across as less place-and-time specific, less parochial, might that be due to a truncation rather than to a disrobing? Russell's paradox proves classical set theory to be inconsistent. Prior to the paradox's discovery, a set theorist who advanced a size-restricting axiom would have been pelted with sarcasm. "What part of 'all' don't you understand?" Might cultures that seem more catholic than the Bible-based one seem so only because *they* omit some fundamental, so that their adherents are guilty of the fallacy of misplaced concreteness?

Philosophy and Ontology

Two issues require remark before we pass beyond the preliminaries. The first has to do with philosophy's origins; the second concerns philosophy's character. I'll describe both in the company of Bernard Williams.

"Plato," Williams writes, "invented … philosophy as we know it."[18] Of Plato's massive influence on subsequent philosophical activity there is no doubt. Yet for all his originality, Plato, as I'll confirm in the next section, is *streamlining* the cultural chariot.

The second issue has to do with the term "ontology." It is this. Although the word "ontology" is in philosophy's lexicon, the discipline does not recognize what it names as a compartment in the same way that it recognizes ethics, say, or epistemology.

Williams lists the topics whose philosophical study Plato inaugurated: "knowledge, perception, politics, ethics, art; language and its relations to the world; death, immortality and the nature of the mind; necessity, change and the underlying order of things." On a first pass, "the underlying order of things" might be taken as a synonym of "ontology." It's more accurate to see it as convertible with "metaphysics" – in Plato, the account of the Forms and of the (spatio-temporal) Receptacle and of the relation of participation. None of these is a thing of the sort with which we interact in our daily lives. The Forms and the Receptacle and the link of participation *underlie* the planets, the trees, and the people. But it's the planets, the trees, and the people that constitute the raw material of ontology.

Revealingly, Williams's language is inexact. As I just now stated, the Forms and the Receptacle and the relation of participation *underlie* the order of things. But *pace* Williams, they are *not* the underlying order of things. No one fastidious about such matters would equate "what underlies the order of things" with "the underlying order of things" *unless it made no difference from his or her perspective*. And *that* would be so only if from his or her perspective the things have no philosophically relevant reality apart from what underlies them. That is what the philosopher holds. At the most basic level *philosophy deals with (non-general) things as (ground-level) instances of (general) kinds*. Their status as instances apart, (non-general) things like planets and trees and people are assigned no autonomy. Having identified them as instances, the philosopher has nothing more to say. The metaphysics subsumes the ontology.[19]

A refusal of the subsumption underlies what the Bible says about the issues that Williams enumerates. *The thing-hood of some (ground-level) things is lost if they are processed metaphysically*. So say the Bibleists.

The issue of philosophy's origin and the issue of philosophy's character can be linked. Plato leaves his father Ariston's house. But he departs only for the Garden of Academus, a stone's throw away. There's no comparable exaggeration to Williams's in the Bible's saying that Abraham leaves his father Terah's house. Abraham (or the tradition he fronts in the biblical narrative) did invent monotheism. Monotheism *is* a rupture. The line of thinking of which it is the theological face gives ontology independence from metaphysics.[20]

Some time will pass before the lie of the land is clear. But even at this stage, attention to the character of the culture whose momentum helps Plato take wing brings to light a problem for Maimonides and for Augustine.

Augustine's major work is titled "The City of God Against the Pagans" (De Civitate Dei Contra Paganos). Greek culture was pagan; until Christianization, Roman culture was too. Since the Bible opposes nothing if not paganism, why would a defender of the Bible look to *its* leading thinkers for philosophical resources? I anticipate the answer that those resources *constitute* the discipline of philosophy. The present point isn't however that a different philosophy is native to the Bible. It's that philosophy as we identify it was conceived under a pagan sign.

Philosophy and Paganism

Philosophy came forth in a pagan environment. The biblical position is visible in what Elijah, on the Carmel, presents as a winner-take-all contest with paganism. "If the Lord is God, follow him; but if Baal, then follow him" (1 Kings 18:21). Supposing that merit attaches to the Bible's teachings about fundamentals, the implication is that philosophy is short at least one essential element of being.

What was the link between the Greeks' intellectual activity and paganism?

Plato's criticism of the Homeric portrayal of the gods is informative here. That portrayal, Plato asserts, sets a bad example. "If the gods can bicker among themselves and act on their base impulses in their dealings with men and women, why should *we* restrain ourselves and strive for harmony?" This sounds like a rejection of paganism. It's not. Plato is attempting to mop up pockets of irrationalism (as he sees them) in what would be gathered about paganism from Homer.

The following proportionality is, I think, a good telegram of the link between the Bible and philosophy.

Zeus : Greek-based philosophy :: God : Bible-based philosophy[21]

According to Plato, the world is a unified whole. Homer (this is a second point of criticism) fobs off a misleading approximation.

The criticisms are well-taken. Do I know that Zeus is no philanderer; that Ares isn't a brute; that in her dealings with men and women Aphrodite is a force for bliss and harmony. I do not. Neither, however, do I know that Aphrodite and Ares and Zeus are projections of an infantile cultural imagination. In fact, I know that beyond the cosmetics they are *not*. Their existence is as plain as the wind in your face; the sun on your back; the desire you feel for another, most keenly when you are told that now would not be fair. To be alive is to be under their sway. Think what we might of Olympian religion as religion, it's less problematic in this existential regard than is its biblical counterpart.

Olympian religion is a cognitively mediated response to nature. Its deities personify the governing principles of natural features. Such are the effects of the weather, the seas, and the sun on our lives, that the term "gods" makes excellent sense when applied to Zeus, to Poseidon, and to Apollo.

In agreeing with the second of Plato's criticisms, I am accepting a point about *the multiplicity of deities*. That multiplicity links to what we – misguidedly – call "polytheism."[22] The natural world *is* complex. "But," the reader will ask, "*doesn't* shadowy Nyx tussle with sunny Apollo?" The form of Plato's answer we know: the mythopoets are deceived by the appearances.

With regard to the data used to back up the representation of nature as messy, we side with Plato. The truth in a remark about strife between night and day isn't the truth of strife. Nor, despite how we speak of it over coffee, is seasonal conflict conflict. The lunar phases are phases of one thing; likewise the seasons with respect to that of which *they* are climatic phases.

Plato makes much of what had until then been said sound childish. Nevertheless, what *he* says isn't revolutionary. In giving fixity to a cycle, the myth of the seasons says what he says. It's not as if Hades, who carries Persephone off each fall, will one year decide to lock his embrace. As sure as spring follows winter, Demeter's daughter is sprung. For all his originality, Plato is of his native land and of his father's house.

Why does Plato expend so much energy on Homer? Had Homer been the Shakespeare of the age, Plato might have averted his gaze. But Homer was more to the Greeks than a cultural icon. The epics are *scriptural* – a window onto the nature of things and (therefore) a guide to living. There is also the less atmospheric point that the correction of what Plato identifies as Homer's mistake leads in *Plato's* direction.

How does the intellectual traffic flow? Always, those who manage the movement reduce the number of vehicles to the minimum needed in their estimation to bear the freight. If the number exceeds 1, they arrange the several vehicles in orderly convoy. Thales holds water to be the basis of things. Some who draft in Thales's wake postulate a non-aqueous principle. Others advance a number of coordinate principles. None abandons the idea that the whole is a unity.[23] By the lights of all these more "rational" thinkers, Homer is on the right track, although, like the cave dwellers of Plato's allegory, he only skims the depths.

Philosophy in its adult form bears the marks of its infancy and of its early development. The discipline first sees light under the sign of naturalism, of stress on general principles of explanation. Also, the adolescent phases exhibit a reductionist tendency. Into philosophy's maturity survive both (1) naturalism and generality and (2) reductionism.

To bear out the preceding remarks, I now draw on an expert discussion of philosophy's emergence.

The Presocratics, Jonathan Barnes writes, "invented the very idea of science and philosophy. They hit upon that special way of looking at the world which is the scientific or rational way … The world was not a random collection of bits, its history was not an arbitrary series of events … Still less was it a series of events determined by the will – or the caprice – of the gods."[24] I put up resistance to Williams's claim that Plato invented philosophy. Barnes waters down the companion ascription to the Presocratics of inventor status in regard to science. Of Homer and Hesiod, he later asserts: "All this is myth … but it is, as it were, scientific myth."[25]

Didn't the myth tellers and users hold that fickle gods underlie happenings in the world? Barnes's affirmative trades on an ambiguity. The problem phrase is "the will – or the caprice – of the gods." Do different whims drive each of the gods, or are the events disordered because different gods collide? Reading Homer, we do not find that the gods are severally mercurial. The different gods, we find, have different overall agendas: "our … conflicting wills," as Ares says (*Iliad* 5:1009). Since their natures differ, that's expected.[26] When their several agendas intersect in the world, the results are therefore hard for men and women lacking supercomputational powers to predict.

The Homeric view (like the Hesiodic one) applies the language of motive and purpose to the doings of the gods. Even at that stage the vocabulary is under pressure. Anticipating (in effect) Thales's naturalist and reductionist claim about mind, that "all things are full of gods," the mythopoets are themselves proto-proto-philosophers.

The anthropomorphism in the portrayal of the Olympian deities is veneer. It's empty for men and women to say that Zeus and Apollo and Hera are persons when the attribution to the gods of motives and purposes furnishes no guidance to those who say it. Contained within the portrayal of the residents of Olympus are the seeds of the banishment of the attributed notions.

Science, Philosophy, and the Bible

To do philosophy is to deal reflectively with fundamentals. The fundamentals Roth lists – space, time, form, matter, causation – concern the structure of the physical world. How do *these* come to be singled out? With an eye on the absence from the list of distinctively human characteristics – consciousness, emotional ties, destiny, mortality, morality – let me blueprint an answer.

The notions that Roth lists develop out of a pagan view. The fundamentals of the pagan conception in its undeveloped form are the pagan gods. These deities are the world's foundations and load-bearing pillars. Appeal to them meets explanatory needs. The philosophical positions demythologize the same subject matter that the god-involving representations package.

On the cosmogonical stories that make up the early phases of Greek cosmology (Abraham departs from a pagan culture similar to the Greek one), an initial state of disorder undergoes progressive differentiation, the end result being the world that we experience. First to emerge are the largest regions of the natural world. Like the sub-regions that precipitate out afterward, the heavens and the earth are associated with gods.

Here are the rudiments of Hesiod's account in *Theogony* (ll. 116–18, ll. 126–28).[27]

> Chaos was born first and after it came Gaia
> the broad-breasted, the firm seat of all
> the immortals who hold the peaks of snowy Olympos,
>
> Gaia now first gave birth to starry Ouranos,
> her match in size, to encompass all of her,
> and be the first seat of all the blessed gods.

Since in its earthly disposition and heavenly turnout nature is expressive of *their* natures, what better course than the study of nature to gain information about Ouranos's above-ness, Gaia's below-ness, and what happens at the meeting place? The axiom of early Greek thinking, that the gods manifest themselves through nature, survives in philosophy and in science. Philosophy and science are rational retrofittings of the mythic processor.

The earliest phases of Greek rational processing of the cosmos answer to "proto-monistic naturalism." The gods correspond to aspects/elements of nature when nature is viewed superficially, as a loose unity. More refined rational dealings – controlled observation, advancement of explanatory hypotheses, prediction and testing – move towards monistic naturalism. "Monistic naturalism" approximates to "the scientific world view."

This constellation doesn't jibe with the biblical arrangement. In the latter, God stands apart from the natural world; also, God's creative activity is voluntary. It follows that from the biblical standpoint the systematic study of nature isn't the route to knowledge about the creator.

This "render unto Newton" doesn't equate to saying that from the biblical standpoint the outcome of the creative work is silent about God's nature. Van Gogh's self-portraits are informative about the painter's appearance. Similarly, in bringing men and women into the world, God creates objects in which he is reflected, albeit rarely with a circumcised ear.

Couldn't one argue, then, that we have here a point of comparison between Hesiod and the Bible? The contrast I am bringing out concerns mode, however, not content. The Bible shares Plato's critical attitude towards mythic accounts of the sort found in *Theogony*.

The upshot is as adumbrated. "These are the generations of philosophy: Hesiod begat Thales." Conceived and brought to term in a pagan environment, philosophy continues to show the marks of the pregnancy and the birth.

According to Roth, Jewish philosophy occupies itself with matters definitive of *Jewish* reality. The historical excursus suggests that (general) philosophy's even-handedness depends on a reduction whose success Thales and followers of his lead assume. This leaves open the possibility that the deity of the Bible, or what this deity stands for, is an *excluded* fundamental. If the Bible is first and foremost a work of philosophy, that is exactly what the thinkers behind it would be saying.

The notion of a committed Jewish thinker commenting on the products of pagan thought otherwise than negatively sharpens what I said in criticism of Maimonides's practice. Augustine targets *The City of God* "against the pagans." Yet he leans heavily on Plato. This, *mutatis mutandis*, is the same point. Greek philosophy had its Moses. In placing Plato at Jeremiah's feet, Augustine errs about the Hebrew Scriptures. The Greek Moses is on the slopes of Olympus.[28]

In what is overall an essay of advocacy, "Jewish Thought as a Factor in Civilization," Roth takes one potshot at the Bible. "At its worst," he states, "it is just not interested [in science]."[29] This missile is off-target. Those behind the Bible do not dogmatically devalue the scientific spirit, much less do they lack it. What is true is that through the bulk of the chapters and the verses *other* fish are being fried. We caught a glimpse of the Bible's reasoning for putting the fish on the back-burner in the theologically couched denial that the study of the creation is instructive about God. If the Big Fish is the focus of interest, looking elsewhere makes eminent sense.

The Bible holds that science cannot tell us what we need to know about the reality of men and women. There is another mountain, on which reposes the god of that reality. To secure a sense of the contrast, I shall jot down some observations on the view from Homer's mountain.

A few Homeric characters have a god as one of their parents. Among mortals it is *they*, this genealogical detail says, who exemplify to an extraordinary degree the natural forces the gods represent. Achilles dwarfs the Hellenic counterparts of Joe Bloggs in the same way that Usain Bolt leaves the galumphers in the dust.

On this view, men and women see themselves as do many of us, as parts of nature. The claim that each of us has *some* god in him or her – of Nike, Bloggs a little, Achilles a lot – comes out, naturalized, in Thales's proposition that all things are full of gods. Thales is not a primitive animist. The position he holds is that the principles of animation evident in the human realm are present even in the non-human one. The distinctively human can ultimately be explained on the basis of the non-human. This the Bible gainsays.

Roth's claim about Jewish thought and science is revealing – revealing, that is, about the claimant. Roth too is committed to the Greek view of philosophy. It is to him philosophy entire. Observe, by comparison, how Barnes knots philosophy to science. He doesn't state that the Greeks came up with the idea of science *and also* came up with the idea of philosophy. He doesn't state that the Greeks came up with the *ideas* of science and of philosophy. The Greeks, he states, "invented the very idea of science and philosophy." They "hit upon that special way of looking at the world which is the scientific or rational way." For Barnes, philosophy is one side of a coin of which science is the other.[30] Roth's remark shows that he, philosophically, is *pro paganos*. Little wonder that he finds no philosophy in the Bible!

Can the Bible's attitude *contra paganos* be defended? The attitude is reasoned. A position at odds with the position out of Greece anchors it. Could it be that the Bible, *at its best*, is not interested in science?

As the details of Genesis 1 confirm, those behind the Bible know as much about science as any reflective contemporary. The wonder that inspires scientific inquiry is given its due. Consider these lines from Proverbs (30:18–19):

> Three things are too wonderful for me;
> ...

> the way of an eagle in the sky,
> the way of a snake on a rock,
> the way of a ship on the high seas,
> ...

Each "thing" referred to inhabits one of the sectors into which the story of the creation partitions the natural realm. Each "way" provokes the wonderment that animates scientific inquiry. How does the eagle remain aloft? How does the snake locomote? Why doesn't the ship sink like a stone?

As the ellipses signal, I've suppressed two lines:

> four I do not understand:
> ... the way of a man with a girl.

These lines identify the spur to Bibleism. The thing numbered "four," from the personal sphere, doesn't provoke wonderment. *Perplexity* it engenders.[31] The bafflement, according to the Proverbist, is permanent.

The Proverbist and Aristotle agree: knowledge begins in wonder. But Solomon would add that a region of cognitive activity exists to which on the experiential side science is inappropriate and which on the reflective side philosophy can't handle.

"For it is owing to their wonder that men both now begin and at first began to philosophize."[32] Solomon's counterpart claim? "It is owing to their perplexity that men now begin and at first began to think biblically." In the one case, it's a matter of figuring the subject out and of adjusting one's behaviour accordingly. In the other case, it's a matter of coming up with coping strategies when the subject can't be figured out.

The Theological Isms Untangled

When we pare off the mythic rind, here's what we find. "Polytheism," as it is usually called, is actually pluralism regarding basic natural principles. In this sense of "polytheism," the non-polytheistic position would be *monism*, the position that the number of basic natural principles is one.

The first item of the left-hand pair in the proportionality

> Zeus : Greek-based philosophy :: God : Bible-based philosophy

tends towards monism; the first item of the right-hand pair, towards monotheism. The Bible is not "mono" where the Greek scriptural documents and myths are "poly." Nor is the Bible in agreement with the Greek side when (as in Plato) the Greek side is "mono."

Had Zeus presided alone on Olympus, Olympian religion would have been monotheistic. That's an implication of the usual view. Cued by the view's flaw, I'll now home in on its linguistic accompaniment.

The textual basis for the usual line on the Bible's position is the Shema: "the Lord our God, the Lord is one." But if the Olympian belief system would qualify if Zeus had no company, the Bible, for being monotheistic, wouldn't be revolutionary. Equating the Bible's novelty with its recognition of God as, numerically, the only deity therefore voids "monotheism" of analytic/interpretive utility.

Provided that one attends to both its parts, "monotheism" *is* however of great utility. The Bible's position is *theistic*. Its deity, God, is a personal deity. As such, its deity is what no non-theistic deity could be – a unitary entity, a one.[33]

"Monotheism," in the strict sense, applies exclusively to the Bible's (kind of) position. Since what is not theistic cannot be polytheistic, the usual contrastive characterization of pagan religions as polytheisms muddies the waters.

In the strict sense of "polytheism," the deities of a polytheistic belief system would each of them be, like God, a one. So it's a good question whether the biblical belief system could accommodate more deities. Yes, No, or Maybe, the sharp contrast with pagan systems would remain. The biblical belief system alone would be theistic. If for you this isn't reason enough to reform the taxonomy, the following might do the trick.

Scholarly Confusion

In "Monotheism and Polytheism in Ancient Israel," an appendix to *The Bodies of God and the World of Ancient Israel*, Benjamin Sommer writes: "The term polytheism can either refer to the worship of many deities (which is the typical form of polytheism) or to ... polytheistic monolatry."[34]

Failing to appreciate that the Bible's difference (theologically speaking) has to do with the nature of deity, not with the size of the set of deities, Sommer misunderstands the opposition to paganism. Because they worship both God and El, the Israelites are, he asserts, polytheists. This can't be true. El isn't a theistic deity.

"The ... Bible at once describes and proscribes polytheistic worship among ancient Israelites through the preexilic period." The Bible does nothing of the kind. Described and proscribed is the worship of pagan (non-theistic) deities.[35] Any theistic position has to have the "mono" feature that the Bible endorses. So a poly*theistic* belief system isn't a proper contrast. "One" as asserted in the Shema applies to each of the personal deities whose existence the belief system's adherents affirm.

According to the Bible, paganism is mistaken because it lacks the ontological idea of a one. Ontological one-ness is what the Shema ascribes to (the extra-natural, non-pagan deity) God. "God is one. Because of that God is the deity."

Appendix: Christian Philosophy

Roth singles out Étienne Gilson as a modern exponent of Christian philosophy, by which is meant the Aristotle-based scholasticism of which Aquinas's *Summa Theologiae* is the *fons et origo*. God, on the scholastic way of thinking, is existent in the fullest sense – supremely, ineluctably, existent. It's in terms of this special kind of existence that the biblical God's "I AM" is understood.

A natural suggestion from the modern analytic quarter is that this kind of existence equates to necessary existence as per the possible world analysis. But in the view of those who think of God as existent in the fullest sense, the analysis is overly reductive. God, they would explain, is a being lacking in nothing. Not only is there nothing that he lacks, but he also has nothing in him of nothing. So to say that God is "all" to our "some" is to water down God's plenitude. God *overflows* our general descriptions. God cannot be encompassed by the cognitive capacities of limited and imperfect creatures such as us; indeed, any attempt to so encompass Him would require a movement of thought that goes above and beyond the general as we finite and limited creatures grasp it.[36]

Since a modification of the general – the *super-general*, we might say – is the cognitive ticket to God, there's something to the claim that (Greek-based) philosophy has an internal link to Christianity.[37]

The biblical position also associates God with a distinctive mode of being. The mode – particular being – lies at the other extreme. Moses doesn't beat around the bush. "It is not in heaven ... No, [it] is very near to you." It's by getting beneath the general that this kind of being is understood.[38]

Although the two positions are incommensurate – the idea of God at the centre of the Christian position, we see, has nothing to do with the idea behind the biblical deity's "I AM" – both associate God with a distinctive style of existence. It would have benefited Roth to have pondered the unabashed assignment on the Christian side of philosophical significance to (the idea of) God. Roth's sequestering of (the idea of) God in theology leaves him with no choice but to classify Maimonides as, *au fond*, an apologist for religion, and that classification colours his understanding of Jewish abstract thinking generally. Be Maimonides's philosophical credentials as may be, Roth's "No" to "Is there a Jewish philosophy?" is compromised.

The rabbis of the Talmud oppose not only paganism but also nascent Christianity. Given that Greek-based philosophy developed in the pagan context, and given Greek-based philosophy's influence on Christianity, we have here something of a Trinity. So the rabbinical opposition to Greek-based philosophy and the rabbinical opposition to Christianity are aspects of a single oppositional stance.

2
The Inaugural Lecture

Biblical Philosophy: The Beginning

Verse 33, the next-to-last of chapter 21 of the Book of Genesis, announces Abraham's mission. Here, in the NRSV's rendition, is the verse. "Abraham planted a tamarisk tree in Beer-Sheba, and called there on the name of the Lord, the everlasting God."[1]

After his journey from Ur of the Chaldeans, Abraham puts down roots in Canaan. The man who departed home and native land then begins to spread the word about what he came to understand through the theophany (as it is represented) nine chapters earlier. What was that word? There is a verse 34, but it is – is it not? – epilogue. "And Abraham resided as an alien many days in the land of the Philistines."

It's odd that the word should be mentioned only to be raced past, odder still that the subsequent chapters don't circle back. "Could it be," the reader will muse, "that verses between verse 33 and verse 34 have been lost?"

The oddity is in the eye of the reader. Verse 33 is not epilogue. It is informative about the mission's content.

"בשם"

Depending on how "be-shem" is taken, verse 33 can be read in a pair of ways. On one reading, the verse asserts of Abraham that he *calls out to the world in God's name*. On the other reading, it's being said of Abraham that he *calls out [with] God's name to the world*.[2] Both readings convey that Abraham is beginning to impart the news. But only the first prompts "What does he say?" The question, on the second reading, the text pre-empts: Abraham is advancing the axiom of the Bible's revolutionary system of thought.

"You call out in someone's name. In doing so, don't you speak of that someone?" Not necessarily. Suppose you call out in Albert Einstein's name: you proclaim Relativity to the physicists of the world. In doing this, you don't have to mention the great man, do you? The physical world to whose deep nature Relativity is a key – Einstein himself isn't any more relevant to it than Archimedes is, or than is Isaac Newton.

Suppose Relativity Theory had been a collaborative venture. The change in its genesis wouldn't unbalance "$E = mc^2$." In presenting Special and General on the Science Channel you would however be calling out in the name of Einstein *and* in Adalbert Zweistein's name. But judging from common knowledge about *Abraham*'s case, a duo of deities couldn't have appeared to him back in Mesopotamia. (His insight connects somehow with the position answering to "monotheism.") The implication is that the change to the history of science couldn't have a likeness in the story of religion. *Zweistein? Vielleicht. Zwei Götter? Unmöglich.* The impossibility isn't clear from Genesis 12. True, interpreters are of one mind that a number of deities $n > 1$ wouldn't do. Why however must $n = 1$? As a straight textual matter, a single deity appears to Abraham in Genesis 12. If the number of deities is non-negotiable, why not the place?

At stake is more than the rendering of 21:33. Agreed, God has to figure as part of the Bible's truth-content. Agreed, God cannot be just one more chocolate in the box. To be sure, God's position as the support of the structure could be asserted elsewhere.[3] Still, it's reasonable to expect at least a preview in the first mention of the mission.

The usual reading of chapter 21's final portion indicates that what is at stake eludes the responsible parties. God supports the system. *That* they know. *Why* is God needed? Their attitude towards 21:33 signals an infirm grip.[4] The problems surrounding "monotheism" back up the diagnosis of infirmity. Genesis 1 is in an important respect external to the Bible's message. Failure to appreciate the fact buttresses the reading of 21:33 on which I am prepared to pin at most the silver medal.

Breathing the Word

To continue the recovery of what Abraham said in Beer-Sheba, let's consider the change from "Abram" to "Abraham." The renaming signals that the biological and cultural son of Terah has become God's man

– that God has adopted him, so to speak. More significantly, it conveys that he has taken God into himself. The dropping of "h" into "Abram" is a verbal version of the internalization, as is the shift from "Sarai" to "Sarah." In the opening chapters of Genesis, a special intimacy with God marks men and women off from the rest of the creation. What happens there happens again here. Is it fortuitous that "h" is appropriate for (hot) breath? To warm your hands, you exhale on them open-mouthed: *hhhhh* … For cooling, you purse your lips and blow: *fwwwww* … God's insertion of "h" into the founders' names is a parallel of his breathing life into the first man. In giving himself the new name, Abram expresses his newfound, God-based self-understanding. The point about "be-shem" and the point about "h" can even be linked. "Abraham" speaks God's name, as I claim Abraham is said to do in verse 33. Verse 33, that is, describes Abraham as breathing God's name into a world comprised of men and women who haven't (yet) recognized this deity.[5]

The truth of Relativity doesn't depend on Einstein. Abraham's (sc. God's) view's truth *is* relative to God. The inaccurate rendition of "be-shem" epitomizes failure to appreciate God's axiomatic status here. Although Abraham, as he is depicted in the biblical narrative, stands to the view that he inaugurates in the same way that, in the annals of science, Einstein stands to Relativity, evidence is to hand that *this* proportionality is incidental. Doesn't Sarah undergo the same change of name? More significantly still, what I said about "h" applies to the person in the Bible's story whom we know as "Adam."[6]

This point owes a lot to the imagination. Happily, a cognate point anchored in the part of the text under examination obviates the need to trust overly to fancy.

Chapter 21 describes Abraham calling out his message. Why do nine event-filled chapters pass before he acts into the world on the life-altering experience that Genesis 12 describes? The fact that Abraham *immediately* departs Mesopotamia upon receipt of God's "Go" (12:1) makes the question all the more pointed.

Here's a sketch of what happens in the chapters between 12 and 21. In Haran, midway through the journey, Abraham takes leave of the caravan. At the terminus of his trek, in Canaan, he has a variety of dealings with the inhabitants. He is drawn into an imbroglio in the Jordan Valley. By stages he moves southwards, finally pitching his tent in sparsely populated Beer-Sheba.

Interpreters and users of the Bible don't race past these episodes. They extract from them norms of comportment and ideals of conduct.

Were there no noble, honest, doughty, and open-handed Mesopotamians? Wouldn't Abraham have been selected in the first place because he exhibited these traits in his earlier life?

In fact, our expectation for the bolt from the blue to electrify all that happens afterwards is met. The chapters between 12 and 21 aren't merely edifying situational filler and/or character development.

Abraham's deeds starting with the incoming call from God and continuing to the outgoing call to the world *enact* the Bible's philosophical thrust. In form, Abraham's doings in the human sphere match the happenings in the extra-human sphere that are described in Genesis 1.

To see that this is so, apply a magnifier to the events listed four paragraphs back. Abraham departs, that is, *separates from*, Mesopotamia. Having travelled with his extended family to Haran, he *takes leave of* the bulk of its members. Reaching Canaan, he *shifts from* settled parts of the land to the desert. His nephew, Lot, he *extracts from* the clutches of the warlords. When Lot goes hither, he *goes yon*. From the locals he *distinguishes himself* through transactions that "set apart" (21:28) mine from thine, sometimes in kine (to Abimelech of Gerar seven ewe lambs for rights to a well [21:30]), sometimes in coin (to Ephron the Hittite four hundred shekels of silver for the burial cave of Machpelah [23:15]).

Abraham's doings between the receipt of God's call and the address to the world *don't* lie in a region whose contents are neutral vis-à-vis the call's meaning. The call was to "[g]o from." That's what the episodes depict him doing. I quoted Speiser: "the genesis of the biblical way is bound up with the beginnings of the monotheistic concept; both converge in the age, and presumably also the person, of Abraham." Abraham, through the description of whose actions "the beginnings of the monotheistic concept" are told, isn't a person who happens to do these things. As the narrators make their choices, their eyes are locked on Abraham's philosophical principle. These are the acts of a philosopher.

God appears to Abraham in Genesis 12. "Why does it take until Genesis 21 for Abraham to act on his newfound understanding?" The fact that no one asks the question is to me a further indication that Genesis 12 is misunderstood.[7]

The appearance of God to Abraham in Genesis 12 marks the biblical deity's first self-revelation to (historical) men and women. A hitherto unrecognized (ontological) principle is here acknowledged – a principle that, I am saying, breathes life into the separations that the chapters between 12 and 21 describe. These separations reflect Abraham's new understanding: men and women, the only things in whom the principle is seen, are separate from the natural creatures.

The biblical position, although couched in a theological idiom, is philosophical in character. Abraham's discovery of God may be likened to Wittgenstein's discovery of family resemblance and to Kant's discovery that not all knowledge arises out of the experience that is necessarily its beginning; each of these its discoverer presents as the smashing of an idol – of Platonic universality and of transcendental realism respectively.

A Great Nation or a Great Notion?

Abraham "called … the name of the Lord" (Genesis 21:33). Although Abraham signed on in Babylon, he commences his mission in Beer-Sheba. Shouldn't belief in the message have motivated the choice of a less desolate place than this parched backwater?

We need not take the setting factually. The choice of locale could be a caution to later sowers of the seed against sanguinity about a quick harvest, or a bountiful one.[8] Quite a few generations later, in the arid wastes of Sinai, doesn't God again reveal himself only indirectly?[9]

Although the clientele differ – Abraham addresses the few herders within earshot; Moses orates to more than half a million souls whose recent captivity will have made them all ears – the events constitute a couple. Abraham calls out God's name to the indifferent and accidental few. Moses asks its bearer for that name to supply to the expectant throng. The implication is that the new idea counts, not the national allegiances of the recipients.

On the assumption that the writers are modelling the patriarch's activity after Genesis 2, the specifics of the locale embody a point of theme. The Genesis 2 story begins "when no plant of the field was yet in the earth and no herb of the field had yet sprung up" (2:5). Then "a stream would rise up from the earth, and water the whole face of the ground" (2:6). That the text goes out of its way to say that Abraham "dug this well" (21:30) cements the parallel: God causes the seeds of the dormant world to sprout; Abraham gets the human enterprise going in a culture asleep to it. Abraham's insistence on his rights to the well is more, if so, than a claim to land. The water that *he* divined is unknown in the pagan world. From the biblical perspective, that world is, figuratively, a desert. Abraham's insistence presages a reclamation of land for the human enterprise.[10]

On the assumption that the writers are modelling the patriarch's activity after Genesis 2, it turns out that the last verse of chapter 21 isn't a perfunctory exeunt. "And Abraham resided as an alien many days in the land of the Philistines." The biblical view is that men and women are *permanent aliens* in nature. Since the Philistines among whom Abraham resides conceptualize themselves in natural terms, he is philosophically alien to them. According to the narrative, in Beer-Sheba nothing changes in that regard. The locals remain frozen in their beliefs despite the new resident's efforts "to till the ground" (2:5).

Abraham is promised a future as a great nation. Here are three reasons against taking the covenant as an agreement between parties, one of whom pledges to pay for services that the other pledges to render. One: Donin sees monotheism as a breakthrough. For Speiser, it marks the Bible as a departure from the status quo. Roth falls between the scholar and the believer. God offers what is, arguably, a great notion, either in itself great or great in Abraham's context. What sense does it make to say that I should compensate you for taking such a thing on board? Two: Abraham's theophany arguably gives dramatic form to a Eureka-moment. Like Archimedes in the tub, like Saul on the road to Damascus, like Newton beneath the tree, Abraham in Mesopotamia has a momentous insight. It makes more sense to construe "great nation" as a reference to adopters of the notion than to a nation comprised of Abraham's genetic issue.[11] By incorporating into their lives the new thinking, Abraham's ideological progeny, liberated from falsehood, elevate themselves.[12] Three: Given that God's call requires a total break with home and native land, Abraham's *immediate* compliance has to seem the more impulsive in view of the fact that his annals contain not a sliver of a Mesopotamian Kristallnacht. But if insight in the course of an otherwise humdrum life is the spark, the response makes excellent sense. Dramatized is the situation of a person whose faith in the insight overcomes his hesitations about going public.

The text has "great nation." I cannot grumble too loudly if on that basis readers balk at "great notion." To prevent hesitation from hardening, I will however add a pair of softeners.

Take "great nation" as it comes, and we're driven to conclude that God reneged. How could portraying the deity as reluctant to perform, or as unable, recommend what Abraham wrought, let alone authorize the character named "God"? Yet the redactors described the Temple's fate with all the emotion of a gum-chewing court stenographer. "In the fifth month, on the seventh day of the month – which was the nineteenth year of King Nebuchadnezzar, king of Babylon – Nebuzaradan, the captain of the bodyguard, a servant of the king of Babylon, came to Jerusalem. He burned the House of the Lord, the king's house, and all the houses of Jerusalem; every great house he burned down" (2 Kings 25:8–9). The career of monotheism did not however end with the sack of the Temple and the exile of the notables. Isn't that to say that the bargain wasn't violated?

Often, the Bible links happenings to outcomes like the sides of a coin rather than like causes to their effects. Take Genesis 3:17. "Because you have ... eaten of the tree [of knowledge], cursed is the ground because of you." At the end of the story, the man and the woman are "sent forth" (23) from the Garden. In my understanding of the goings on, God himself could not have obviated the difficult existence associated with the eating. Eden is (=) a place of ignorance of what the fruit of the tree of knowledge imparts. The ignorance consists in not having to give the next meal a thought. So eating of the tree of knowledge doesn't bring about the exclusion. Outside Eden is where(ever) one must work for bread. "Heed," God is saying in analytic mode, "or toil."

The two emollients should reduce resistance to equating (1) the greatness of which God speaks with (2) Abraham's progeny's adhering to the new way. The change *to* their lives is the change *in* their lives. When we elaborate the great notion, its theological content (God and the promise of a gift) is cut back. We are left with, so to speak, an immanent God.

The Inaugural Lecture

What does Abraham's inaugural address contain? The expected answer is that he asserts, and then elaborates, that God stands behind all things, "heaven, the heaven of heavens, with all their host, the earth and all that is on it, the seas and all that is in them" (Nehemiah 9:6).

To the degree that the answer reflects what the writers of the narrative believe, they need correction. Had Abraham begun with Genesis 1:1, the audience would have protested. "Apart from the introduction of the character named 'God,' we've heard it all before. What's more, functional equivalents of this character are found in the other stories to which we are alluding."

The first story isn't the Bible's – it isn't Abraham's – story. The reference to God apart, Genesis 1 resembles the cosmogonies of Greece and of Babylon. "The world that we know takes shape as a primordial chaos becomes increasingly differentiated."[13] Moreover, relative to our experience of things, the story has a lot to recommend it. As to God's presence in what is essentially a God-less story, a broadly political explanation is available. To those who accept the Bible, everything happens on God's watch. A form like "Elizabeth I defeated the Armada" comes naturally.[14]

Abram of Mesopotamian Ur could have declaimed Genesis 1. In the day that Abraham the covenanter arises in Beer-Sheba, what does he declaim? His opening words are Genesis 2:4: "In the day that the Lord God made the earth and the heavens ..." *This* story had never before been told. It is the Bible's – Abraham's – story.[15] It introduces monotheism, of which no one prior to Abraham knew. What however does monotheism have to do with the natural creation? The question is especially pointed given that the cosmogonic story of Genesis 1 is so plausible.

These issues we now explore. Monotheism, I'll show, has nothing to do with the natural creation. It's only with the advent of the first man in an act of artificial respiration that the significance of "one god" emerges.

3
Natural Philosophy: System and Humankind

Genesis 1

The philosophical core of the Bible comprises (1) Genesis 1, and (2) Genesis 2 and its continuation.[1] Because of an error to which the writers are party, it's less clear in their presentation than it should be that Genesis 1 takes a back seat to Genesis 2. In preparation for correcting the error, I'll link the current phase of the discussion with what I said at the outset.

The Bible is a philosophical work. Its centre is a thesis of philosophical anthropology: men and women belong to a distinctive category of being.

Fortuitously, the 1:1 of Rashi's commentary echoes my position on Genesis 1. Rabbi Isaac, Rashi reports, suggests that the Bible should have begun with Exodus 12:2, not with the all-time No. 1 1:1. "This month shall mark for you the beginning of months; it shall be the first month of the year for you." How does Rabbi Isaac rationalize so radical a revision to his most sacred document? Rashi spools out the reasoning.[2] "The Bible is the charter of the children of Israel, and the first law specifically for this group is enacted in Exodus 12. Being by and of and for the children of Israel, the Bible shouldn't pretend to be catholic."

The Bible revolves around the children of Israel. On that, the Rabbis agree. But holding as he does that the biblical narrative is consistent and coherent, Rashi denies that Genesis should be Exodus. As we therefore expect, he furnishes a construal that connects Genesis 1 internally with Exodus 12.

To defend the textual status quo consistently with maintaining that the Bible is Israelite-centric, Rashi has to fix the cosmogonic beginning as a satellite of the Star of David. He reasons: "Had the Bible not commenced with Genesis 1, the nations would have quoted the Book to challenge the territorial claims of the people of the Book. 'The world came into being independently of the deity who chose you. Your occupancy of the Promised Land is illegitimate.' But since the world as a whole is God's product, it is God's prerogative to parcel it out *ad libitum*. Thus Leviticus 25:23: '[T]he land is mine; with me you are but aliens and tenants.'"

That in a few salient respects the Bible *is* a partisan text doesn't make it Israelite-centric. Yet I agree that the positioning of Genesis 1 obstructs understanding. It's not because it skews the Bible's Israelite-centricity that the positioning gets in the way. Rather, as perceptive contemporaries would have seen, the contents of Genesis 1 infringe a copyright held by paganism. Contrary to what both Rabbi Isaac and Rashi maintain, Genesis 2 is the centre.

The Bible is not Israelite-centric, and Genesis 2 is its centre. According to those behind the text, the deity upon whom Abraham calls is superfluous to what Genesis 1 narrates. Not that Genesis 1 can simply be excised. Its account of the physical world supplies a contrast vital for bringing out what is philosophically unprecedented in the Bible. Unless the *contrastive* nature of this function is clear to us, we will have a difficult time with the Bible.

DH and the Two Creation Stories

The start of Genesis 1 most have by memory. Here is the start of Genesis 2: "These are the generations of the heavens and the earth when they were created." The sentence is the first part of verse 4. Verse 4 also includes the opening clause of the next sentence: "In the day that the Lord God made the earth and the heavens." Isn't this yesterday's news – a stylistic variant of Genesis 1:1?

In analyzing the two creation stories, many scholars make use of the Documentary Hypothesis. DH has it that the Tanakh's core part descends from a text that at a late stage in the early history of the children of Israel was fashioned from a number of yet earlier texts ("documents"). On various of the grounds that proponents of DH appeal to, Genesis 1 and Genesis 2, both of which tackle the primordial beginning, get assigned to different sources.

Many DH-ers view its implications for interpretation as catastrophic. "Different hands composed the constituent parts, each hand guided by the pressures exerted within its own sector of the Israelite world. It would be miraculous if the product were unitary in meaning." My dealings with the text lead me to conclude that whoever compiled the whole had a single idea in mind.[3] That is what I'm arguing here in regard to Genesis 1 and Genesis 2. The chapters fulfil *distinct but complementary* functions.

But although the chapters complement, they are joined in a way that is sure to confuse. Specifically, Genesis 1's subordinate status is not made clear. Those responsible for the product *think* what they set down to be more tightly unitary than it is. As a result, Genesis 2 is bound too closely to Genesis 1, which is not especially biblical. An error that, before Darwin, everyone made props the thinking up. On the basis of other things the product contains, it's possible to see that the fashioners would welcome a rewrite.

The Purpose of Genesis 1

Genesis 1 tells what happens during the first week – of seven days.[4] The days, except for the sabbath, are divided in two: from sunrise to noon, let's say, and from noon to sundown.

The first phase is an account of the creation of the physical world up to sundown on Day 4. From a condition of total disorder, separate regions precipitate out. Of these, a few undergo further differentiation. On Day 5 and Day 6 the organic things that occupy/inhabit the regions come into being.[5]

On Day 2, the watery area beneath the heavens is parted into an upper and a lower region. God inserts "a dome" (1:6) in the middle,[6] one that has variable spillways that manage the descent of the waters above onto, *inter alia*, the waters below. On Day 5, marine creatures come into being for the lower waters (the oceans, the lakes, the rivers), and birds for the region in between (the sky).

When the Bible's story is placed alongside Hesiod's ("Chaos was born first and after it came Gaia"), it is, we see, more rational or intelligible. Its basis is clear; the line of development too.

chaos → regions differentiated → inhabitants supplied for the regions

Of myth there is none. Consider Genesis 1:1's pairing: "the heavens and the earth." Doesn't an upper region entail a lower? By contrast, Hesiod's story of Ouranos (the heavens) coming into being from Gaia (the earth) courts incoherence.[7] Intending praise, Barnes characterizes Greek myth as "scientific." The Bible, clear of fantasy embellishment, would seem more worthy.

Although most readers would give the Bible the nod once its eschewal of myth is pointed out, there's a weightier respect in which, as they see it, Hesiod's story prevails. "The feature of the physical realm that the Bible's alignment of the first three days with the next three brings out, namely systematic integration, is explained by appeal to purpose or design."

In composing Genesis 1, the Bible's writers have in their minds' eyes the construction of a house. Unlike a bird nest or a beaver lodge, a house is the product of design.[8] In a house, the faucet is in the bath because that's where the plumber has installed it. The plumber has installed it there because it's where the builder has run the pipes. The location is intended for the thing. The garage entrance is more than eight feet wide because fin-to-fin the automobile measures almost six. The front entrance is narrower because it is meant to serve as a portal for people on foot. If the work goes according to plan, each thing ends up in its allotted place. Observe the vocabulary: "design," "purpose," "intention."

None of this survives in Darwin. Doesn't it follow that the Bible *can't* be praised over *Theogony*? Not that Hesiod knows aught about random mutation and situational advantage. Rather, his modelling of primordial coming-into-being in sexual terms gives design a wide berth. This avoidance might even be deliberate. Suspicion of the idea of purpose has an ancestry. A feature of Hesiod's story of generational strife is that the chief male gods are driven from the loins. The forward-looking motives of love have no part in it.

That is how it seems. In reality, the Bible's use of purpose and design in Genesis 1 is equivocal.

Design Decommissioned

A slight switch, and the Bible's account of the emergence of the natural world takes on a different look than a purpose-employing or design-invoking one.

The sky teems with birds. How is that? Here's a plausible story. Birds have the wherewithal – porous bones and feathers – for that habitat. Had they lacked the features, they wouldn't *ceteris paribus* have got there in the first place. If some other thing had been better suited to the location, birds would have been displaced.

The story supplies the germ for Darwinian adaptation. Does the Bible contain that germ? Here are verses 11 and 12 of Genesis 1: "Then God said, 'Let the earth put forth vegetation …' And it was so. The earth brought forth vegetation …" Verse 20 runs thus: "And God said, 'Let the waters bring forth swarms of living creatures …'" The sense of verses 11 and 12 is that *the earth* brings forth plant life;[9] of verse 20, that *the waters* churn out marine dwellers. In a few cases (in verse 11 for instance) the text uses the *cognate accusative* construction, a paradigm example of which is "dance a dance." Independently of the gyrations on the floor there is no dance. Just so, the biblical idea is that an internal program (the laws of nature) has the physical world forming from a condition of formlessness.

The composers do not extend the pattern through the whole of Genesis 1. The story they tell isn't allowed to outrun their actual experience by much. But, in a telltale manner, they are gesturing at an extension.

A few paragraphs hence, I'll discuss the separation of the waters into upper and lower. God, it is said in this regard, "made" (6) the dome. The same verb is used in verse 25 with regard to land animals. Observe that in reference to sea creatures and birds, "create" (21), which figures in verse 1, appears. One *could* read the story of the emergence of sea creatures and of birds as a story of the creation naturally bringing them forth: the conditions as they were sufficed. That's a not implausible deflationary reading of "So God created" (ibid.).

The greater difficulty of imagining land animals emerging on terra firma along the lines of fish in churning waters and birds in turbulent air, let alone imagining them springing up on the barren earth as does vegetation, makes reasonable the distinction both from the case of plants, where neither "made" nor "created" is used, and also from the case of marine animals and birds, with its "created." The writers are arranging the cases of the emergence of life from the simple (plants) to the more complex (fish, birds), to the most complex (land animals).

The implication? If they could they would extend to the complex the pattern of the simple. But they can't. This leaves in the story the idea of deliberate intervention – making. The generation of overall order is thought of in terms of purpose. "How else," it might be asked, "can an integrated system of this complexity come about than deliberately?" In

Genesis 1 the writers therefore characterize the whole as the product of a designing intelligence. The system is treated as an *artefact*.

Although Genesis 1 cannot be *accurately* reconstructed unless the reconstructor appeals to the idea of purpose,[10] reading along the preceding lines discloses the presence of internal resistance to the idea. So Genesis 1 might be *rationally* reconstructed without the appeal.

The world of Genesis 1 is a system: a place for everything and everything in its place. The narrative tracks the system onwards from a formless beginning. Distinct regions emerge: heavens and earth, upper and lower waters, wet areas on earth and dry land. Then, inhabitants emerge for the regions: celestial bodies, plants, marine creatures and birds, land animals; finally, men and women. The thinkers maintain that internal principles govern the differentiation of the chaos and (some of) the formation of (some of) the inhabitants, like the principle, of which Big Bang theorists speak, that as temperature decreases, the energy soup congeals into more discrete objects.

When in Genesis 1 the narrators describe the creation, they therefore employ a *deistic* pattern: the result comes about in accordance with the principles. God may preside, but he isn't active. What about the instances where God intervenes? By comparing the separation of upper and lower waters, where God steps in, with the separation of watery and dry areas on earth, where God stands apart, I'll argue that the deistic pattern is the default one.

Here, in verses 6 and 7, is the first separation:

> And God said, "Let there be a dome in the midst of the waters, and let it separate the waters from the waters." So God made the dome and separated the waters that were under the dome from the waters that were above the dome.

Here, in verse 9, is the second:

> And God said, "Let the waters under the [dome] be gathered together into one place, and let the dry land appear." And it was so.

In the second separation, God doesn't pull on his boots. As the waters on earth collect, dry areas appear. Why, then, should God be said to have "made" the dome in the first case? Waters we see pooling, for example, after a downpour. In our experience, the separation of upper liquids from lower liquids requires by contrast *the insertion* of barriers.[11]

When the Bible departs the deistic pattern, it's not that the thinkers see that the true story isn't a deistic one. It's that they can't see how to tell the story deistically. Look again at verses 6 and 7. You might not now feel disinclined to go along with me in expanding verse 7 thus. "So, having waited in vain for it to congeal in the midst of the waters, God made the dome &c."

The deistic pattern is pressed as far as the writers can see it going; and then it is pressed an inch or two into the dark. It follows that the thinkers would welcome its extension.[12] Here's an illuminating one.

God's "Let there be light" (3) is invariably held up as divine activity at its purest: God asks; the world answers. But the statement, one verse later, that God "separated the light from the dark" indicates that extrusion from a dusky amalgam is necessary before the final word can be spoken. It follows that "Let there be light" is a *summary* of what's in the offing, not a play-by-play of its being offered. The starting condition with respect to light is, then, comparable to the initial waste and void; more relevantly to our comparison, it's like the initial condition with respect to dry land.

Of dry land to plant our feet on none exists at the start. It is not the case, however, that terra firma has to be added from the outside. The implication is that although initially there is no light to see by, the makings of it are present.

Sense is easily made of the mixed condition for the wet and the dry: the moist – mud, marsh, mire. The idea of separation is therefore intelligible. A sodden sponge is wrung over a glass. Done the wringing, the glass is half full, the sponge dry. What however corresponds to the drenched sponge for light and dark?

Caleb is pawing at the back door. Flashlight in hand, you proceed for the evening walk.[13] "Light," you say, switching on the beam. Light there is. But a fog blankets the neighbourhood, so you are still groping. A milky volume of space, a mixture of light and dark, envelops you. (Recall Thomas Mann's "white darkness.") For the beam to be effective, the particles constituting the aerosol need first to coagulate. How might this come about? It might, if the cohesive forces between them cause the particles to agglomerate as they lose energy. The result of the clumping? A (greater) separation of light from dark.

Many take "'Let there be light'; and there was light" as the paradigm of divine creative activity. The fit of the preceding way of handling the words with the wider text is therefore significant. The naturalization of the magical-looking case (light and dark emerge from a mixed condition, as do dry and wet) gives greater unity to the whole – an interpretive plus.

As to the inhabiting of the differentiated regions, we again find the contrast between what happens on its own and what comes about through active intervention. "[T]he earth brought forth vegetation" (12). Because the writers are in the dark as to how natural processes of the sort they experience could generate fish, birds, and land animals, they supplement God's commands, "Let the waters bring forth" (20) and "Let the earth bring forth" (24), with, respectively, "God created … every living creature … with which the waters swarm" (21) and "God made the wild animals of the earth of every kind" (25).

For wet and dry, for light and dark, for plants of the field, appeal to God's active contribution isn't needed. In these cases no doubt is present, as doubt is present in the case of upper and lower, where one can say either that the dome separates upper from lower or that God makes the dome separate the two. And it's clear why. The story tracks everyday experience.

Integrated system is a broader concept than *artefact*.[14] The story in Genesis 1 is predicated on the physical world's being (as it is) a system. The story is misleading in its details because the model of an artefact's emergence guides the tellers, and artefacts are designed systems. The concepts – *system, design* – coalesce. Our discussion confirms that so far as Genesis 1 goes the writers would prefer to avoid the notion of purpose. The cognate accusative construction is a signal. The second member of <location, occupant> comes to be in accordance with the principles operative within the first. Since prior to Darwin no one could have told a credible purpose-free story, it's not surprising that most interpreters treat the signal like static on the radio. Nevertheless, given that resistance is put up within the text to allowing the category of artefact to engulf integrated systems – that is, resistance to classifying all integrated systems in the category of the made – lending the Bible writers our hard-won knowledge wouldn't be anachronistic.

The Bible frequently serves for target practice in the boot camps of science *because* the fabric of its cosmogony displays the idea of design. But the idea's presence is due to the fact that when the writers think of systems their models are products of design.[15] That is why God (the only deity the writers are prepared to appeal to) is part of this part of the tale. God's presence in Genesis 1, it may be inferred, is for them *faute de mieux*. The implication of our having *mieux*-ed is that Genesis 1 is secondary to the Bible's thrust.

Similar remarks apply to philosophers, many of whom on their more reflective plane challenge the postulation that there is a designer behind the natural world. David Hume, an astute critic of *natural religion*, doesn't deny that that world is a system. Matter, he conjectures, is instinct with a principle whose operation accounts for the system's emergence.[16] If what I've said is credible, the writers of the Bible could have conjectured the same. In fact, it's possible to read them as surmising Hume's surmise. My claim that God is not creative with respect to the physical world is, then, the claim that the Bible teaches natural *ir*religion.

Men and Women: The Origin of the Species in Genesis 1

At least up to and including verse 25, Genesis 1, in its description of the development of the physical realm, resembles pagan works such as *Theogony*.[17] But on the afternoon of Day 6, a part of the physical realm is represented as bearing a special relationship to the Bible's deity. Here is verse 26.

> Then God said, "Let us make humankind in our image, according to our likeness; and let them have dominion over the fish of the sea, and over the birds of the air, and over the cattle, and over all the wild animals of the earth, and over every creeping thing that creeps upon the earth."

In Genesis 1's description of the creation of the heavens and the earth, are the heavens stated to be nearer the creator? They aren't. Nor are either the heavens or the earth designated as bearing to God a unique resemblance. Nor yet are plants, and non-human animals said when *they* emerge to have a distinctive likeness to the deity.

That verse 26 should attract attention is, then, no surprise. It's not that in the verse the world's creatures that interest us most are first referred to. Were it just a matter of Xs' fascination with pictures of Xs, then verse 20, not verse 26, would, *per impossibile*, attract the attention of fish. Rather, verse 26 breaks with the pattern that up until then has been followed. The Bible seems to be telling of *discontinuity* in the world's organic part – discontinuity, moreover, in that one element of the creation does have a greater proximity or likeness to the creator. This, certainly, is an attention grabber, as much, *per impossibile*, to fish as to men and women.

Invariably, interpreters view the mention of divine intervention as indicating that the thinkers behind verse 26 held that some creatures are unlike others in more than just anatomical respects. But although it's true that verse 26 sets men and women apart, it's not true that it sets them sharply apart.[18] The key to wisdom here is recognizing that God doesn't first create humankind and only afterwards bestow dominion. To have made fox or bear beneficiaries of the bestowal, God would have had to bring them into the world on the afternoon of Day 6, in which event they would have been vulpine and ursine men and women. Since "for Xs to have been be like Ys, they would have had to"-connections between Xs and Ys are senseless, not just counterfactual, unless X-type things and Y-type things have a common denominator, the claim that the Xs and the Ys in this case are being set sharply apart is falsified.[19]

Verse 26 turns out to say the reverse of what it is always understood to say. It does not deny continuity. A grasp of how dominion relates to God-likeness will bring out the continuity that it defends.

Ecologists find the biblical position repellent. "Holy Writ gives men and women licence to stomp upon the natural world, to subdue it." True, the Hebrew word translated "dominion" sounds harsh. Think of "dominate" as used in sports. "Ali dominated Liston." Yet English "dominion," fairly neutral to our ears, turns out partly for that reason to be inspired. "Dominion" has more to it than "domination." That more, as I'll now explain, doesn't imply "subdue," "trample," "lord it over," "despoil."

Why, and how sharply, are men and women, "humankind" in the NRSV's rendering, set apart?

And a second question: Prior to the advent of humankind, did a dominant creature walk the earth? The familiar idea that the lion tops the (non-human) chain of predation – the food chain – supports an affirmative. Since animals dominate plants, doesn't the unpredated predator have dominion over all else?

Here's the reasoning behind the affirmative: "A finite vertical series has to have a top. In investing the lion (or, in their ages, the trilobite and the dinosaur), we are saying that it occupies the highest position."

"When men and women arrive they *take over* top spot, deposing the incumbent." If this were so, why should God be represented as *bestowing* upon them the place of honour? From the Bible's description, the correct inference is that when men and women are characterized as having dominion they are *not* being said to be uneaten eaters. Otherwise, a different species would have worn ermine prior to noon of Day 6. This, however, is not biblically possible. God created land animals on the morning of Day 5. No talk is heard of image and likeness. Bestowal isn't mentioned.

What does "image and likeness" mean? The word "dominion" is, I repeat, an inspired choice.

"Dominus" is Latin for "God." Use of the word plugs the image and likeness claim (henceforth "the likeness claim") into the dominion claim. In the following sense, to be in God's image and likeness is to have dominion. It's being like God, *similis Domino esse*. As we shall see, creatures who are said to have dominion *are* like God.

Alone in the natural creation, men and women are God-like. Many understand the affinity in religious terms: God-likeness signals that men and women are partly extra-natural.[20] Genesis 1 supplies no more than an excuse for such an understanding.

However like God men and women are, identical to God they are not. The pertinent respect of likeness has nothing to do with physical properties.[21] God's *non-physicality* is what counts. Putting some physical language to figurative use, we might usefully say that God is *outside* the world of space and time, or that God *occupies no place* in that world, or that God is *above and beyond*. Outsideness, above-and-beyondness, placelessness, is the common denominator. God, being uncreated, is displaced from all creatures. That's axiomatic. Men and women, among creatures, are displaced. That's the anthropological thesis of Genesis 1.

"The mountain dominates the valley." "The skyscrapers dominate the downtown core." The dominator of the dominator/dominated pair is not being applauded, nor is pity being expressed towards the dominated. Since God is above, or outside, or beyond, why not say that God, Dominus, dominates in this *neutral* sense?

The Bible says that men and women have dominion. The neutral sense of "dominion" *is* the term's sense in Genesis 1. Men and women are above; they are beyond; they are outside. Such being the case, endorsing the position doesn't oblige us to shut our eyes to a fact that back then was even more apparent: men and women do not bestride the natural world like kings and queens. As for the colossus of glass and steel that dominates the downtown core, can't it be under threat – of collapse – due to the restlessness of the earth far below?

"What does it mean when we say that men and women are above, outside, beyond?" The clause needs explaining. Taken as it comes, it does however seem to state a truth. When we excavate the earlier part of the story, textual support for the truth it seems to state is unearthed.

The Blessing of the Fish

Day 5. Afternoon. Up to now, if a reaction of God's is reported to the stocking of a vacant region, it is the reaction of seeing that it is good. Then, closing out the phase, the refrain "And there was evening and there was morning" is sounded. In *this* case, between the seeing (21) and the sounding (23) God is said to lift his countenance to the fish (22).

> God blessed them, saying "Be fruitful and multiply and fill the waters of the seas."

"A blessing? What kind of fish story is that?" The composers of verse 22 intend to generate puzzlement. Observe that apart from its application here, "be fruitful and multiply" figures only in the case of humankind (28). There too God gives a blessing. What parallel are the writers drawing?

Robert Sacks furnishes an answer.

> How is this kinship to be understood? The denizens of the seas indeed live a kind of watery existence. They neither follow the ecliptic as does the sun nor are they restricted in the direction of their motion as are the other animals ... Man shares this openness of direction with the fish. The way was not marked for him in the beginning. It had to develop, and even then he was apt to wander from his path. Since man could err, he too required a blessing.[22]

In their watery domain, fish move in every direction. Up. Down. Left. Right. Forward. Backward. Diagonally. At any location, a fish can remain stationary too. Land animals are by contrast restricted to the two-dimensional surface. Leap? What goes up must come down. Birds too can move in every direction in *their* ocean. But should it cease to flap its wings, a bird will plummet. Nor, unlike a squid in water, does a bird, except when the headwinds are violent, move in reverse. And that movement, like an uprooted tree's spiralling in a twister's vortex, is not its own.

I cannot give my blessing to Sacks's reading. Still, what he says supplies wherewithal for sustaining the claim that God-likeness plugs into dominion.

It's by aligning them with fish that the Bible makes the point that men and women do not fit as seamlessly as the other creatures into the woof of creation as woven in the first five and a half days. And it makes the point *without representing men and women as having been parachuted onto the pattern from the outside*, like a Lacoste crocodile onto a knitted garment. "Fish deviate" is an alert not to take the human case's involving a dropped stitch as ground for concluding that men and women aren't part of the natural fabric. Had Sacks stated that the validity of the

Bible's point requires *only a figurative likeness* with fish, he would have noticed that, compatibly with what he says the Bible is saying, men and women might stand in *no literal relation of likeness* to God. Here too, the link ("kinship") might be figurative. Since, in the Genesis 1 story, the likeness claim differentiates us from the other creatures, Sacks's construal of verse 22 is refuted. To understand the Bible, we must go beyond the parallel between men and women and fish (men and women need to be blessed; fish also need a blessing) and look at the parallel between men and women and God (men and women are made in God's image and likeness). *Must*, for it's false to say, as Sacks does, that men and women "too" require a blessing. If applicable, the "too" could only apply to God, blessed be he.

Certainly, fish are incidental to the point about the blessing. That's not the present objection, though. The objection is that on Sacks's reading the assertion of God-likeness is incidental to the Bible's argument. But it's utterly counterintuitive when working out the argument to elevate the obviously figurative "fish are like men and women" over the importantly informative "men and women are like God."[23]

Aficionados would cite their field-and-stream observations to refute Sacks's assertion about the marine dwellers. This confirms that the sense of the assertion is ichthyological; Sacks's interpretation of the blessing ends where it starts: under water. The claim that men and women are made in God's image and likeness is as a result interpretively gutted. "Didn't you yourself assert that God plays no *indispensable* role in the Bible's opening chapter?" I did. "Dispensable" isn't however synonymous with "interpretively irrelevant." If the Bible's mention of God gives us a handle on something elusive about men and women, the deity contributes more basically to the argument than do Sacks's fish.

Needed is a construal on which what is said about fish relates to what is said about men and women as closely as the two relate on Sacks's reading, and on which, also, the assertion that men and women are God-like contributes to bringing out the relationship.

"Dominion"

Fish are in the sea; birds, in the air; planets wheel in solar orbits. But when it comes to us, men and women of the world, a niche is lacking. *Alone among the species, we have no domain*. Being domain-bound is (=) not having dominion. Having dominion has naught to do with polluting, trampling, despoiling.[24] The ecological critics are not without a leg to stand on. But here they limp. Kinship with God, as the Bible presents it, isn't kingship over all (else) that God made.[25]

God is extra-natural. Not occupying any natural place, God, *a fortiori*, hasn't a special one. We men and women, then, are like God, literally so. Also, our being God-like in this aspect does not require that God give us what he has. The talk of God-likeness *makes clear* the (special) character of the human case. It doesn't *present its truth-basis*. In addition, the God-likeness claim now connects internally to the dominion claim.

That men and women have no domain is known on the positive level. Illustrations comprehensible apart from any of the Bible's preoccupations are legion in the text. The first man and the first woman get uprooted from the Garden. Cain, the settler, supplants Abel, the wanderer. Lot strays from shepherding ways for city life. Looking to the future, *we* envisage lifting off to the planets.

We have no domain. *That's* what is being said of us. "If the point is clear on the positive level, why link it to God-likeness?" The fact that God has no place in the whole is clearer than the same fact about us.

Some might think that they hear in the God-likeness assertion this stronger claim. "Men and women participate in God's nature." Let me neutralize the thought.

Consider two cakes from the same batch. The truth of "cake A is like cake B" is not due to A's giving B its ingredients. Just so, it doesn't have to result from God's sharing himself with them that men and women, like the biblical deity, are outside the whole. One who insists on applying the language of participation to Genesis 1's likeness claim has to put "God participates in the nature of men and women" on an equal footing with "Men and women participate in God's nature."[26]

The Genesis 1 story, the ascription of dominion included, is down-to-earth. Far less in it is susceptible of relevant theological elaboration than all non-scholarly readers see – indeed, far less than most secular critics and professional interpreters see.

The Bible cannot be saying that on the afternoon of Day 6 dominion is alienated to humankind from a creature already on the prowl. The creature frequently designated the loser when the sun crosses the meridian never had dominion. "Aren't lions atop the food chain?" By contrast with antelopes, lions on the Serengeti do seem nonchalant. Still, the idea of a food chain is an artificial idea.

According to Genesis 1, nature is a system. Thus the conjunctive phrase in the chapter's first verse: "the heavens and the earth." The position is not that the heavens usurped the place of honour that had previously been the earth's. Rather, the two go together. Just so, it is as true to say that lions depend on antelopes as to say that lions dominate antelopes.

Nature is a system that develops through stages of increasing differentiation. A stage is not static. It's a condition in which equilibrium is maintained. Some quantities are conserved through the exchanges characteristic of the stage.[27]

In everyday thought and talk, we readily enough distinguish changes internal to a system (the party proceeds from cocktails to dinner) from changes due to outside factors (party crashers overturn the sweet table). Often, however, especially in our dealings with the extra-human world, the line we draw leaves too little inside. Consider a herd of animals. Head counts reveal that the number of adult males is stable, as are the numbers of adult females and of juveniles. The herd, we conclude, is in equilibrium. Obviously, birth at the front end and death from wear and tear at the back aren't the only things that keep the ratios constant. Without predation, the size of the herd might increase unchecked. How indeed can one speak intelligibly of natural life expectancy without factoring in endings in the jaws of a predator? From the vantage point of the herd how does predation differ from immunological deficiency within an individual? What about the availability of food? The herd itself is not the system. The predators belong too. It's falsifying to liken them to party crashers.

The impact of an asteroid was, we are told, the flood of the dinosaurs. Isn't the earth part of a whole that encompasses the asteroid belt? So isn't the natural ascription of the extinction to an outside factor incorrect?

Are we doing what we think when we think in (what we naturally think are) natural terms? These remarks suggest that a statistical meaning alone attaches to a phrase like "natural life expectancy." Kant's transcendental idealism bears some similarities to the Bible's deepest view on this, a view at odds with the thought that everyday's "natural" means what we think it means.

In likening them to God, the Bible is not excluding men and women from nature. The position is that men and women lack a natural domain. Unlike the niche-bound, they aren't constituted primed for the interaction with the system that is (non-human) nature. Their lives are therefore, in a distinctive way, risky. That's why a blessing is appropriate. Intending a contrast, Sacks says, rightly enough, that men and women have no set way. But he goes wrong in inferring that men and woman can go wrong. (It's inconsequent to pass from "X lacks a set way" to "X is apt to be wayward.") The related point suggests itself that, usually, the giver of a blessing is wishing *bonne chance* to the getter. If staying on the rails were the wished-for thing, a grounding would follow the parental benediction. The point is not that men and women can go wrong. The issue of depravity belongs to Genesis 2. The blessing is in Genesis 1.

Sacks's gloss on verse 22 – "The way was not marked for him in the beginning" – confirms the criticism. "Him" is third person singular. But Genesis 1 is about *humankind*. Verse 26 describes *humankind*'s creation. What is blessed in Genesis 1? The plural "them" appears in verse 22. It appears in verse 28. My reading makes sense of the blessing where Genesis 1 locates it: on the level of the species. Talk of niches is species talk. When we come to Genesis 2 we'll see that Sacks is heedless of what turns out to be the crucial distinction with Genesis 1.

I am confident in the reading. The supporting point has to do with the adjective "good" that through nearly the whole of Genesis 1 is used to express God's view of what has been wrought. "Good" does not function in a moral sense. "X is good" means "X is as it should be."

"Nearly the whole." At the close of the chapter, the litany changes. "God saw everything that he had made, and indeed, it was very good" (31). If nature were a single system, unmodified "good" would suffice. Humankind, however, is separate. The human part of the creation does not fit in. So, "very good."

"Isn't the suggestion of 'very good' that it's better that way?" It remains true, though, that the idea of a contrast is unlikely to occur to the reader before he or she comes upon the intensifier. Encountering "very good," he or she will think of a lesser amount of the commodity, even of its absence. This points in the direction of Genesis 2, where "bad" stands alongside "good."[28]

Mortality is a preoccupation in the Book of Genesis. According to casual readers, most scholars too, it figures from the start. In fact, it doesn't enter until Genesis 2. Because Genesis 1 describes the creation of the world entire, a world whose (living) creatures exit with the same frequency that they enter, this should puzzle skimmers and delvers both.

Mortality enters along with the fruit of the tree of knowledge of good *and* bad. "Bad" is absent from Genesis 1. It doesn't belong. So mortality is absent because *it* doesn't belong. This confirms that the world of Genesis 1 is a system. It isn't death that has the final say in it. It's recycling. And recycling's say, as its name indicates, isn't as final. I can recycle Weinberg: "the disappearance, sc. the death, of Peter is not accompanied by the appearance, sc. the birth, of Paul." No "quantity" is conserved, as is the sum of H_2O molecules and OH ions in a glass of water.

How is it that Peter and Paul are located within the sweep of the reaper's scythe? The nominal answer is that they are particulars. "According to you, doesn't God transmit the particularity to the man in Genesis 2, and doesn't the particularity, according to you, get communicated to each of us? Isn't God immortal?" According to me, twice yes. But the Bible's answer to the last question isn't a categorical affirmative. Suffice it for the moment to say that although particularity may not rule immortality out, of mortality it is a precondition. Augustine makes this point – from the sower's side. "Ut initium esset, homo creatus est."[29] Not " ... mundus creatus est." Not " ... natura creata est." Not even "humanitas creata est."

A second point has to do with a standing issue of discussion for the religious and for the anti-religious both: theodicy. If God's appearance in Genesis 1 is inessential, then natural evil (as it is naturally denominated) does not challenge God's justice. A cancerous growth invades the body. The "programs" of the cancer and of the immune system conflict. The "victory" of the tumour can no more be characterized as "bad" than the body's "repulse" of it can be called "good." Whatever happens accords with the laws governing the various things. Cancerous tissue and non-cancerous tissue are like sun and rain. To be sure, we are homers in this matter. But the favouritism isn't objectively justified. Asked to line up the two pairs, a desert dweller might link downpour rather than radiation to cancer.

Let's take stock. One: Save for a few vague, possibly proleptic, gestures towards the (irreducibly) non-natural, Genesis 1 tells a natural story. Nature is represented as a physical system. Two: While purpose figures in the story of the creation, it doesn't figure ineluctably. The representation of God actively intervening is a *pis aller*. Three: The likeness to God that is used to mark humankind off from the rest enfolds no theological commitments. The writers are making this God-independent point: among natural things, non-human ones have niches; men and women don't. The human component of nature is part of nature.

4
Philosophical Anthropology: First Person, Singular

"Elohim" and "Yahweh"

What Roth sees as the Bible's lack of interest in science leads him to enter a complaint. The lack of interest he regards as indicative of an immature philosophical impulse. In point of fact, the Bible is guiltless. Genesis 1 is a response of the scientific type to the natural world. In the manner of effective inquiry of this type, the response transmutes wonder into understanding. "Upper waters separated from lower waters by a dome. *That's* what rain's all about!" That processes of evaporation and condensation have taken over explanatorily from the physical barrier is immaterial. Newton's explanations too have been overtaken. Yet those who wondered about the motion of the planets were certainly helped by his laws. "Their momentum. The pull of the sun. Like a stone in a sling." In a sense, though, Roth is right. Vis-à-vis the Bible's core message, Genesis 1 *is* peripheral. "Doesn't this sustain the charge of dogmatism?" It doesn't. The Bibleists have reasons for looking in a different direction. It's Abram the Mesopotamian who is doing the talking in Genesis 1. Abraham the monotheist has other fry, blessing-needing fry, to fish.

Roth sees Jewish thinking through lenses ground to a (Western) philosopher's prescription. Some scholars who, like Roth, come at the Bible from philosophy appreciate what he misses.

In their commentary on the Presocratics, G.S. Kirk and J.E. Raven discuss the similarities and differences between, on the one side, Greek and Babylonian cosmogonies, and, on the other side, the Bible's account of beginnings. Of the latter, they assert that

> the abstract Elohim of the first chapter [of Genesis] is replaced by the fully anthropomorphic and much cruder [Y]ahweh of the second, and the vague "God created man in his own image" of chapter 1 is repeated in a far more graphic and more primitive form in the second chapter, where [Y]ahweh creates man out of dust and breathes life into his nostrils.[1]

Because Greek thinking has an affinity for the general and the abstract, the commentators find the god of Genesis 2 "cruder" and "more primitive."

Contrary to the thinking of Kirk and Raven, Genesis 1 and Genesis 2 aren't windows on the same scene. The natural world of Genesis 1 is devoid of genuine particulars. It's the act of adding particulars to the system that makes the deity of Genesis 2 *the* deity of the Bible. *The making of the man is the making of the deity of the Bible.* On its critical side, monotheism is therefore the view, targeting worshippers of the "other gods," that the natural realm leaves each one of us absent and unaccounted for.[2]

Kirk and Raven observe that the deity is referred to as "Elohim" in Genesis 1, as "Yahweh" in Genesis 2. But although the chapters are to them more than stylistic variants, they fail to appreciate how sharply the two differ. The likeness claim makes full sense in natural terms. Not so the breath-of-life claim. Also, fundamental in the opening chapter are the features that I identified as central to the Greek proto-philosophical accounts: naturalism and generality. Small wonder Kirk and Raven prefer Genesis 1.

Genesis 2's epochal novelty should by now be sensed. This is the place to amplify the animadversions regarding "polytheism."

The analysis of Genesis 1 revealed a cosmogony of the pagan sort. The implication is that the one-deity/more-than-one-deity distinction boils down to a distinction between a unified system and a looser assembly. The second position is better labelled "pluralistic naturalism." An apt denomination for the first is "monistic naturalism." Monistic naturalism? This is the modern scientific ideal.

Abraham turned his caravan south upon exiting Mesopotamia. The children of Israel did not sojourn among the pagans of Hellas. There is however an Egyptian context for what I am saying.

Some specialists opine that monotheism had a brief spring on the banks of the Nile. Against the extant form of worship, Akhenaten, whose dates overlap the conjectured date of the exodus of the Israelites from the land of the pharaohs,[3] promoted the sun deity to sole sovereignty. In the light of our discussion of Plato and of Olympian religion, this looks like a shift to monism. James P. Allen quotes Egyptologist Jan Assmann's support: "We stand here at the origin less of the monotheistic world religions than of natural philosophy. If [Akhenaten's] religion had succeeded, we should have expected it to produce a Thales [sc. a material monist] rather than a Moses [sc. a monotheist]."[4]

The contrast between Genesis 1's (plural form) "Elohim" and Genesis 2's (singular form) "Yahweh" correlates with the distinction between the chapters.[5] Whether or not the verbal contrast is deliberately adjusted to the substantive one, the singular form suits the god of Abraham, Isaac, and Israel.

Why is it wrong to say of Abraham that at the gathering in Beer-Sheba he calls out Genesis 1? It's wrong because Genesis 1 asserts something that Abram believed.

The difference between Genesis 1's story and the story of Genesis 2 is hard to miss. *How* the verses up to the middle of Genesis 2's verse 4 relate to the chapter as a whole is a topic of debate. Most commentators hold that the four and a half verses constitute a backwards-looking summary. Be this as may be, the patch of text from the middle of verse 4 to the end of verse 7 departs Genesis 1. Rather than an undifferentiated chaos, we have stasis, "for the Lord God had not caused it to rain upon the earth, and there was no one to till the ground" (5). Of the two pertinent points here, the second supports my argument about God's (in)activity in the Genesis 1 story. Point 1: The writers/thinkers are deliberately eschewing the model of chaos-and-differentiation. (Many English translations begin 2:6 with "instead.") Point 2: In this case, internal processes can't account for what comes about. For there are none. God's "plant[ing] a garden" (8) leaves little doubt that this is the text's point.

The parallel between the garden-making and the man-making of verse 7 – "the Lord God formed [the] man from the dust of the ground" – raises the key question. What is it about the human case that precludes a natural story?

Genesis 2

The full-scale treatment of Genesis 2 I'll begin by drawing attention to a widespread variation in how a few biblical verses are rendered into English. That different translators translate differently will surprise no one. But the relaxed attitude to the lack of uniformity in this case has a deeper explanation. In advance, Genesis 1 and Genesis 2 are run together thematically.

Important for our examination are three verses: verse 26 from chapter 1, and verses 7 and 8 from chapter 2. The translation is the NRSV.

1:26	Then God said, "Let us make humankind in our image and likeness; and let them have dominion over the fish of the sea, and over the birds of the air. And over the cattle, and over all the wild animals of the earth, and over every creeping thing that creeps upon the earth."	ויאמר אלוהים נאשה אדם בצלמנו כדמותנו וירדו בדגת הים ובעוף השמים ובבהמה ובכל הארץ ובכל הרמש הרמש על הארץ.
2:7	then the Lord God formed man from the dust of the ground, and breathed into his nostrils the breath of life; and the man became a living being.	וייצר יהוה אלוהים את האדם עפר מן האדמה ויפח באפיו נשמת חיים ויהי האדם לנפש חיה.
2:8	And the Lord God planted a garden in Eden, in the east; and there he put the man whom he had formed.	ויטע יהוה אלוהים גן בעדן מקדם וישם שם את האדם אשר יצר.

I've highlighted (by enlarging) several words. Two are key. The key word in 1:26 is "אדם." This is the common noun "man." In 2:7, and again in 2:8, the key word is "האדם." Here, the definite article is attached to the common noun. For reasons that will become clear, I have also enlarged two other words.

Here is how a number of English versions translate the two key-words.[6]

	1:26 אדם	2:7 האדם	2:8 האדם
NRSV	humankind	man	the man
Mechon-Mamre	man	man	the man
NET Bible (Bible.org)	humankind	the man	the man
King James	man	man	the man
New International Version	mankind	a man	the man
New Life Version	man	man	the man
English Standard Version	man	the man	the man
Young's Literal Translation	man	the man	the man
Jewish Publication Society	man	man	the man
Speiser	man	man	the man
Sacks	man	the man	Man
Alter	a human	the human	the human

The key word in 2:7 is the same as in 2:8. The key word in 1:26 is different. Yet the second column is as often identical to the first as it is to the third.

Framed *in my terms*, here is the thinking of those who render the (different) keywords of 2:7 and of 1:26 identically:

> Both chapters describe the emergence of men and women. By contrast with the treatments of the coming-into-being of everything else, these descriptions feature an extra-natural infusion. In Genesis 1, God's image and likeness are projected onto nature. In Genesis 2, God's breath of life is breathed into nature. If 1:26 and 2:7 were not translated uniformly, readers might ask, irrelevantly: "Where do we find ourselves? Are we in the world of the Genesis 1 story, or in the world of the Genesis 2 story?"

As for the translators who render the key word of 2:7 identically with the key word of 2:8, they would never have allowed the departure from the letter of the text unless they equated the subject matter of the chapters.[7]

The translators see themselves as having to choose between two equally acceptable options. The thinking behind that perception is erroneous. The differences on the linguistic level carry thematic significance, which the uniform rendering obliterates.

Verse 2:8 describes God putting a person into the Garden. The dramatics in Genesis 2 require a particular. Isn't this particular the person whose creation 2:7 describes? 2:8 has definite article + common noun: "the man." 2:7 has the same.[8] So doesn't the rendering of the key word of 2:7 require "the"?

The form "definite article + common noun" is available for a type. "The lion is king of the beasts." Since the common noun on its own can also function as a type term – "Man is the most intelligent of the creatures" – a first translation of the key word of 2:7 might easily be "man." Again, the conjecture that the translators want to keep 2:7 connected to 1:26 explains the rendering. Since both "the man" and "man" are available as type terms, and since "man" is used in 1:26, and since "the man" is used as a referring expression in 2:8, the translators revert in translating the key word of 2:7 to what they employed in rendering 1:26.[9]

The standoff over "man" and "the man" can be broken. The second enlarged word in 1:26 is the third person plural of the verb "dominate." Unmodified "man" is used with the plural.[10] The accompaniments (verbs and pronouns) in Genesis 2 are *all* singular,[11] and 2:7 is no exception. The second enlarged word, corresponding to "became," is the verb's third person singular. Only a translator numb to content could adjust 2:7 to 1:26. As the verbs verbalize and as the pronouns pronounce, the verses don't have the same subject matter.

Genesis 1 and Genesis 2 both deal with men and women. Created in Genesis 1 are systems and sub-systems. In Genesis 2, a particular man and a particular woman come into being.[12] Aren't systems made up of particulars? Like the "Shall Nots" of the Decalogue, the answer, "No," brings us close to the Bible's philosophical heart.[13]

Q & A

Q1: What is it that is said of our sector of the creation in 2:7 that isn't said in 1:26? A1: Verse 2:7 says we are particulars. Q2: How does 2:7 say this? A2: By saying that some part of the natural world (a lump of clay) is inspired with God's breath of life. Q3: Why say this in terms of God? A3: The natural world, *qua* system, has in it no particulars. The advent of particulars cannot be explained on the natural basis. Q4: But why

God? A4: God, the deity of the Bible, is not only non-natural. God is also a genuine particular: God is one. In fact, particularity, the ontological idea, is, I would say, prior to monotheism, the theological idea. So God has one-ness. That one-ness is communicated. The result of God's surgery in creating the woman is a (second) separate particular. Q5: What is the basic expression of the biblical position? A5: The Shema Yisrael. The Shema asserts God's one-ness. That one-ness is compatible with the existence of any number of entities having it. Adam is one entity. Eve is a second. According to the Bible, each of them, inspired with God's breath of life, has God's one-ness. One-ness itself is not what sustains the theological view that one and only one deity exists. In its standard theological use, the label "monotheism" is therefore misleading. The Bible's point is not that the class of deities is a singleton. It's that the deity is a particular.

The resources of paganism are unequal to the particularity of men and women. Platonism, a rational development of paganism, speaks of the items in the world participating in the Forms. This sounds a bit like God's particularity being shared with the man of Genesis 2. In the penultimate section of this chapter I'll explain the deep difference between the links. Here, it should be enough to say that Plato's realm of Forms, constituting a system like the system that is nature, contains no particularity for items in the world to participate in.

Taking the "h," Abram becomes God's man Abraham. In the spirit of that taking, and also – literally – in the letter, I note that from a more purely linguistic point of view, mankind ("adam") becomes particularized ("ha-adam") by the addition of an "h."

All of this confirms that Genesis 1 must be kept apart from Genesis 2; that Genesis 1 is not especially biblical; and that monotheism is, or is closely connected with, ontology. Explained at the same time is why mortality makes its entrance in Genesis 2.

"Why haven't you brought the Documentary Hypothesis to bear on Genesis 1 and Genesis 2?" In the preceding chapter, it was established that the tellers want their story to be a natural one. The references to God in Genesis 1 either are courtesy references or else are *faute de mieux*. By contrast, God's presence in Genesis 2 carries commitments to the non-natural. When the Genesis 1 story resumes, in Genesis 11, the development is a counterpart of the unfolding in the intervening chapters of the Genesis 2 story. This substantiates that the text's fashioners had unity in mind. It follows that Genesis 11 is part of the Bible's answer to "How should we arrange our communal affairs?"[14]

"Don't 'man' and 'the man,' or 'humankind' and 'the man' differ only verbally? Isn't humankind the collection of particular men and women?" Technically, the issue is whether claims like "The wolf is a pack animal" can be translated without loss of content into claims about particular wolves. I'll deal with the issue non-technically.

Some years back, a reduction in the number of bison in Canada's Wood Buffalo National Park was determined to be necessary for the health of the herd. Park rangers culled 30 per cent of the animals.

Imagine demographers recommending a prophylactic thinning of the human population of Bangladesh. Sooner colonize Mars.

The arithmetic of men and women differs from that of non-human animals. Non-human animals we think of in group or species terms. For men and women, the particulars count.

The Upshot

Nature is a system. This is the Bible's natural philosophy. Humankind, albeit in a somewhat irregular way, is part of the system. Men and women, each man in his particularity and each woman in hers, aren't parts of the system, regular or irregular. Our separateness, yours and mine, is basic to the Bible's philosophical anthropology. The affinity of men and women with God, conveyed in Genesis 2 via the image of an act of artificial respiration, is affinity with an extra-natural being. "Mightn't 'God' name nothing?" What counts is the kind of being God is: particular, *hence* extra-natural. When God self-identifies – "I AM WHO I AM" – the point is that by contrast with the pagan deities, the biblical deity is incommensurate with nature.

The following contrasts and similarities are revealing:

Man that is born of woman hath but a short time to live, and is full of misery. He cometh up, and is cut down, like a flower; he fleeth as it were a shadow, and never continueth in one stay. *Job* 14:1–2	Like the generations of leaves, the lives of mortal men. / Now the wind scatters the old leaves across the earth, / now the living timber bursts with the new buds / and spring comes round again. And so with men: / as one generation comes to life, another dies away. *Iliad* 5:171–5

What do people gain from all the toil at which they toil under the sun? / A generation goes, and a generation comes, but the earth remains forever. / The sun rises and the sun goes down, and hurries to the place where it rises. / The wind blows to the south, and goes round to the north; round and round goes the wind, and on its circuits the wind returns *Ecclesiastes* 1:3–6	God of the earthquake – you'd think me hardly sane / if I fought with you for the sake of wretched mortals … / like leaves, no sooner flourishing, full of the sun's fire, / feeding on earth's gifts, than they waste away and die. *Iliad* 21:527–30

The passages from Job and from Book 5 of the *Iliad* could be swapped. But while the Bible is stressing the mortality of men and women against the backdrop of nature, in which neither birth nor death is found, the Greek texts see men and women as part of the natural system. The flower in the Book of Job is an analogy. To the speaker in *Iliad* 21, the budding tree captures a genuine likeness. The difference is implicit in the "born of woman" phrase in Job. It's not that the Bible writers know nothing of stamens and pistils. It's that birth and death are distinctively human. For the Greeks, the finitude of men and women is a deficiency. The Bible treats it as ineluctable.

Holy Ground

Moses has *his* first theophany on "Horeb, the mountain of God" (Exodus 3:1). From "a flame of fire out of a bush" (2), God instructs him to remove his sandals, "for the place on which you are standing is holy ground" (5). Then, God tells Moses his name: "I AM" (14). God, the holy one, is the principle of particularity. He is wholly one. Moses is confronting the basic truth about himself, the truth that Abraham had divined at the genesis of the biblical way.[15] The ground on which he stands, the ground of his being, is not natural. In *that* sense it's holy. The bush, "blazing, yet … not consumed" (2): a perfect emblem of God *qua* not bound up with the cycle of nature.[16]

Horeb is not the meeting point of the immanent and the transcendent. It is where the natural and the non-natural intersect.

After centuries in Egypt, enslaved to a pagan culture, the children of Israel have lost the patriarch Abraham's insight. It matters not that the bondage is probably fictional. The insight can be lost in a matter of years. One can be in theoretical bondage to nature.

Genesis 2 describes an act of disobedience. The Christian tradition has worked up a story of original sin. Pinning the tale on its endorsers, the Bible's critics run riot in the Garden. "We are created stained, and the tyrannical deity damns us for the spot. General Motors, having manufactured a lemon, may force the purchasers to sue for a fix. Happily, GM, by contrast with GOD, isn't too big to fail." But although the conduct of men and women does invite the imputation of stain, that Genesis 2 issues any such invitation doesn't follow. Genesis 2's is more philosophical an idea: particular men and particular women aren't parts of the natural system. The act of disobedience dramatizes the apartness. Being a sinner, if so, is no bad thing. Provided that we swim like the squid, we can award a few marks here to Sacks's take on the blessing of the fish. For being able to go against the flow, we are blessed. Genesis 2's story of deviation reveals something about (the biblical view of) us: we are particulars. Only the holy can deviate. Isn't it a conceptual truth that the holy is deviant?

"If this is the point of the Genesis 2 story, why does God explode in anger upon discovering that the man and the woman have eaten?" To the woman he says (3:16): "I will greatly increase your pangs in childbearing." To the man: "By the sweat of your face you shall eat bread" (19).

Does God explode? Might the reaction not be concerned resignation? "Goodness me! Look what you've gone and done." As to the pains of labour: are these punishments? To not be part of nature, to dominate, is to not be part of the equilibrium. That, while a gain, is likely also to be a source of pain. Consistently with the preceding assertion of equality, "I will greatly increase your pangs" can even be glossed thus: "Your sense of yourselves as 'I's is a sense of something about yourselves that connects internally to the difficulties you will have to face."

In *mis*behaving, the man and the woman are performing the *imitatio Dei* that their (God-given) nature mandates. They are being themselves.

The nature of men and women as extra-natural, as particulars, needn't come out in acts of defiance. Important is that *they* author their doings.[17] But although the conceptual content would be the same if they did their duty *because they chose to*, a story of voluntary compliance would smudge the line between men and women and the rest in a case where clarity is at a premium.[18]

"What about 'to dust you shall return'? Doesn't that pay out the wages of sin?"

Nothing of the kind. Only particulars can have (true) beginnings and ends. That's the Bible's point. God says "out of [the ground] you were taken; you are dust, and to dust you shall return" (19). For being a particular, no person is part of the ground. Throughout *their* existences, the other creatures are permutations and combinations of dust in equilibrium, nothing more. God is not part of nature. Neither are God-like men and women. But since men and women are taken out of the ground, returning to it is for them possible.[19]

As we now see, *the same treatment is not meted out to the animals. They never leave the dust.* That's why the issue of mortality is absent from Genesis 1.

Particular doesn't stand to *mortal* as *bachelor* does to *male*. Nevertheless, the proximity of the idea of an immortal person to science fiction entitles the Bible to treat the link as non-contingent. That the longest-lived of the Bible's mortals expires at nine hundred sixty-nine gestures at a ceiling: a thousand years effectively counts as immortality.

At this point, I expect that readers will have lost patience. "God is immortal! Look at Genesis 3:22."

> Then the Lord God said, "See, the man has become like one of us, knowing good and bad;[20] and now, he might reach out his hand and take also from the tree of life, and eat, and live forever."

But where, pray, does it say here that to be like God is to live forever? Having eaten of the tree of knowledge, the man and the woman, now knowing good and bad, resemble the speaker in this respect. That's what the first part of the verse says. Should they eat of the other tree, immortality will be theirs. That's what the second part says. The verse as a whole doesn't say that eating of the other tree will result in their becoming "[even more] like ... us." If anything, the implication is that the new acquisition will knock out a respect of resemblance.[21]

The idea of particularity is salient in the Bible's treatment of mortality. Here, in more philosophical terms, is a summary.

The fundamentals of paganism, the natural forces, are general in character. The difference between the wind that blows here and the wind that blows there is not the difference between one wind and another wind but the difference between here and there. The difference between the wind that blows now and the wind that blew then is not the difference between two winds but the difference between now and then. "To which wind are you referring?" can therefore blow us off course. The wind that filled Columbus's sails is the wind that cools your face. More perspicuously put: both the sail-filling and the face-cooling are due to wind. According to the pagan view, instantiations of general properties populate the level on which we pass our lives. The idea of instantiation introduces a yet higher-level generality, namely *falling under a concept*, or, in material mode, *having a property*. The characterization of ground-level things as instantiators of properties therefore introduces no new category at the bottom – it only ascends a rung on the ladder of generality. Philosophy is committed to this same view. It trades in necessary truth. Necessary truth, anchored in (timeless) relations – entailment, compatibility, inconsistency – of general properties, is carried by concepts that express those properties.

Accepting the particular as basic, as not just the instantiation of some general property or properties, biblical thinking breaks with the structure of general properties and instances.[22]

Ontology, Metaphysics, and the Shema

When Maimonides looks to Aristotle to philosophize the Torah, he subordinates God to the Stagirite's metaphysical categories. For Plato, the Form of the Good is, functionally, a replacement for God. In philosophy as constituted in the West, metaphysics subsumes ontology. Due to that, philosophy as so constituted has a native tendency thusly to subordinate and to replace. Jewish thought is what it is because it *refuses* the subsumption. This is its act of transgression in the Garden of Academus. "You shall have no other gods before [God]." Ontology, that is, is needed to make full sense of reality.

This is a good place to have a look at several translations of the Shema, as it is stated in Deuteronomy 6:4.

NRSV	Hear O Israel, the Lord is our God, the Lord alone.
Mechon-Mamre	Hear, O Israel: the LORD our God, the LORD is one.
NET Bible (Bible.org)	Listen, Israel: The Lord is our God, the Lord is one!
King James	Hear, O Israel: The LORD our God is one LORD.
New International Version	Hear, O Israel: The LORD our God, the LORD is one.
New Life Version	Hear, O Israel! The Lord our God is one Lord!
English Standard Version	Hear, O Israel: The LORD our God, the LORD is one.
Young's Literal Translation	Hear, O Israel, Jehovah our God [is] one Jehovah.

While avoiding the phrase, the translators are trying to get the text to suggest "one and only." So why not the conjunction? There's a good reason. The Hebrew has "one." Since the biblical repertoire includes "one and only" – see Genesis 22:2 – the translators should have been provoked to head-scratching. The meaning, in their view, is "God is our deity. God alone is our deity."[23] In other words: "There is one and only one deity. God is that deity." "One" gets detached from "God" and gets connected to "deity." With this the translators feel comfortable. It's true that in everyday discourse "one" is seldom attached to a proper name. We readily say that Gord is the one and only student in the class. We readily say that there is exactly one student in the class, Gord. Unless "Gord" is the telescoped general term "bearer of the proper name 'Gord,'" "one Gord" is most unlikely to emanate from our lips. The text does however say "The Lord is one" without using a general term. *My* reading of this is known. "The Lord is a true one." That is: "God is a particular." The Bible is making an ontological claim, a claim about the (level 0) thing. It isn't making a claim about a (higher-level) type of thing, for example, the concept *deity*. The variation in the translations attests that the translators, while speaking Hebrew, are thinking in Greek.

Between Pure and Applied

"Without doubt," writes Charles R. Gianotti, "the tetragrammaton, 'YHWH,' is the most significant name in the old Testament."[24] "To understand the meaning of the divine name is to understand the character of God as revealed by that name." Before applying the preceding results to show the relevance of the biblical principle to mainline philosophical issues, I will sample the fruits of scholarship in a region of the Bible, the region that Gianotti is referring to, where my thesis about God comes directly into play.

Organized religions' appropriation of the one-and-only-one god view creates the impression that the basic desire of monotheism's originators is to institute a belief-system with a new deity at its centre. This poke about the maze of biblical scholarship will support the proposition that rooting out error about the nature of men and women is the originators' animating intention.

Behind the uniformity of renderings of "אדם" and "האדם" in Genesis 1 and in Genesis 2 is the renderers' thought that the chapters are conceptually/theoretically uniform. The thought is mistaken. Translating uniformly smudges the textual expression of the Bible's basic point.

How does God's self-naming get interpreted? Observe that "YHWH" doesn't put in an appearance in Genesis 1. Consistently with what I've said throughout, I'll argue that the theological approach misses the mark. The issue is men and women; men and women as they are described in the *second* chapter of Genesis, where "YHWH" does appear.

Compressing Abraham's inaugural lecture down to four letters, the Bible says that he calls out God's name. What are we to make of the assertion at Exodus 6:2–3 that "YHWH" was unknown until the time of Moses? Non-devout readers might sniff an attempt to elevate a Mosaic tradition over an Abrahamic one. Our examination of Abraham's career suggests a non-political construction: what the patriarch exemplifies in action, the lawgiver puts into words.

Needing to be factored in from the start of any discussion of "YHWH" is that the issue of God's self-identification has to do with more than "the character of [a hitherto unknown deity,] God." It has to do also with setting up a hitherto unknown way, based on a changed understanding of human nature. Interpretations of "YHWH" from a theological angle conflict with my point that Abraham was telegraphing the new way via the telegraphic "YHWH."

There are a number of prevalent readings of "YHWH." *The inscrutability reading* has it that the tetragrammaton is deliberately baffling. God is a mystery to men and women. Proponents enter in support that Jacob's request of God, "Please tell your name?" (32:29), is evaded.[25] "Why is it that you ask my name?" (Ibid.)

Explaining "YHWH" isn't easy. Nonetheless, the-difficulty-is-the-answer answer limps in this case. If Jacob's sponsor remained mysterious, the protégé would have to respond to a curious party's "Who has sent you?" with "Who, indeed?" Jacob concludes the encounter thus: "I have seen God face to face, and yet my life is preserved" (30). "Face to face." That's hardly an expression of inscrutability. A reading proposes itself from our perspective. "The way of life based in God is viable. I still have a life." I would put it more strongly. To see God is to appreciate that one has a life of the human kind. That Jacob is lamed during the wrestling match conveys that the new life won't be smooth going. This new word is not, in the literal sense, a gospel. The character named "God" is asking a hard question: "Are you prepared to live with the answer?" Nor are we speaking only of the expected difficulties of living alongside those who do not find the answer to their liking. The point is philosophical. A lamed person walks out of step not only with the crowd but also with the ground. Jacob understands that he will not fit in with the natural world.[26]

The point has to do not with God's mysteriousness but with the unnatural character of men and women. Each of them (like God) is a particular.

The idea of the unnatural bears on the interpretation of "YHWH." God's character isn't part of the natural sphere. Moreover, the encounter between Jacob and God converges with the encounter between the first man and God and with Moses's theophany on the mountain. In the encounter, the man is given his being, his life; in the theophany, the giver's identity is disclosed to the people's conduit. One expects the convergence to bear on the name.

Another view of "YHWH," Greek in stimulus, has it that God is the principle of pure being. Supporters of this, *the being-theoretic view*, focus on the verb in God's response to Moses. "But the verb," detractors object, "hasn't the timelessness that pure being requires." *What about the pronoun?* God instructs Moses to "say to the Israelites, 'I AM has sent me to you.'" Recur to the inscrutability view. One might cite the non-optimality of cognitive access to X to back up the assertion that X is hard to make out. Our side of paradise, whose conceptual repertoire is limitless? This sort of ground for asserting inscrutability might indeed be principled. Couldn't some properties exceed the grasp of subjects constituted as we are? When we link inscrutability to predicates, recourse is unavoidable to the idea of some cognitive deficit. Inscrutability, as this shows, does not *naturally* connect to property-expressing predicates. It does however go *logically* with the pronoun. The object of "I" is as such not expandable predicatively.[27]

This leads to a second point. Metaphysics, exhausted by general properties and instantiation, has no separate principle of particularity. The many particulars do not share particularity as the many red things share redness. Red things instantiate redness. Particulars aren't instances of particularity. So while redness is an abstract thing, particularity is an abstraction.

Greek thinking and biblical thinking differ. That is widely understood. Often enough, it is said that God is not a static principle of being, but has a process-character. Again, however, predicates and pronouns differ more than do timeless states and events. God is the emblem of pure thinghood, "I." God is the emblem of the unpredicable. It's not only I *AM*. It's also *I* AM. Scholarly focus on the verb is off-topic.[28]

The issue of the name is not, if so, primarily theological. It is anthropological. The name functions to express the view that each of us is an I. Your being, or mine, cannot be captured in predicates representative of shareable properties. It cannot be captured metaphysically. Men and women are the basic unpredicables.

Other views exist. "YHWH" can be read as future-tensed. On *the efficacy view*, God is indicating that he will manifest himself in his actions through history. To me, "I will be what I will be" sounds more like "*Que sera sera*" than like "Stay tuned. I will reveal what I am."

Although each of the readings has critics among biblical scholars, many of them intersect the truth. (a) *Inscrutability* is connected to not being a predicable. (b) A special kind of *being* is particular being. (c) The idea that God is speaking of his *efficacy* in action is also relevant. For parts of systems are not independently effective. (d) The point that God is not pure being is also anchored in particularity.

Understanding the name "YHWH" is getting a line on God's character. That's Gianotti's view. My position is that the name is not revelatory, primarily, of God's character. Theology here is in the service of anthropology.[29]

1:30 and 2:7

	1:30 אשר בו נפש חיה	2:7 נשמת חיים
NRSV	that has the breath of life	the breath of life
Mechon-Mamre	wherein there is a living soul	the breath of life
NET Bible (Bible.org)	has the breath of life	the breath of life
King James	wherein there is life	the breath of life
New International Version	that has the breath of life in it	the breath of life
New Life Version	everything … that has life	the breath of life
English Standard Version	that has the breath of life	the breath of life
Young's Literal Translation	in which is breath of life	breath of life
Jewish Publication Society	wherein there is a living soul	the breath of life
Speiser	all the living creatures	the breath of life
Sacks	which has a living soul in it	the breath of life
Alter	which has the breath of life	the breath of life

PART TWO

Topics

5
Moral Philosophy: The Commandments

Truth and True Believers

Those within the circle of faith find their answer to "Why be moral?" in the opener of the Ten Commandments: "I am the Lord your God …; you shall have no other gods before me" (Deuteronomy 5:6–7).[1] Looking in from the outside, the majority are hard-pressed to locate in the Declaration of Independence from Polytheism a reason for being moral.[2] Not that students of Scripture contest the proposition that it's in the Bible that the idea of a moral law gets introduced to the world. But as they see it this last is newspaper copy, no more. Since the code of conduct that good people abide by is packaged with the position, monotheism, of which the Bible is the charter, we are, these students will grant, indebted to the theological innovators whose ghostly presence is felt on Sinai. "To the innovators. Not to their theological innovation. The law in its moral content," they will add, "could have been handed down from some other high place."

I will defend two theses, one about the text, one about the truth. The ordinally first commandment has cardinal firstness too; the other commandments, including the moral ones, depend on it for their validity. The true believers, it turns out, are right to hold that morality is based in the first commandment.

Preliminaries

The following abbreviations will come in handy.

1G = Accept God as the one and only god.
NIW = No making or worshipping of idols.

NV = No taking of the Lord's name in vain.
OS = Observe the sabbath.
HFM = Honour father and mother.
NM = No murder.
NA = No adultery.
NS = No stealing.
NFW = No bearing false witness.
NC = No coveting.

Since the commandments do not come numbered, and since we are not presented with a list of syntactically imperatival sentences, two questions of clarification arise.

Are the commandments ten in number? The fingers don't suffice for the imperatives in the relevant portions of Exodus and of Deuteronomy. "Ten" at Exodus 34:28, Deuteronomy 4:13, and Deuteronomy 10:4 seem like insertions, added, perhaps, to quell a schismatic irruption within the Israelite communion. Abandonment of the number would unsettle *us*. Imagine finding out that it was really Cecil B. DeNeuf-Cent who produced *The Ten Commandments*! But had those behind the biblical text spoken throughout of thrice three commandments, "Ennealogue" would be standard scholarese. On Orthodox Christian practice, to which I default when speaking informally, the first commandment, 1G, is found in verses 6 and 7 of Deuteronomy 5; the second, NIW, in verses 8 to 10; the third, NV, in verse 11; the fourth, OS, in verses 12 to 15; HFM, the fifth, in verse 16, and so on. Other identifications prove more appealing once we delve. When it comes to interpretation, the relative position of a commandment is more important than its number.[3]

Are the items commandments? The Bible's term is something like "pronouncement." In fact, isn't "I am the Lord your God" declarative? Some will sense an implicit "Accept that ..." My feeling is that the words express a condition for all that follows: "Given that I am your God ... ." If so, the first part of 1G is akin to the preamble of the American Declaration of Independence, whose almost as famous second sentence resembles it.

Two Pentalogues

One architectural feature of the biblical set of "statutes and ordinances" (5:1) is plain – a division down the middle.[4]

A	B
1G	NM
NIW	NA
NV	NS
OS	NFW
HFM	NC

Any even-numbered collection partitions into equal-numbered halves. An examination of a representative item from each confirms that the Decalogue comprises two Pentalogues otherwise than in this formal sense.

From the first five, OS: "Observe the sabbath and keep it holy, as the Lord your God commanded you. Six days you shall labour and do all your work" (5:12–13). Had these words been the whole of it, you and I, passing to "Honour your father and your mother" (16), would have wrinkled our brows. "Why a sabbath? Why the seventh day?" Anticipating the furrows, the presenters add a reference to God's primordial doings: "the seventh day is a sabbath to the Lord your God" (14). The corresponding verse in Exodus is explicit: "For in six days the Lord made the heavens and earth, the sea and all that is in them, but rested the seventh day; therefore the Lord blessed the sabbath day and consecrated it" (20:11).

From the second quintet, NM: "You shall not murder" (17). No God-based motivation is offered.

Textual markers signal the partition into Fives. Like the representative OS, each of 1G to HFM mentions God. Like the representative NS, none of NM to NC does. Each of NM to NC is shorter and more sharply imperatival than is any of 1G to HFM. For none of NM to NC is outside motivation furnished.[5]

"Doesn't the partition clash with the thesis that 1G governs the other commandments?" The impression of conflict has its source in what initially comes over as a meeting of minds between latter-day thinkers and the Bible.

The Religious and the Moral: Now versus Then

Latter-day readers see in the commandments as laid out in the table a partition between *religious* ordinances and *moral* imperatives. OS has to do with God-inspired ritual; NS, with interpersonal conduct. Since latter-day readers are likely to be secular, the perception harmonizes with an independent belief that religion and morality are animals of different stripes. This – the meeting of minds – has got however to be a source of interpretive discomfort. Had the propounders of the commandments believed that the imperatives divide into groups the taking of either of which is consistent with the leaving of the other, would they have twice formally enunciated the set in one go, each time advancing the members as binding *en bloc*?

"*Doesn't* its way of stating OS support the application of the labels 'religious' and 'moral,' understood to be unlinked in meaning, to the Bible?" True, appeal is made to God's post-creation breather to motivate sabbath observance. But the appeal itself is what needs interpreting. The Bible's manner of composition suggests that the composers see the God-based motivations connected with the first five commandments as underpinning the imperatives of the second set. Even if the composers are confused, we would still have to agree that in treating the absence of a link as self-evident, the secular hobble their capacity to deliver an accurate interpretation. "Dixie" can be whistled out of tune.

"What about sabbath observance's being a matter of *imitatio Dei*?" We can agree that mimicry of God has something to do with moral instruction. Moral training often consists in trainers (parents) getting trainees (children) to copy their acts of kindness, promise-keeping, and so forth. Yet why can't those who transact business on the sabbath use accurate weights and measures? Contrariwise, what prevents a person who keeps it from lying on the sabbath? True, the seventh day prevaricator would not be following the creator's lead. Neither however when tools were downed did God engage in the other physical delights that are encouraged. Nor is it clear why ignoring the day of rest should more obliquely foster immorality.

The Decalogue (to recapitulate) comprises a pair of Pentalogues. Although latter-day usage of "religious" and "moral" implies mutual independence, Scripture's sense is that *failure* to partition would leave the reader in the dark as to why the moral commandments are binding. "Why is killing wrong? Why should you not steal? I'll tell you why. The Lord is God."

The Logic of the Link

1G, the chief religious commandment, *underpins* the rest. As a matter both of interpretation and of truth, that is what I am arguing.

The position isn't that 1G *entails* the other commandments. Also: in saying that the basis for the moral ordinances is located in a commandment on the religious side, I am focusing only on an aspect of Commandment One. That aspect, despite having to do with monotheism's distinctiveness among theological positions, is separable from the matter of God's existence. To be a moral agent, must one subscribe to the biblical faith? The position is only that morality wouldn't be possible if not for a part of what men and women of biblical faith subscribe to.

How *does* 1G relate to the other commandments? 1G specifies a condition the satisfaction of which is logically necessary for NM, NS, and so on, to have truth-value. The moral commandments *presuppose* the religious one.[6]

Command Structure

Teasing out further structure among the commandments is the next step in establishing that morality as Scripture understands it presupposes 1G. To this end, let us reset the previous table.[7]

	A	B
1	1G	NM
2	NIW	NA
3	NV	NS
4	OS	NFW
5	HFM	NC

With respect to several of the horizontal pairs, connections of content serve themselves up. A little Edenic tilling brings them out with respect to several of the remaining pairs. One of these connections bears on our thesis.

PAIR 1

[A1] God is the creator, bringing things into existence. [B1] Murder reverses an act of creation. The murderer takes things out of existence. Coupled to the idea that God's doings are normative for those of God's creatures capable of a cognitive grasp of those doings,[8] 1G links internally to NM.

PAIR 2

[B2] The adulterer violates a bond between two people who have chosen each other. [A2] The worship of other gods also violates the bond, often figured as connubial, between God and his chosen people. NIW and NA are, therefore, a couple. What moreover is worship of idols if not thievery of the obeisance that is God's due? NIW weakly implicates NS.

Adulterous behaviour being a kind of thievery, shouldn't NS precede NA? Isn't the natural ordering from general to specific? Adultery links more closely to the worship of idols, the latter being a breach of the bond between God and his people. If we assume that those behind the presentation of the commandments have the affinity in mind, NA's adjacency to NIW falls into line.

PAIR 3

[B4] Bearers of false witness violate a formal verbal vow to tell the truth. False witness is a species of [A3] verbal taking-in-vain. Non-observance of the horizontal line is thus explained. Being so central to moral conduct, NS, respect for others' property, has to be dealt with independently. But since NS is linked to adultery *qua* species of thievery, NS (on the right side) is more closely associated with NIW (on the left) than with NV.

The stray from the horizontal in rows 3 and 4 could be a sign that *we've* gone astray. In the presentation of the commandments only the order is positive. Provided that relative position is preserved, adjustments won't automatically attract the charge of trampling. The manner in which NA and NS line up vis-à-vis a generic notion of taking what is not yours suggests binding the two. Four commandments end up in the B-column. To restore numerical balance, HFM could be shifted to its top. The repositioning, rather than attesting to a symmetry fetish, taps into the roots of biblical thinking.

Some blurring occurs in the region of HFM. The appeal to God vis-à-vis HFM – "Honour your father and your mother … so that your days may be long and it may go well with you" (16) – is unlike the appeal vis-à-vis OS, the commandment that precedes. Rather, it's identical to the appeal to God vis-à-vis the commandments *en bloc*. The people, God explains to Moses shortly after the enunciation is complete (29), are "to keep all my commandments always, so that it might go well with them and their children forever!"

A shift of gears occurs in the move from OS to HFM. So it's reasonable to see HFM as more distant from OS than OS is from *its* predecessors.

As for raising HFM to the top of the B-column: in the following deeper respect than the respect identified a moment ago, HFM stands to the B-commandments as 1G does to the A-ones. God is our creator in the elemental sense. Our parents create us in the personal one. Accordingly:

	A	B HFM
1	1G	NM
2	NIW	NA/NS
3	NV	NFW
4	OS	
5		NC

Some further tinkering, and almost full horizontality is restored. As per Anglican and Reformed exegesis, 1G can be divided into 1Ga, the assertion "I am the Lord &c.," and 1Gb, the imperative "you shall have no other gods &c."

	A 1Ga	B HFM
1	1Gb	NM
2	NIW	NA/NS
3	NV	NFW
4	OS	
5		NC

Two non-aesthetic reasons recommend the partition of 1G. 1Ga isn't imperatival in form. The alignment of (at least some of) 1G with HFM is supported by "God : humankind :: parents : child."[9]

The internal connections are instructive. NIW's resemblance to NA, and NV's resemblance to NFW, strengthen the impression of careful composition. The implication? To understand an A-commandment, the corresponding B-one should be examined. We see, also, that the order *does* trump the numbering. As to the division into Pentalogues: appreciating the three things together – the intricacy of the links; the capacity of the standard numbering to obscure the intricacy; the greater significance of order – breaks the tendency to characterize the A/B-partition as religious/moral. It's a near certainty that the commandment against lying, say, is regarded as valid because of something about God.

"It's a near certainty ..." Most modern readers think it's a clear uncertainty. "The writers of the Bible formulate the A-commandments as they do *because* they accept the B-ones. God is introduced to certify the moral imperatives, which might otherwise be questioned." Assuming that the explanatory toolbox does not contain revelation, it's reasonable to assert that an independent sense of morality actuates the writers. What I say in the pages following will support the view that their assertions about God aren't merely a way of annexing to what they independently accept an authority that people at the time wouldn't have acknowledged.

1Ga ≈ HFM

"Parent" entails "offspring." The referent of "God" in 1Ga's "I am the Lord your God" has done all manner of things to the referent of "your": chosen forefathers, delivered from bondage, promised a homeland. To see why 1G implicates the creative doings of a parent, let us think about the term "before" in the enunciation of its b-part.

1Gb is naturally read as prohibiting the raising of other gods over God. "Before" is understood to function metaphorically: "in preference to." What comes naturally should be resisted. The preposition in 1Gb has to be taken more literally.

Pagan religions accept that there *is* a temporal "before" with respect to the gods. The pagan deities, despite possessing the deathlessness that distinguishes gods from men and women, are not uncreated.

As Hesiod tells it in *Theogony*, the first deity properly speaking emerges from a primordial chaos. "Chaos was born ... and after it came Gaia." It's impossible to miss the parallel with Genesis 1. Too, the difference. In Genesis 1's story God imposes order *on* the initial waste and void. Gaia, in Hesiod's story, emerges *from* it. The god's emergence *is* the emergence of cosmic order. Ouranos comes from Gaia.

The two correspond to "the heavens and the earth" of Genesis 1:1. Unlike Gaia, God, standing outside the natural order, has no (natural) beginning.

The upshot is to hand: making other (sc. pagan) gods prior to ("before") the god of the Bible tramples a truth about being.[10] Among deities, only the biblical kind is "before" the natural world – not enmeshed in space and time. Putting Zeus or Marduk before God draws fire irrespective of the existential issue. Assigning antecedence to the former is tantamount to placing 7 before 5 in the ordering of the numbers. 1Gb follows directly then from 1Ga.

The Torah addresses the commandments to 1G-accepters. The ordinances spell out the implications of acceptance. By violating NIW, the addressees evince confusion about their undertaking. As I'll explain later, provided that they know what they are doing, those who reject 1G are free of NIW. The present point is that failure to accept 1G (or 1G's falsehood) has consequences for morality.

We have sought and we have found. God is "before" all created things, which means: all other things. Parents are "before" children, whom they create. Placement of HFM next to 1Ga has conceptual underpinning.[11]

The ontological foundation of moral conduct is heaving into view. In the Bible's judgment, morality presupposes something that is linked to God's beforeness, something that is absent from pagan belief systems. This does not mean that statutes identical to NM and NS cannot figure in pagan contexts. It means that when present they have all the force of our rules of etiquette.

To prepare for discussing NIW, in whose connection the foundational thing emerges most clearly, I return to the characterization of Commandment One as the Declaration of Independence from Polytheism. Understanding as we now do that the assertion of God's before-ness in 1G is a repudiation of pagan views, the issue of polytheism becomes relevant.

Before What?

How did the natural world come about? The inability of the writers of the Bible effectively to defend the cosmogonic view that they favour does not affect the truth-quotient of Genesis's early phases. Although most non-scholarly readers, and many interpreters too, fall to the temptation, the Bible's *In Principio* is improperly measured against Hoyle, Hubble, and Hawking.[12]

HFM is inestimably important in this regard. Before I state the reason, I'll again underscore the oddity of its presence.

What's an imperative about family ties doing among the commandments? Isn't it hazardous to morality for principles designed to adjust relations between social beings who have no particular interest in one another to give status to the parental bond? From the other side, why no HS? Is honouring a spouse less important than respecting a parent?

The parallel with 1Ga illuminates HFM's presence. A problem affects 1Ga: God's cognitive inaccessibility. No small liability, this, given that the deity is represented as anchoring the commanded conduct. HFM plugs the information gap.

The creative activity explicit in the language of HFM is of the world of experience. That parents are before children is no more a mystery than that eggs-in-shells precede an omelette. By contrast, the assertion that God created the world is opaque on the "before" side. The link of HFM to 1G atop the Pentalogues therefore keeps the text from reducing to "Tralalala, so be moral." At the same time, HFM singles out the relevant aspect of God's before-ness: the creative activity on the afternoon of Day 6. This is the same activity as that of fathers and mothers. In thinking of parents bringing children into the world, we aren't thinking of the emergence of non-human animals.[13] The beings in question are inspired with the same sort of life that each of the parents has, the life of a particular.

"Aren't the offspring of any non-human animal related similarly to *their* mothers and fathers?" The speed with which the casual reader nods assent is an index of how easily the Bible's meaning is missed.

In the language of the Bible as in English, "mother" and "father" lack literal non-human application.[14] Parenthood is an inter*personal* thing. Planets and oceans are not persons. Nor are salmon and bear. The association with HFM implies that the creative activity implicit in 1G concerns the compartment comprised of men and women. This activity is not the scientist's province. The relationship of parents to a child is for the scientist of a piece with that of a foal's sire and dam to the foal. The biological organism is the subject. The scientist's vocabulary runs the personal pronouns "who," "his," and "hers" together into the more impersonal "that" and the impersonal "its."

The active ingredient of the before-ness that is asserted of God in 1Gb belongs to philosophical anthropology: the apartness of men and women from the rest of the *natural* creation, which is the part that contains no parents who are (potential) objects of honour and respect in the same way that, *mutatis mutandis*, God is an object of worship.[15] To accept God is to accept the uniqueness of men and women among creatures. The genesis of the extra-human world is incidental here. That its existence has to be acknowledged doesn't make it the subject matter.[16]

HFM is significant to 1G for locating the point of difference between men and women and other creatures in the world. Attributing uniqueness to men and women generates no commitment to a trans-spatial and/or extra-temporal sphere. The Bible is saying that a person differs more from a non-human creature than non-human creatures differ among themselves. Its way of putting this – by withholding the vocabulary of "parent" and "child" from the (extra-human) natural realm – puts God in the picture because more than generative activity is at issue. That which fixes you and me in the field of "father," "mother," "son," and "daughter" is a presupposition of morality. We, the only creatures who are children and can be parents, have a kind of being that makes morality possible.

From HFM a corollary, RSD, might therefore be extracted: respect your sons and daughters.

These facts separate the Bible from accounts that explain the origins of men and women in the same terms as are used for salmon, bear, and cedar. Restricted as it is to the human sphere, the concept of a parent is alien to pagan thought. Consider Hesiod's easy application of sexual imagery in describing how the heavens, Ouranos, and the earth, Gaia, create the second generation of deities, the Titans. "[T]hen / [Gaia] did couple with Ouranos to bear &c."[17] Hesiod is not sexualizing a non-sexual process. He is depersonalizing the process whereby men and women come into being. That the Bible differs is self-evident. Among the myriad creatures, men and women alone are inspired with "[God's] breath of life" (Genesis 2:7).

The phraseology in the narration of the alternative line of Seth echoes that of Genesis 1's account of God's creation of humankind. This vacuums up residual doubt that the Bible is thinking of the creation of men and of women in the special terms. At the same time, it confirms the tight association of 1Ga and HFM.

> When Adam had lived one hundred thirty years, he became the father of a son in his likeness, according to his image, and named him Seth. (5:3)[18]

Hesiod's script is flipped. The process that brings men and women into existence is desexualized. It is personalized.

Declaring independence from polytheism, the Bible is declaring that persons from the standpoint of paganism are surds. It's not with the intention of filling a blank canvas labelled "The Origin of Our Species" that the thinkers behind the text paint the picture of the man being thrown like a pot and of the woman emerging by an animal version of a plant cutting. Although the thinkers are in the dark about the physical basis of life, the difference between persons and the rest they understand. The prominence of the creation of men and women in Genesis responds to a point of general agreement: men and women do not fit seamlessly in with the rest. Men and women have parents and nothing else does. HFM is relevant to them. (So 1G is relevant to them.)

Theology and Taxonomy

In the preceding pages, "polytheism" and "paganism" have functioned as synonyms. From early in this essay, the term "polytheism" has been under attack. The alignment of 1Ga and HFM supports the attack from the flank.

Two parents create a child. Couldn't a multiplicity of gods have created the world? Polytheism, why isn't it an option here? If we take the label strictly, it *does* constitute an equal possibility. It's *paganism* that doesn't constitute an equal possibility. Paganism is not theistic.

Theism views deities as persons – as having our psychic make-up and personality structure.[19] Pare away the anthropomorphic rind, and the reality of the pagan gods is revealed: the principles behind natural forces. "Polytheism" is therefore misleading as a label for a pagan system. Yet the label is invariably applied. Language that trips off our tongues thus abets the misunderstanding of monotheism. Carelessly, 1G might easily be denominated "the Declaration of Independence from Polytheism."

Typically, monotheism is identified as the doctrine that there is only one deity. That identification is at once too broad and too narrow. Too broad: Monotheism is the doctrine that there is only one *personal* deity.[20] Because non-theistic systems characteristically contain many higher beings, the possibility of a multiplicity of gods – personal ones – on the non-pagan side gets passed over.[21] Too narrow: Although it's natural to call the position endorsed on the non-pagan side "monotheism," denying the existence of a multiplicity of non-personal deities is compatible with affirming the existence of a number of personal ones. The monotheist cannot assume that the number of personal gods is one.[22] The Bible acknowledges the need to argue for the reduction through its association of HFM with 1Ga. That there can be more than one personal creator is a truth testified to by each breath that each of us draws.

Important about monotheism is not the *number* of gods. The (special) unity of the person is important – a one-ness like the one-ness of God. This one-ness is also vital from the moral perspective. As for the contrast with paganism: the idea of a number of pagan deities isn't the idea of an irreducible multiplicity.

The pagan deities constitute a system. A pantheon of polytheism, in the ism's strict sense, would be a collection.

On the usual understanding of the isms, there are, then, a couple of curious reversals. Paganism gravitates towards its mono- form, since forces like the wind and the sun are aspects of the system called "nature." Theism tilts in the direction of its poly- form, since the core idea is that the deity, God, is a separate and self-contained being.

Here is the correct typological scheme, the cells filled in with the presumptive inmates.

	Theism	Non-theism
Poly	Liberal democracy on high	Olympian religion
Mono	Explicit biblical position	Science (Plato, Spinoza)

No Graven Images?

Obeisance, to be done, must be done somewhere. Why not in the shadow of a graven image? Provided that steps are taken to make clear that the thing has no common denominator with God, and provided that the thing itself isn't worshipped, the practice might be tolerated.[23] "Isn't there a danger that the provisos won't be provided?" As a Maimonidean position in a related connection indicates, that doesn't settle the matter.

According to Maimonides, the sacrifice of edibles to God – grain and meat – is thrown as a sop to the Israelites, whose members the Egyptian practice had captivated during their sojourn in Goshen.[24] Is this a correct account? As the case may be, the burning of offerings – the centre of Temple ritual – could inculcate the attitude of mindful worship. A cost/benefit analysis might have persuaded the authorities to risk it.

Maimonides denies that God has physical attributes. Yet he condones sacrifice. Isn't it inconsistent of him to adduce God's non-physicality to justify the ban on graven images?

It isn't Moses son of Maimon who condones sacrifice. Moses son of Amram does. *The Guide for the Perplexed* and the *Mishneh Torah* don't ban graven imagery. The nation's guide, the Torah, forbids it. Why NIW? Obviously, idolatry bespeaks misunderstanding of God. A grievous thing from the Bible's perspective, it's the theological face of an ill graver still. Idolaters evince misunderstanding of their own natures.[25] Since one's treatment of others is a function of what one understands them to be, *justified* immorality can result. The Talmud (Tractate Sanhedrin 37a) says that saving a single life is equivalent to saving the world entire. This, we now understand, is not a loose analogy from the standpoint of the Bible's anthropology.

Theism, Paganism, and Self-Understanding

What self-misunderstanding accompanies the denial that men and women are distinctively God's creatures? Pagan accounts figure the world as a system with weak internal differentiations. In *Theogony*, Chaos differentiates Gaia, and Gaia fissions Ouranos, as in Genesis the waters divide into upper and lower. Men and women could not emerge in the Bible along such lines. Lacking a place for particularity, the biblical epitome of which is the single deity who breathes life into the man, God-less accounts are dumb in the face of morality.

1G isn't just a way of attaching authority to the commandments. Nor is it that God literally created us. Rather: if we think of ourselves in natural terms, our particularity is mysterious. "What makes us what we are cannot be captured" equates to "Our natures have an extra-natural basis." That, couched in a theological idiom, is the Bible's claim.

Men and women are (potential) moral agents. In the Ten Commandments, capacity for morality is a function of the special relationship to God. The list headed "I am the Lord your God" includes central moral imperatives. As the quotation about the line of Seth verifies, the relationship of men and women (as creators) to *their* children matches, in part, that relationship.

The point has to do with an issue of causation – the metaphysical face of the idea of agency. Paganism's problem, which comes out in the plurals that the Bible uses when dealing with it, is that the causal source cannot be isolated. The remarks about the family of words containing "mother," "father," and "parent" touched on the matter. To firm up our grip, let's look at a case of idol worship.

Elijah on Mount Carmel

In the story (1 Kings 18) of the showdown between Elijah and the prophets of the Baal, the Bible heaps scorn on the latter. Saying that pagan gods cannot answer is how the Bible says they are not persons.[26]

Although the scorn is overdone – scientists interrogate nature and get answers from it – the underlying point is sound. From the scientific vantage point, persons are missing from the causal field. But morality requires agents made in God's image and likeness, agents inspired with God's breath.

What's so foolish about bowing down to sticks and stones? God is the kind of thing that can *respond*. This is the gravamen of the match on the Carmel. From *their* deity, the prophets of the Baal are unable to elicit a flame.

"Aren't petitioners of God answered with the same frequency as are men and women who twiddle their thumbs?"[27] Should the secular turn Elijah's mockery back on the devout as failure succeeds failure – "Cry aloud! Surely [the Lord] is a god; either he is meditating, or he has wandered away, or he is on a journey, or perhaps he is asleep and must be awakened" (1 Kings 18:27) – they only display their misunderstanding. If there is no one to take the call, it's pointless to talk at the wall. But talking *at the wall* isn't talking *to the wall*. The first is futile. The second is idiotic.[28]

Along these lines, what many see as biblical barbarism at its hardest can be softened. It's the worshippers of the nature gods whom the Bible accuses of not knowing God. Pagans conceive themselves as (small) parts of nature. As they see it, their gods express themselves through, *inter alia*, stones. Stoning for sabbath violation is therefore a return to what, in the pagans' own understanding, their condition is. Which is the justice that David, poetically, pronounces: "Those who make [the idols] / and all who trust them / shall become like them" (Psalm 135:18).

What about conceptually careful polytheists? In their case the problem is the position's inability to sustain morality. No singular agent is present who puts his or her shoulder to the wheel and on whom responsibility ultimately falls. Thus the panic about fate. Thus the resort to the likes of horoscopy. "The fault ... is ... in our stars." Monotheism is an assertion of a presupposition of morality as we understand it: the reality of the agent.

Famously, the Code of Hammurabi contains a version of "eye for eye, tooth for tooth" (Exodus 21:23). Given the dates,[29] a basis exists for seeing the origins of the Bible's moral code in Mesopotamia. But even if we grant the code an influence, the preceding remarks absolve Abraham and Moses of trampling the eighth commandment and then of violating the ninth. Thinking of things in terms of system, paganism can make no more than pragmatic sense of moral conduct. To accept the principles of such conduct on the basis that selfish men and women get along worse is to relativize the obligation to outcomes.

1Ga, the foundation for morality, underpins the status of men and women as agents, a status that is required for being a moral being. Not that the pagan view denies the capacity of men and of women to act. But paganism has a problem (evident in the panic over fate) with regard to effectiveness and responsibility. In the (purely) physical world, the conservation laws hold. Change there is aplenty. For substantial termination to be possible, God's breath is needed. The principle of pagan interpersonality is exchange. Is a person who moves money from one pocket to another a thief? Murder, the taking of another's life, is however a species of thievery. In the absence of a substantial other, no theft – of life or of anything – can occur.

Many instructors of first courses in ethics teach that the biblical view succumbs to Plato's critique of the divine command theory of moral value. "Is some action good on the basis that a deity approves it, or does it qualify apart from the attitudes of a higher being?" The criticism of the Bible on the ground that it bases goodness on God's positive attitude is grounded in a misunderstanding. The Bible does not subordinate to God's decree. Nevertheless, since morality depends on a specific conception of the agents and patients of moral conduct, good *is* contingent on God. The Bible, in a fashion that can easily mislead, moves too fast from "each person is a particular" to "the conduct required is moral conduct." Still, the focus being on paganism's inability to sustain moral principles, the transition makes contextual sense. Also, other thinkers about morality who are on our side of the antiquity/modernity divide accept the inference. Kant argues that their extra-natural status requires treating each man and each woman as an end.[30]

I spoke of conceptually careful polytheists. Many moral philosophers walk among us. Most assume what needs defence. Take *utilitarians.*

It makes sense to ground moral good in this or that sort of life-enhancing utility. Good is as good does. But in the utilitarian's handling of it, the ground seems to levitate above the men and women the goodness of whose lives is the basic concern. The majority in a country with an impressive GDP may be living hand to mouth. True, some utilitarians provide a patterned treatment. Whence the idea, the idea of the individual person, whose accommodation motivates and guides the patterning?

Brian Ellis writes:

> The conception of morality involved in social contractual utilitarianism does not depend on our having an innate moral sense. Nor does it depend on our being metaphysically free to act as we please, as some have argued that it should. It depends only on our being social agents, with prima facie social rights, obligations and responsibilities.[31]

For Ellis, moral principles are idealized social principles. "Social principles"? There are (at least) two different ideas of society: the liberal one and the collectivist one.

When a theorist speaks of a collectivist morality, I fill my mouth with water, despite that the talk does violence to what "moral" means for me. It behooves Ellis to justify his basic ideas. Given that he is a humanist, basic to him is the (particular) human being. Had Ellis looked at Plato, he would have seen that others count as abstract what for him is basic.

In the case of utilitarians, the problem is patent. Utility seems too impersonal a notion. In the *Rawlsian* context, the problem is latent. In Rawls's analysis, the individual person is placed behind the veil of ignorance. Why not a group? Isn't there some unacknowledged metaphysics here? Isn't Rawls preaching to the converted?

Sabbath

In the Gospel of John, Jesus is described as rebuking the Pharisees for their rigid observance of the day of rest, their eyes blind to the needs of others. "My father is still working [to sustain the world on the sabbath], and I also am working" (5:17).

On the sabbath, the world-sustaining processes of Genesis 1 are not on sabbatical. The winds continue to blow. The rivers flow on. Does that justify "my father is still working"? The *natural* processes aren't expressions of God. The biblical representation of (God) resting on the sabbath connects to (God's) *non-natural* status. In the (purely) natural order, no day is of rest. Lolling in the shade, which animals do, is a metabolic thing. The sabbath is available only to beings who aren't completely natural, beings to whose creation Genesis 2 is devoted. The seventh day is the occasion for exhibiting mindfulness of non-natural status. OS thus belongs on the A-side of the Pentalogues. By enacting God-likeness, sabbath observers acknowledge the presupposition of the moral modes of conduct that make up the B-side.

Is lending a hand to a needy person destructive of that mindfulness? Need I say more in response than that non-human creatures do not lend a hand, and not out of stupidity or selfishness?

From the perspective we've gained, the Akedah contrasts with the structurally similar myth of Iphigenia. However distressed Clytemnestra is about Agamemnon's sacrifice of the girl,[32] the offering, as a way of getting the wind to pick up, is, in principle, sensible. Don't we flick the blade of a stalled fan? Men and women as natural beings are like the sun and the wind, only more complex. Within the pagan conceptualization, Agamemnon's relationships to the elements and to his issue are of a piece. Neither he nor Clytemnestra is a parent in our sense. As to the Akedah: the death of a person in the biblical frame is unlike the death of a person in the Greek frame, where it's more like recycling. Recyclers we reward for ensuring that "the place where the streams flow, there they continue to flow" (Ecclesiastes 1:7).

Commencing *Paradise Lost*, John Milton signalizes the misbehaviour that "[b]rought death into the world" (bk I, 3). This Christian view misses the deeper truth. From a natural perspective, men and women count as misbehavers. They are unnatural. They do not fit in. By bringing a man into the world, God brought not only beginning into the world, but ending too.

Sabbath Observance: Rest *from* or Rest *for*?

Men and women rest. Nature doesn't. Genesis 1 tells a natural story, implying that the commandments don't apply in its world. Indeed, or so I argued, God is present in name in Genesis 1, not in act.[33] What need then of an easy chair? Consider more closely the versatile logic of "rest." One can (take a) rest from X. One can (simply) rest. One can rest (in preparation) for Y. In addition to defending the claim that the sabbath doesn't belong to the story of Genesis 1, I'll argue that the Bible doesn't represent it as belonging.

I hear the reader's agitated rustling of this OS-motivating text:

> Six days you shall labour and do all your work. But the seventh day is a sabbath to the Lord your God; you shall not do any work ... For in six days the Lord made heaven and earth, but rested on the seventh day. (Exodus 20:9–10)

In point of fact the words don't say that God rested *because he created.* Observance is needed, they say, *because God rested.* "For" easily replaces "because" in 1:3. "So God blessed the seventh day and hallowed it, because on it God rested from all the work that he had done in creation."

It's simple logic that if a busy person is in repose, he or she will have left off doing what busied him or her. But it's simple illogic to infer that the state of repose marks, let alone celebrates, the cessation.

The issue is joined technically by the fact that the sabbath is first mentioned in Genesis 2. Endorsers of the usual line will point out that the chapter divisions are editorial additions. "The first verses of Genesis 2," they will say, "summarize the creation of Genesis 1." To Robert Alter, it's self-evident that they do: "the first Creation story concludes with [a] summarizing phrase."[34]

There are signs in the text that the chapter division is thematically right; that the sabbath belongs to Genesis 2, not to Genesis 1.

SIGN 1

Verse 2 of Genesis 2 seems to repeat verse 1. Verse 1: "the heavens and the earth were finished." Verse 2: "God finished the work that he had done." Verse 1 would be a suitable ending for Genesis 1. It looks back. Verse 2 adds something: the sabbath. If the sabbath ends the first phrase, why does it appear only in verse 2? Verse 2 says that the work was completed in six days. Verse 3 could be read as "And then, on the seventh day ..." Read this way, the verse stresses that the end of Day 6 is the end. The idea of completion is present, if so, apart from the seventh day. "Since a week has seven days, isn't ending on Day 6 ending with a sequel-less cliffhanger?" Some jobs take one day; some, like Sisyphus's, are never done. In our efforts to pacify the text, we should resist appealing interpretively to the fact that we regard the week as a natural unit.

SIGN 2

During the first six days, God half a dozen times perceives/judges what emerges as good. In Genesis 1, "X is good" means "X does its appointed job; X functions as it should." The intensified form, "very good," the reaction at the end of Day 6, expresses satisfaction at finding that *all* the parts mesh. The general contractor's thumbs-up after surveying the work of the various subcontractors is a suitable internal ending for Genesis 1. Suppose the overseer now enplanes for Bora Bora. Might the trip not have been planned years ago?

SIGN 3

Verse 3 describes God blessing and hallowing the sabbath. Of the two performances, the act of blessing is familiar. We encountered it in Genesis 1. Sanctification is unprecedented. Again the suggestion is that verse 3 doesn't belong with Genesis 1. Also suggested is that the world of Genesis 1 has nothing sacred about it, though it be God's handiwork. The more granular implication is that there is nothing holy about qualifying in Genesis 1's sense as "good." Adherents to the Bible-based faith might find this unsettling. Yet where's the sanctity in a glass's holding water? A glass that leaks may be holey, but one that doesn't is hardly holy. As to the fact that there is no sanctity in the world of Genesis 1: the distinction with Genesis 2 supplies a ground for understanding the disconnection of blessings from holiness. Again we have that pivotal feature. The blessing connects with what has passed; the sanctification raises something new. This treatment, moreover, solves another obvious problem. If the sabbath is holy because on it God rests, why aren't the other days holy because on them God acts? "Therefore shall you light your lights on Sunday; for on that day God created light."

SIGN 4

The fourth sign is from later in the Torah. The Ten Commandments are prefaced with "the Lord God" (i.e., "YHWH" is used). But the treatment of the sabbath in Genesis 2 has "God." Doesn't this testify that the sabbath's affinity for the topic of Genesis 2 is as great as it is for the topic of Genesis 1?

The signs support the proposition that the sabbath is rest for what is to follow. It's a way of saying that there's nothing hallowed about the natural processes. "Thank goodness that's over. The real work begins." The discussion of the blessings in Genesis 1 confirms this. The blessing of the sabbath is of a piece with the other blessings. In each case, we have something that lacks a natural niche. But in this case there is holiness. It's the holiness of the particular, the holiness of those who can, each one of them, say "I AM." (Resting, so understood, is like the unconsumed fire of God. Here as there, a process doesn't pro-cess. Nothing accumulates. Nothing depletes. The fire doesn't need feeding. No ash heaps up.) The sabbath must not only be blessed. It must also be (indicated to be) sanctified.

The sabbath is central among the patterns of practice associated with the Bible. It makes a difference if it's understood not as marking the end of the natural creation but as prefiguring the creation of the first person. Could it be that driving the halakhic prohibition on sabbath driving is a substitution of the first for the second?

We have here, in fine, a test of the distinction between Genesis 1 and Genesis 2. Conformably to the reading I am offering, it's apposite that the sabbath be referred to as *God's breather*. With the natural world up and running, God is preparing to breathe his breath of particular life into some piece of it. God's rest, then, is *for*, not *from*.

Roth on Monotheism and Morality

Monotheism has to do with a presupposition of morality. It will be instructive to look at Roth's position on the link.

For Roth, monotheism is the theological doctrine that one and only one deity – God – exists. Immediately after observing that the doctrine and the teachings of polytheism clash, Roth makes a *differential* link between monotheism and morality: "[Monotheism] means the setting up of one standard for all. What one god disapproves of another god can always be found to approve."[35]

To back this reading up, Roth comments on a few episodes in which the Bible deals with interpersonal duties. Of God's confrontation with Cain, he writes: "This confrontation is only possible under a monotheism. Only under a monotheism is there no opening for evasion, no dodging the issue, no appeal from one divine power to another."

Paris could plead before Zeus that the Merchant of Venus procured Helen's flesh for his bed. Cain has no Demeter to summon to justify the grim reaping of his brother, nor is there a Pan to pipe up for Abel.

It's true that Cain's attempt to evade God's criticism fails. That, I mean, is how the story is written. Why however should we defer to the authority figure of the piece?

The mildest criticism of Roth for not answering the question would be that his understanding is incomplete. But something more serious is amiss. Look at what Roth writes immediately following the first quotation in this section.

> As a logical argument against polytheism this is sound and can be found repeatedly in Plato; but logical arguments have little effect on the emotions. The Jewish contribution is not a theory of morals but its practice, and practice depends on feeling.

That *Plato* makes the point about polytheism and standards provokes these obvious questions. Is Plato (who is a pagan) a monotheist? Does he have monotheistic tendencies? As I'll explain, Plato's positive theory of morality does not correspond to the Bible's *because* the answer (in both cases) is "No,"[36] not because Plato is a cold fish.

Roth was quoted to say that Judaism "is not a theory of morals." Let me extend the critical discussion from this starting point.

"Not only a theory of morals" would have been unobjectionable. "Not a theory or morals" is wrong. Roth takes no steps to back up the proposition that in and of itself our emotional economy is moral. Nathan's admonition of David does work on us ("You are that man!"), as does Elijah's admonition of Ahab ("Have you killed, and also taken possession?"). This is because we are *independently* committed. Moreover, the commitment is expressible in abstract terms domestic to the Bible. "Do not do unto others &c." A good thing too that it is. David bows to the rebuke ("I have sinned"); Ahab issues a licence to kill. Has Ahab anaesthetized his moral feelings? Has his emotional life been annexed to predatory values? Without benefit of the more abstract terms, we be unable to say.

Roth's chief point I'll quote again: "there is no opening for evasion." One god, one message. What about the message's content? It's in response to God's instruction that Abraham abandons Ishmael. Could God not have encouraged Cain to avert his gaze from Abel?[37]

It's in this sense only, we see, that Roth connects monotheism to morality: the one deity enjoins obedience to the dictates of the moral code. Must the enjoiner enjoin morality? If the answer is affirmative, a further question arises: What, if anything, does the morality have to do with the one-ness?

How valid a point is it anyway? If the Bible sought converts through conversion of "many deities, many messages" into "one deity, one message," the logical would charge *modus volens*. In the Bible's telling, moreover, God is frequently conflicted. "And the Lord was sorry that he had made humankind on earth, and it grieved him to his heart" (Genesis 6:6). How does a set of feuding deities differ from a single deity who is of two minds? The response that God is single-minded about morality would return us to Plato's point, in the *Euthyphro*, that the mindedness doesn't determine the goodness. Anyway, the response is false. "If you do well," God says to the fratricide Cain (4:7), "will you not be accepted?"[38] In the debate over the inhabitants of Sodom, God, more clearly still, shifts.[39]

"The logical connection between monotheism and ethics is not difficult to trace. It means the setting up of one standard for all." If the higher beings are in charge, monotheism, mistakenly understood as postulating one higher being, does mean a single arbiter. Can't that arbiter be arbitrary, or changeable? Roth moves to disarm the objection: "God is not capricious."[40] But since Roth is arguing *from* monotheism *to* morality, this denial alters the subject – from sets to mindsets. In any case, the psychology of the Bible's **deity** *isn't* rock solid. Why, from the standpoint of monotheism correctly understood, would one have expected it to be? "Capricious" is question-begging in this connection. Caprice is changing when the circumstances don't.

Roth's remark about the Ten Commandments thrusts up a related problem. "[The Ten Commandments] comprise," he writes, "both religious and social ethics."[41] If, as per the standard plastic representation of the Tablets of Law, the Decalogue has this two-partness, do the parts dovetail? If they fly apart unless clamped, socially ethical (= moral) action is consistent with apostasy. If "a monotheism" like the Bible's is not to fracture, the fact that "God cares for the conduct of individual men" had better be locked to the conduct's morality. That both enunciations of the commandments begin "I am the Lord your God ...; you shall have no other gods before me" (Exodus 20:2–3; Deuteronomy 5:6–7) suggests inseparability.

Roth has many sound intuitions. He comes *this* close to asserting that the Bible is reflective anthropology. "If the Hebrew Bible has given the world a doctrine of God, it has given it no less a doctrine of man."[42] He highlights the fact that the Bible is a cornucopia of individualized men and women. "The Hebrew Bible is ... a world of individuals, and what a gallery it presents." He underscores that science is not the Bible's issue. "At its worst, it is just not interested." On all these counts, he appreciates the contrast with Greek thinking. He is however too standard a Western philosopher for the several intuitions to constitute a package.

Because of Roth's status as an observant Jew, extra authority seems to attach to his "No" to "Is there a Jewish Philosophy?" Seeing the issue from both sides, isn't he advantageously placed to answer?

Indubitably, many of one's doings as a member of a cultural group lie in a region about which philosophy is silent. But adherence to Judaism is life-pervading. Views about fundamentals have got to be engaged. One is apt to wonder how Roth "combined philosophical rationalism with religion, Plato with the Bible, universalism with the Jewish legacy. It appeared," reports Mordecai Roshwald, "that he avoided the issue of religious belief and focused on the ethical teachings of Judaism."[43] This cordoning off of religion from ethics is, we now understand, problematic. At the base of the Bible's ethics lies its (distinctive) *philosophical* principle. 1G asserts it.

Roth follows Julius Guttmann on the relations between Judaism and philosophy. "[In the Bible's] opposition between man and nature ... there is ... no hint of an opposition between the world of the senses and a suprasensual world. Man is a creature of this world, and it is only his character as a person that raises him above what is natural."[44] The quoted assertion abuts the truth regarding Genesis 1 and Genesis 2. However, as the formulation makes clear – "only" speaks volumes – a commitment to philosophy as constituted in Greece clouds the formulator's vision.

Morality in Auschwitz

In *Survival in Auschwitz*, a book we are grateful to have while regretting the circumstances that gave it to us, Primo Levi quotes some Bible-echoing lines from the Canto of Ulysses of Dante's *Inferno*: "and over our heads the hollow seas closed up." Implicitly, Levi's title is interrogative. *Can the inmates retain God's breath of life? Must they drown, or might they – might their humanity – be saved*?[45]

There are ethical norms and there are moral norms. Ethos is a matter of doing the thing rightly; morality, of doing the right thing. That which attracts ethical approval can be morally neutral, even immoral.

Auschwitz had an ethos. The life of the inmate depended on figuring out which behaviours were likely to attract special punishments, and then avoiding them. Morality in Auschwitz? It would seem that moral standards were absent. That was not Levi's view. It was not sin or sink. "Survival" in the relevant sense was possible.

A tension in Levi's presentation is a good entry point. Levi speaks of keeping clean as an "instrument of moral survival": "I must confess it: after only one week of prison, the instinct for cleanliness disappeared in me. I wander aimlessly around the washroom, when I suddenly see

Steinlauf, my friend aged almost fifty, with nude torso, scrub his neck and shoulders with little success (he has no soap) but great energy."[46]

Levi's questions – "Why should I wash? Would I be better off than I am? Would I please someone more? Would I live a day, an hour longer?" – Steinlauf refuses to take rhetorically:

> precisely because the Lager [the concentration camp] was a great machine to reduce us to beasts, we must not become beasts: that even in this place one can survive ... We are slaves, deprived of every right, exposed to every insult, condemned to certain death, but we still possess one power, and we must defend it with all our strength because it is the last – the power to refuse our consent. So we must certainly wash our faces without soap in dirty water and dry ourselves on our jackets.

Yet after describing the economy of pilferage in the camp, Levi again asks us to consider "how much of our ordinary moral world could survive."[47] On the strength of his claim that the charade of washing conduces to *moral* survival "on this side of the barbed wire" may we not infer that, for Levi, some portion of that moral world could live on? Judging from the descriptions of the inmates' other-disregarding conduct, the conclusion would seem however to lack firm grounding.

"Moral survival." Is Levi talking of *morale* survival? The near-homonym is revealing.

Levi's characterization of maintaining cleanliness as an *instrument* of moral survival invites the following construal. A *precondition* for a person's not drowning in the turbulence of the camp is the person's maintaining the sense of his or her agency; the sense that he or she is the initiator, the author, of courses of action.[48] One's efficacy in this regard must not be overstated. In the Lager, such is the arbitrary manner of treatment that all bets are off about later today, let alone tomorrow. For any number of reasons the most buoyant can easily be submerged.[49]

In presenting the point about cleanliness, Levi is saying that through such efforts those who made them gave expression to resistance to dissolution. Levi uses the word "vitality." The drowned lacked the quality that it expresses. By them, every doing in the camp was seen as futile. This, sheer luck apart, probably affected their physical longevity.

Those who stood a chance were those who, in advance, had sufficient vitality. They continued to think of themselves as agents. Members of this group contrast to the "non-men who march and labor in silence, the divine spark dead in them."[50]

What does "stood a chance" mean? It sounds like "stood a chance to prolong their lives." Standing that chance is not however the same as standing the chance to survive morally.

At first sight, the commodity labelled "vitality" resembles Jean-Jacques Rousseau's *amour de soi*. But this, the instinct of self-preservation, is an organic constant, possessed to the full by the lowliest creature. Levi's trait comes in degrees. For the types who require a prod, drowning is predictable. It's less *amour de soi* than the thing we call "dignity." Lack of dignity has little to do with survival in the ordinary world, where "it rarely happens that a man loses himself. A man is normally not alone, and in his rise or fall is tied to the destinies of his neighbours."[51] Note the claim that among the mass of men in what is in effect a sea of death, each man is alone. This bears on our question.

The survival value that attaches to dignity shouldn't be overestimated. Through some "banal incident,"[52] the divine spark could be snuffed out. And couldn't a dignified bearing be construed as insolence?

A precondition of being among the saved, an instrument of moral survival, has been identified. It's a carry-over from "ordinary" life. So far, though, *how* the instrument makes for moral survival is unclear. What's moral about Steinlauf's conduct?

Types are found in the Lager who operate effectively but who on any plausible construal of "moral" are beyond the pale. "To see [the dwarf] Elias at work is a disconcerting spectacle; the Polish *Meister*, even the Germans sometimes stop to admire Elias at work. Nothing seems impossible to him. While we barely carry one sack of cement, Elias carries two, then three, then four."[53] "Elias has survived the destruction from outside because he is physically indestructible; he has resisted annihilation from within because he is insane. So, in the first place, he is [literally] a survivor." Levi proceeds to explain that such a one, capable of doing "well" within the Lager, is impossible in the ordinary world. As for Henri, a sociopath whose ongoing exploitativeness would, if spread about, corrode normal social cohesion, he is well suited to flourish (so to speak) in the conditions of the Lager. The thesis was however that a trait accounted normal *outside* the Lager made for membership in the company of the saved *inside* it. The things that Levi says about Elias and about Henri are therefore consistent with the thesis. But we still are without an answer to our question.

Camp-like conditions are Elias's element. Henri is predatory inside and outside. These facts bear on the question.

It's not that doing unto others is impossible. Still, under the circumstances, who could ask it? In the Lager, staying alive for an hour, a day, longer, is the objective behind every choice. In Levi's chilling words: any course other than the course that serves that objective is inconceivable. There is however all the difference between following that course for the life that happens to be one's own, and following it selfishly. Doings that outside are paradigmatically immoral (e.g., stealing an item when that dooms the victim) therefore have a moral quality inside provided that it's for the life's sake, not just for staying alive, that they're done. Elias isn't aware. Henri doesn't care.

People in the workaday world do things for many reasons. Budget for the fact that actions in the Lager have but one reason and we begin to see why morality isn't abolished. Also, we understand why its survival in the Lager will evade us unless in assessing the inmates' behaviour our stereotypes are disarmed.

The Nazis' goal was to make non-men of men. Those inmates who retained the divine spark defeated the goal. Under the conditions of the Lager, actions anchored in a sense of one's worth qualified as moral. This anchorage could be present in respect of actions that, to the observer, might come across as self-interested.[54] *All* rational doings in the Lager appeared self-regarding. But when a sense of the worth of that for which it is done informs what is done, what is done is moral. Acting in the interest of the self, when that self is one's own, must not be confused with acting in disregard of the interests of others.

As could be expected, in the Lager other-regarding behaviours were the province of the saintly. "In the face of driving necessity and physical disabilities many social habits and instincts are reduced to silence."[55] Although no inmate *seemed* to be moral, those whose actions embodied a sense of the dignity of life were moral survivors. *They* retained their humanity. In these cases, then, the absence of choice didn't snuff out the possibility of merit.

What difference about the Lager explains the difference in the Lager? It's rational to assume that where only scarcity was plentiful the advance of one was locked to the retreat of another. "If I give you some of my ration, you'll live (longer) and I'll perish (sooner)." It was therefore no mark of immorality to act in a way that outside the Lager would have been viewed as selfish. In acting selfishly, one might be acknowledging the value of life generally. In the Lager, the only self which you could be expected to be true to was your own. Acting for the sake of oneself (= one's self) was what moral behaviour had to become. Had other selves entered the calculation, withholding from them would have been immoral.

In the Lager, the moral community had contracted to one. We have morality degree-1. "I AM." Unto the only relevant "other" in that context (and hence, in a sense, unto all others), Steinlauf was doing what morality required. In Auschwitz, morality came out in how one did unto *oneself*.

An astonishing piece of literary chemistry: Steinlauf, a man with a name built on "stone," was anointing himself. On *this* stone, God's house, beth-el, is built.

When a chemist decomposes table salt, its familiar features do not survive. In its elemental condition sodium is a volatile metal; chlorine, a poisonous gas. The test tube that was Auschwitz decomposed men on the social and psychological side before they were selected for literal decomposition. Bringing his eye as a chemist to the environment, Levi observed how the human material reacted in the dissolutive medium of the camp. He noted that although the corrosivity was so great that toxicity was set loose in many, the salt of the earth could in principle survive.

Was moral survival possible in Auschwitz? The moral remnant in the Lager comprised those who retained a sense of themselves (each for himself) as having value and who acted to preserve themselves (each to preserve himself) out of that sense. They could do little in the ordinary moral way with that sense of themselves. Obeying the commandments of truth-telling, of respecting property, and so forth, was a fast track to death. Yet a person who retained that sense differed morally from a person who had been stripped of it. Although it was not general*ized* in that context, the sense was general*izable*. Thus we had a moral community – *a community of one*. As to those lacking the sense of self-worth: we cannot expect them to have behaved morally even in that manner. The personality one brought to the Lager was unlikely to be morally deepened inside the barbed wire. Hunger and exhaustion and fear and pain are cruel masters. Still, it is only in rare kinds of cases that, after the fact, one can level criticism.

We have kept company in these pages with another Levi. Moses, of the tribe of Levi, led the Israelites through the Red Sea. Had Primo Levi known Holy Writ as well as he knew Dante, he could for his imagery have stuck with the book from which the metaphor of drowning and being saved derives. Wasn't the bondage in Egypt a version of servitude in the Lager? The Egyptians, whose culture represented men and women as mixed up in the system, perished in the Red Sea. "The floods covered them; they went down into the depths like a stone" (Exodus 15:5).

Two Jewish Philosophers, and a Russian

Levi is better versed in Dante than he is in Abraham, Moses, David, and Solomon. Yet what he says captures the ontological basis of biblical thinking. He is also in synchrony with the Bible in denying that saintliness is commanded of men and women.

This is the place to take up the Jewish philosophers who, although they by contrast with Levi are well-versed in Scripture, appeal in their thinking to post-Enlightenment resources.

Martin Buber's "I–it"/"I–thou" distinction has biblical resonance. I have presented the biblical correlate as individuals versus particulars. The personal pronoun is appropriate to (the particulars of) Genesis 2, not to (the individuals of) Genesis 1. The biblical position is not at base *dialogical*, however. When the biblical philosophers first get to particulars, they give a single one. This is deliberately in contrast to Genesis 1's system of (interrelated) individuals. Moses's theophany too is a dramatization of the Bible's *ontological* point. "Where are you?" When God asks this, the question is to be understood as requiring an answer different from the one – "I am nowhere" – that a pagan would give to his or her deity.[56] The moral level in the Bible has greater generality than Buber's dialogic level. "Thou shalt not kill." The basis for this is the one-ness of those in the field of moral imperatives.

Emmanuel Levinas, like Primo Levi, was interned, although in a prisoner-of-war camp. In view of Levinas's philosophical professionalism, for us the contrast with Levi on these matters is therefore multiply interesting.

Levinas asks probing questions about "Love your neighbour as yourself" (Leviticus 19:18). He maintains, surely correctly, that the biblical injunction is not to be interpreted as rating self-love primary. But Levinas rejects Hillel's plausible reciprocity reading. Supporting "the dissymmetry of the interpersonal relationship,"[57] he glosses "as yourself" thus: "Love your neighbour; he is yourself." The primary duty is to the other.

Levinas is entitled to advance his own philosophical account of morality. But Levi's friend Steinlauf at the end of *his* journey is a better Virgil through the biblical universe. Steinlauf does not place the other first in the Lager. That isn't because he places *himself* first. Steinlauf places *the self* first. In this environment, however, the only self in play morally is the actor's self. The ambiguity of the situation to the naked eye is captured by the homonymy of "one's self" and "oneself." Let me add that the sequel of the verse, "I am the Lord," is expected from the vantage point we've gained, a fact that ranks the reading above Levinas's. The Lord is an I. So is each man and each woman inspired with his breath of life an I.

This contrast between Levinas's view and the Bible's can be brought out by riffing on a statement of Moses's that I quoted several times. "It is not in heaven … No, [it] is very near to you." Let God say this, and then let God elaborate *à la* Levinas: "I AM not in heaven … No, I AM very near to you. Indeed, I AM you."

Your neighbour, like you, is an I AM. So is the stranger among you. Equality of treatment is therefore indicated. This, if we must choose philosophers, is Kant, not Levinas.

Levinas's position, as I see it, lays atop the biblical point matters connected to the Holocaust: the encounter with others whose condition is pure neediness.[58] That the case of a helpless infant *is* like that suggests Levinas's ethics to be too narrowly focused. The biblical understanding doesn't accord with it. Levi's description, which in the circumstances might have been expected to accord with it, doesn't either.

Levinas contrasts Greek philosophy, *the love of wisdom*, with *the wisdom of love*. A wonderful mirroring, this, of Jerusalem's relation to Athens. But Levinas's analysis of "love your neighbour," a distillation of his philosophical position, misses the Bible's point.

Love has an ontological significance illuminative of the denial that the biblical position is metaphysical. More powerfully than any other human-directed stance, love goes to the particular. Nothing can replace the beloved. Not that the beloved, and only the beloved, has a specific suite of properties. Rather, *the lover doesn't love for a reason*.[59] The specialness of the beloved, it's easy therefore to see, can turn the lovers inward. At the same time, the reason-insensitive nature of love opens the beloved to disasters against which effective measures cannot be taken. From the philosophical truth (as we see it to be) of Shakespeare's "Love is not love / Which alters when it alteration finds," love's constancy doesn't follow. The emotion comes calling in a gust; and it can depart in one too. On the positive side, the destructive jealousy of unrequited love should cede to a more manageable disappointment if the broken-of-heart do a little philosophy.

The thinkers behind the Bible are sensitive both to the special ontological force of love (it goes to the particular) and also to the attendant dangers (it can have anti-social effects). In the story of Jacob and Rachel, they identify the former, and move to discipline the latter. Thus "love your neighbour as yourself."

Jewish philosophers focus on ethics. Judging from the examples of Buber and Levinas, they are out of touch with the Bible's basic principle.

Diagnosing the predicament of reflective post-Enlightenment Jews, Levinas observes that the antecedent sense of justice that informed their commitment to the European movements of liberation "found itself deprived of its own language."[60] "It [therefore] turned to a borrowed system of thought to understand itself." The resulting moral position "seems anaemic and emptied of all specifically religious substance."

Strong words. When we look in Levinas for positive backing, all we find is a rhetorical question – "Can one still be a Jew without Kierkegaard?" – and a swipe at the Jewish intellectuals who construct upon Hassidic enthusiasm. Levinas is missing something. He is missing the Bible, understood philosophically. "Talmudic science," Levinas writes, "is the continual unfolding of the ethical order, leading to the salvation of the individual [sc. particular] soul." If talmudic science draws out the Bible's conception of things, why doesn't Levinas say so? If what is drawn out is indefensible, what truth about salvation could the Talmudists have got hold of that turns Nietzchean mockery aside? I don't see how Levinas can resist the anaemic religiosity of Kant. But *we* can resist it. To Kant's roster of dialectical errors, I have added the absorption of ontology by metaphysics.

To close, I'll read into the record Dostoyevsky's dramatization of (in effect) the contrast between ontology and metaphysics – between particular and individual. The scene, from *The Possessed*, contrasts the responses of the novel's tragic figure and of a cynical midwife to a birth. Duplicated is an exchange that one imagines would occur between God and Zeus at the appearance of the first man.

> ... suddenly he heard a cry, a new cry, which made Shatov start and jump up from his knees, the cry of a baby, a weak discordant cry. He crossed himself and rushed into the room. Arina Prohorovna held in her hands a little red wrinkled creature, screaming, and moving its little arms and legs, fearfully helpless, and looking as though it could be blown away by a puff of wind, but screaming and seeming to assert its full right to live. Marie was lying as though insensible, but a minute later she opened her

> eyes, and bent a strange, strange look on Shatov: it was something quite new, that look. What it meant exactly he was not able to understand yet, but he had never known such a look on her face before.
>
> "Is it a boy? Is it a boy?" she asked Arina Prohorovna in an exhausted voice.
>
> "It is a boy," the latter shouted in reply, as she bound up the child.
>
> When she had bound him up and was about to lay him across the bed between the two pillows, she gave him to Shatov for a minute to hold. Marie signed to him on the sly as though afraid of Arina Prohorovna. He understood at once and brought the baby to show her.
>
> "How ... pretty he is," she whispered weakly with a smile.
>
> "Foo, what does he look like," Arina Prohorovna laughed gaily in triumph, glancing at Shatov's face. "What a funny face!"
>
> "You may be merry, Arina Prohorovna ... It's a great joy," Shatov faltered with an expression of idiotic bliss, radiant at the phrase Marie had uttered about the child.
>
> "Where does the great joy come in?" said Arina Prohorovna good-humouredly, bustling about, clearing up, and working like a convict.
>
> "The mysterious coming of a new creature, a great and inexplicable mystery; and what a pity it is, Arina Prohorovna, that you don't understand it."
>
> Shatov spoke in an incoherent, stupefied and ecstatic way. Something seemed to be tottering in his head and welling up from his soul apart from his own will.
>
> "There were two and now there's a third human being, a new spirit, finished and complete, unlike the handiwork of man; a new thought and a new love ... it's positively frightening ... And there's nothing grander in the world."
>
> "Ech, what nonsense he talks! It's simply a further development of the organism, and there's nothing else in it, no mystery," said Arina Prohorovna with genuine and good-humoured laughter. "If you talk like that, every fly is a mystery. But I tell you what: superfluous people ought not to be born. We must first remould everything so that they won't be superfluous and then bring them into the world. As it is, we shall have to take him to the Foundling, the day after to-morrow.... Though that's as it should be."

"There were two and now there's a third human being, a new spirit, finished and complete, unlike the handiwork of man." The Bible writers would have applauded. It's not first, second, and third. It's one, one, and one. Exactly what the first man said: "this one shall be called Woman, for out of Man this one was taken" (Genesis 2:23).

6
Axiology and Ecology

One Leg or Two?

"... and please," the would-be convert says to Shammai, to whom he's applied for an explanation of the Torah, "do the explaining while I stand on one leg." Brandishing "a builder's cubit,"[1] the rabbi shows the man the door. Unfazed, the man then presents himself to Hillel. No less authoritative on the Bible-based creed than is Shammai, and as genial as the latter is prickly, Hillel rises to the challenge. "What is hateful to you, do not do to your neighbour: that is the whole Torah, while the rest is the commentary thereof; go and learn it."

It's no surprise that the talmudic anecdote is recounted from many a pulpit as a monitory illustration of power's insolence towards truth. Mightn't this be unfair to the would-be convert? After the first bum's rush, would a man who wasn't on a quest have put himself in the way of a second?

"How else to interpret the postural figure?" Here's how. Rather than being the timekeeper's point that a person cannot stand on one leg for long, the point could be the kinesiologist's: such is the body's centre of gravity that a person who stands so stands unstably. In glossing the anecdote, why not focus on the instability? Why not, since a genuine issue arises here for those who adhere to the Torah?

The would-be convert, who is he after all? In the context of the anecdote, a person weighing departure from a different religion/belief system must be coming from the direction of paganism.

Pagans worship at different altars than do adherents to the Bible-based faith. To adhere to the latter is to put the pagan deities aside. As it is written at the head of the Decalogue: "you shall have no other gods before me" (Exodus 20:3, Deuteronomy 5:7).

In my construction on the talmudic vignette, the would-be convert is likening the foundation of a religious belief system to the supporting legs of, say, a table. Why should the unsteadiness of a table, one-legged or otherwise, transpose to a one-principle belief system? True, it's only an analogy. The analogy directs attention, however, to a *prima facie* problematic feature of the Torah's view.

It's from the pagan part of town that the man arrives at the doors of the seminaries. Isn't it only reasonable for a reflective person weighing so consequential a move to ask the experts *how it is that their belief system can rest stably on God and on nothing else*. Isn't the man's way of asking wittily consonant with his harbouring such a doubt?

The issue about stability is real for all who situate themselves on God's side of the theological line or whose culture traces back to the shift across the line that the Bible tracks. Most of us are numbered among this "all": the devout in both groups, the secular – usually without awareness of inclusion – in the second.

The issue has two parts. One: What point are monotheists making? Where is *paganism*, the position rejected as idolatrous, being said to fall short? Two: Assuming that adherents to the Bible are correct in imputing shortfall, what about the rest that paganism has to offer? Might monotheism's basis not have to be eked out from the pagan side?

Early on, I said that the Bible's philosophy is misunderstood because the dialectical connection between biblical thinking and pagan thinking passes unappreciated. Pagan thinking, from the Bible's standpoint, isn't a complete write-off. If the Bible's position looks less conciliatory, its self-promoting rhetoric is to blame. I will show in this chapter that a grasp of the dialectical connection gives a perspective on the Bible's ecological position.

"Uncle Sam Wants You!"

"I am the Lord your God; you shall have no other gods before me." Had God's uniqueness as deity been the point, why not "I am the one and only deity; the only object of worship"? What is said, in both parts, stresses "you." This isn't just to add drama. The mention of liberation from Egypt in Exodus 20:2 and in Deuteronomy 5:6 will suggest that the point of "you" lies in the fact that the target audience is a particular group. But this can't be the whole of it. ("You" is second person singular, not second person plural.) The point of the chapters is to enjoin the imperatives upon each and every person, not to report a supposedly historical promulgation that only a few witnessed.

The thrust of what the Bible calls "liberation from Egypt" is ontological. The bondage is to be understood as bondage to a pagan view. Conversion to the Bible-based faith is therefore appropriately represented as a Red Sea crossing to Sinai's side.

The point is not that God is the one and only deity. That misses the point. "I am the Lord your God" means "I am the deity of persons. You are a person. I am your god." By the lights of the thinkers behind the Bible, if men and women who do not accept God possess a proper self-understanding, they cannot justify the possession.

Reality is high and deep and wide: "the heaven of heavens, with all their host, the earth and all that is on it, the seas and all that is in them." The human world is but a part. Another part is the (extra-human) natural world. "God may be the deity of persons. Who is the god of the creatures of the other part, the animals, the plants, the inorganic constituents of the world?"

The would-be convert doesn't have to be seen as taking issue with monotheism's position on the "you"-side. Of concern to him is the rejection of pagan deities. Don't their devotees get explanatory mileage out of the belief system? So it makes sense to question whether monotheism, solely with its proprietary principle, God, can do what needs to be done in accounting for the condition of men and women. My argument will be that the Bible is up to the challenge. *The Bible* is receptive. *The inheritors of the biblical position* have lost touch. One of the casualties is the Bible's ecological position. There's a good deal more to the position than a mixture of enlightened self-interest, a modicum of benevolence, and stewardship.

Hillel and Hazony

"I am the Lord your God &c.," the commandment of commandments, is detachable from the historical experience of the Israelites. Liberation from Egypt stands for liberation from falsehood. Liberation from falsehood all rational persons seek. In his recent book *The Philosophy of Hebrew Scripture*, Yoram Hazony makes this point.[2]

> [T]he teaching offered by the Hebrew Scriptures … has recourse to concepts of a general nature … Because of their generality, such concepts require no prior commitment to the historic Jewish alliance with the God of Israel to be understood. Thus while they were written for the instruction of the Jews, there is no reason why the standpoint and argument they make should not be heard and debated among all nations.

> [I]n Abraham, God is looking for a man whose name can become great, and of whom a great nation can arise. God's concern here is not merely to find a just man, but to raise up an individual who can lay the foundations for a just society.

The Bible tells of a "creator of the entire earth, whose concern is for the good of all his creatures." '*[T]he Israelite cause is worthy because it is, in fact, the cause of all mankind.*" In other words, the Bible is in its key parts speaking – albeit in an ethnic accent – to all. It's basic truths hold equally for the progeny of Moab. Ethnically accented their presentation is; but they are not ethnic truths.

From the fact that the Bible is in its key parts speaking to all it cannot however be inferred that it speaks about all the things that those who look to such a book expect. Hazony's "creator of the entire earth" obscures the invalidity. "Entire earth" implicates the (non-human) physical world. But men and women are the only ones among "[God's] creatures" that he discusses.

Hazony's narrow focus passes problematic. The book contains no substantial reference to the Bible's basic and proprietary ism. But monotheism is the theological face of the biblical basis for the distinctively human side of the creation, a basis that does not extend to the natural realm, not even the natural realm taken to include the biological species to which we belong.

Hillel's focus in the anecdote is the same. He doesn't say what many will have expected him to say, that God gives life to the world and to all its contents. As I see it, the interpersonal focus puts us on the relevant "one leg" footing from the standpoint of the potential proselyte's request. It zeroes in on the principle that paganism is missing. What about the impersonal part of the creation? Does Hillel's distillation have its anchorage in God's cosmogonic activity? If not, then the Bible has two hubs. One hub is the principle that underlies the (natural) world's character, the other is the principle that underlies the character of a single set of creatures. Monotheism, if so, is not a comprehensive alternative to paganism.

The second of Hazony's sentences quoted earlier, the sentence regarding Abraham, ends as follows: "… lay the foundations of a just society with the ability to survive in a sea of injustice." As we'll learn in exploring the Tower of Babel episode, the Bible ponders how politics is likely to look in a world where God does not preside. Accordingly, the truth of the general truths to which Hazony refers in the other sentences is relative to (acceptance of) the deity mentioned in Commandment One. Although, subject to this relativization, moral value is the only positive kind in the interpersonal sphere, it doesn't follow that what counts as immoral from the biblical perspective is unprincipled – a roiling sea. For the other kind of value may apply not to individual persons but to the collective. The objection extends to Hillel. His "Do not do unto others ... " also suggests a Hobbesian free-for-all out of the range of the Bible's principle.

Unless the biblical principle is grasped, none of this will be clear. Social values at odds with the Bible's norms will be characterized as unprincipled. This, in turn, will foster the misimpression that the extra-personal sphere cannot be the locus of positive value. One casualty of this misimpression will be the Bible's ecological position.

Dominion Revisited

> Then God said, "Let us make humankind in our image, according to our likeness; and let them have dominion over the fish of the sea, and over the birds of the air, and over the cattle, and over all the wild animals of the earth, and over every creeping thing that creeps upon the earth."

Then Lynn White, Jr, said, "A main root of current environmental problems is Judeo-Christian arrogance towards nature."[3]

Genesis 1:26 is White's Exhibit A. The prosecutorial summoning of the verse is however a mistake. The bestowal of dominion upon men and women makes good analytic sense. Moreover, the Bible's notion of dominion, understood aright, has no affinity for the attitudes that the environmentalists denounce. The primary association is with "domain."

Here are two annotations on the text of *The New Oxford Annotated Bible* – a distillate of the underlying misunderstanding here. The first summarizes Genesis's opening chapter; the second glosses Genesis 1:26–7.[4]

> Out of original chaos God created an orderly world, assigning a preeminent place to human beings.

> The solemn divine declaration ["Let us make humankind ... and let them have"] emphasizes humanity's supreme place at the climax of God's creative work.

Pace the annotators, men and women don't have a *pre-eminent* place. They have a *different* one. "Supreme place at the climax of God's creative work" piles hyperbole on inaccuracy. In its descriptive sense, "climax" does apply to the emergence of humankind. But the meaning isn't that humankind is in a substantive way special. If the quotation's authors believe that "last" is convertible with "best," they are afoul of the fact that fish get a blessing! The emergence of humankind in Genesis 1 is from the Bible's final perspective a coda to the chapter's theme, not a fanfare. "We're more of the same." Genesis 2, which tells the biblically more important story of the emergence of men and women – "more important" because the story is a biblical departure, not because men and women are more important – has no climax. The man, and then the woman, are the only things whose creation is described.

Here is another illustration of the degree of misunderstanding in the forums of more hermetic biblical thought.

J. B. Soloveitchik distinguishes a utilitarian attitude towards the world, the attitude he claims to find in Genesis 1, from an attitude of faith, geared to redemption, which, he says, is present in Genesis 2.[5] The man of Genesis 1 Soloveitchik calls "Adam I"; the man of Genesis 2 he labels "Adam II." Between Adam I, created in God's image and likeness, and Adam II, vivified with God's breath, *no ontological difference is drawn.* The elision is disastrous. Soloveitchik asserts that Adam I is mandated "to exercise mastery and to ... subdue the garden." *But Genesis 1 is not a Garden, and dominion has little to do with mastery.* Absent from Soloveitchik's treatment is the principle that makes the Bible the Bible.

My readings are not self-certifying. They are however of Genesis itself. An external driver, the appeal to God's creative activity in Genesis 1 as a template for what counts as normative in the human sphere, is central *to Soloveitchik's defence of halakhah.* In comporting themselves halakhically, men and women in *their* affairs are ordering what would otherwise be chaotic. The claim that Genesis 1 is a pagan story runs counter.[6] As for Genesis 2, the ultimate approval therein of the transgressive character of men and women is tough to reconcile with Soloveitchik's needs.

Hazony and Soloveitchik are missing the same thing, as are the annotators of *The New Oxford Annotated Bible.* The principle that applies in Genesis 2 is inapplicable in Genesis 1. Monotheism, a theological form of the Bible's principle, isn't operative in the creation story that Genesis 1 tells.

This criticism of Hazony and Soloveitchik extends beyond the Jewish circle. Non-human animals, Aquinas points out, make use of nature. It is as it should be, he says, that men and women do the same.

A first problem with this reasoning is the mistaken thought that in the matter of dominion God determines the situation of men and women. Dominion is *conceptually* concomitant to the niche-freedom of the human species. The Bible doesn't explain the niche-freedom through the appeal to God, but only clarifies it. A second problem is the representation of the creatures of Genesis 1 as "making use" asymmetrically of the natural world. It is as true to say that the flowers use the bees to get pollinated as to say that the bees use the flowers to get honey. Aquinas, not distinguishing the man and the woman of Genesis 2 from Genesis 1's humankind, writes anthropocentrically. Genesis 1 isn't anthropocentric. As to anthropocentrism in Genesis 2: in the sequel I defend the Bible against attack on this point.

White's criticism gathers force from the Bible's readers' and advocates' textual misunderstandings. To have dominion, in the Bible's sense, is not to be non-green. It's to not have a specific domain. The cut between the niche-bound and the non-niche-bound does not hive off what is natural from what isn't. The Bible stresses the feature of omnivorousness in the case of men and women: "every plant yielding seed ... and every tree with seed in its fruit ... for food." A varied menu would be expected for a cosmopolitan. Would you not say about a niche-bound creature with a need for nourishment unavailable in that niche that extinction would soon put things right?

Appeal to God is not needed to make full sense of Genesis 1's characterization of men and women as having dominion. So it's a mistake to read "let them have" as a bestowal. Starting with the niche-bound (cactuses, polar bears), we move to (natural) things with a more versatile mode of presence (men and women), and then to God, who, being extra-natural, has no (physical) domain. The characterization of men and women is therefore as it should be. At any rate, men and women perceive themselves to be niche-free. God, *qua* having no domain in the natural world, is not appealed to in order to account for the difference.

The repudiation of idolatrous practices doesn't separate the biblical view from the view of non-mystical environmentalists. The objection is only to worshipful reverence of ("bowing down to") nature. Also, and to its credit, the Bible sees the natural world as more tightly unitary. The system-character is asserted, "very good" sealing the deal. The idea of understanding things from the standpoint of the whole does not therefore fall to the objection that, the gods being at odds, "whole" is misleading.

This, then, is the Bible's ontology of the natural world. (1) It's a system of interconnected parts: upper and lower, day and night, the seasons, dry and wet regions. The integrity of the parts depends on the order of the whole. (2) Humankind is part of the system, albeit with the difference that its constituents are niche-free.[7] (3) In the last analysis, humankind's being in his image and likeness in Genesis 1 isn't a doing of God's. (4) What humanity's dominion implies for conduct isn't what White decries. The capacity of the niche-free constituents to cross paths with the niche-bound ones is equilibrium-disrupting. In this there is no more for the defender of nature to object to than there is in an antelope's death in the jaws of a lion. (The death of a bird when it smashes into a plate-glass window is something else, though.) The "problem" goes both ways. Non-human animals are not more fearful of humans than they are of other non-human animals. Nonetheless, God's asymmetrical claim to Noah that "[t]he fear and dread of you shall rest on every animal of the earth, and on every bird of the air, on everything that creeps on the ground, and on all the fish of the sea" (9:2) is sensible in view of the difference – that is, sensible without seeing the ascription of God-likeness to men and women as differentiating them sharply from the rest.[8]

In fine: the natural world has its own character. So does the world of individual men and women. Each world has its governing principle, of system in the one case, of particular in the other. The standpoint of neither is a basis for devaluing the other.

Black and White and Green

From White and Green, I turn to Black and Green – "Black" here referring to Steven S. Schwarzschild, a biblical insider.

My criticism of Schwarzschild is the same as my criticism of Hillel, of Aquinas, and of Hazony. Schwarzschild reads the Genesis 1 story as if it were an adjunct of the Genesis 2 story when in fact it is similar in ontological character – really, *non*-ontological character – to paganism.

Criticizing Soloveitchik's view that there are two Adams – one aesthetic (Genesis 1), the other practical (Genesis 2) – Schwarzschild turns conciliatory only when he finds Soloveitchik subordinating the former to the latter. In support of the subordination Schwarzschild quotes Leviticus Rabbah: "the first man was created for God's use and the disk of the sun for human use."[9] These words repeat the error. The sun comes into existence in Genesis 1. The first man does not. *Humankind* does. Moreover, no issue of use arises in Genesis 1; only an issue of systematic interrelation and reciprocal interchange.

The first man, "Adam" we call him, is created in Genesis 2. Because of the conflation, Schwarzschild is blind to the textual basis for reconciling White to Scripture. Not seeing that Genesis 1's humankind is essentially part of the greenery, Schwarzschild misses what White also misses. From the Bible's perspective the consideration of humankind's well-being requires seeing things – *humankind's* seeing things – from the standpoint of the whole.[10]

Schwarzschild sees in the early part of the Bible only the man of Genesis 2. The attitudes towards the world in the story of the man and the woman in the Garden he takes as biblically normative. This omits the Genesis 1 attitudes. Here, nature is not a garden and humanity is not singled out. A garden is a *cultivated* piece of the world. How could a position about the wilds of Borneo be extracted from Capability Brown's Blenheim? The thinkers/writers responsible for the Bible perform no such magic trick.

Schwarzschild's essay is "The Unnatural Jew." "Unnatural" does not mean "non-natural." The former is a term of abuse; the latter is evaluatively neutral.

The essay's opening anecdote is as provocative as its title. Schwarzschild reports, impishly, that he doesn't get invited to the annual departmental picnic. His colleagues learned early on that he, the unnatural Jew, is a picnic pooper. *The annual departmental picnic, for heaven's sake!* Had *Hillel* been a wielder of the builder's cubit, he might have been tempted. "Don't separate yourself from the community." To be sure, principles are principles. But why should Schwarzschild assume that his colleagues' activity is summer Stravinsky?[11] Genesis 2 features a garden. A picnic is, like a garden, not natural. Also, among Torah-based Jewish festivals are Tu B'shvat, the new year of the trees, and Lag Ba'Omer, on which the celebrants go into nature and, often, picnic. Doesn't God himself (Genesis 3:8) take a "walk ... in the garden at the time of the evening breeze"?

Let's let Schwarzschild have his fun. The flashing of the word "anthropocentric" as a badge of honour cannot similarly be let pass. "This," Schwarzschild writes (351), referring to the Bible, "is anthropocentrism ... long before Kant." The claim that nature hasn't any value in itself anchors Schwarzschild's position on the environment. The denial of value to it, defensible or not, is misdescribed as anthropocentric. It is some stripe of (quasi-Kantian, non-Hegelian) idealism.[12]

Parts of the Bible are hospitable to the idealist construction. God's invitation to the man to name the animals sounds like saying that human cognitive processing of the world is peculiar to the human perspective. But the defence of a bona fide Kantian position isn't a defence of the Bible. The world of Genesis 1 is not a world understood from the perspective of human consciousness. Yet it is, for the Bible, intelligible. Genesis 1 tells us what it's like.[13]

A final provocation is Schwarzschild's use of "pagan." Although hostile to paganism, the Bible is receptive to the naturalism that underlies it, *provided that the naturalism isn't extended into Genesis 2.* "Paganism" in Schwarzschild's hands is therefore tendentious. When he speaks of pagans, it's implied that they bow down to nature. But the Bible's "you shall have no other gods before me" isn't a denial that nature has intrinsic value, and hence is compatible with attitudes such as admiration, respect, and concern for integrity.

Schwarzschild's position is distilled in these lines:

> The biblical and Jewish God is, indeed, absolutely transcendent. Nature is never in any way identical with him. It can serve him, as it can serve human beings made in the "image of God." What makes humans "images of God" is that they share with him the "will," the rational and the ethical.[14]

What a farrago! "Image and likeness" is in Genesis 1. Explaining the phrase, I never used the word "will."Also, I showed how, without bringing in God, to explain what is said when it is said that humankind is made in God's image and likeness. The Genesis 2 story is the story that involves transgression and (therefore) choice. Genesis 2's story is the story from which reference to God is ineliminable.

When, in the Book of Job, God says he plays with Leviathan, when he rhetorically asks whether Job "[c]an … draw out Leviathan with a fishhook" (41:5), he is not saying that the natural thing serves him. Our playmates do not render us a service.[15]

The crucial distinction between Genesis 1 and Genesis 2 passes unnoticed for another reason. The whole of the core of the Bible, the first four books of the Torah and the Deuteronomistic History that concludes with 2 Kings, pursues the Genesis 2 agenda. The interest of the writers/thinkers is in the relations between men and women, personal, family, social, national, and international.[16] That is not surprising, the Bible's novelty being the man of Genesis 2. Paganism's incapacity in this regard is what spurs the Bibleists. When Abraham called out the name of the Lord in Beer-Sheba, he called out Genesis 2, not Genesis 1. At the Bible's core is a philosophical anthropology.

Schwarzschild's confused understanding of the Bible's relationship to the naturalism that suffuses paganism has troubling anti-ecumenical side effects. To the self-proclaimed champion of the Bible, paganism is the foe. Singling out the Christian idea of incarnation, Schwarzschild charges Christians with crypto-paganism. "Nature is never in any way identical with [God]." This threatens to make nonsense of a common denominator between the deity and men and women. Provided that Schwarzschild averts his gaze from an obvious difficulty with this uncompromising assertion, namely that it is as part of the physical world that men and women are fashioned in God's image and likeness, he might think to help himself here to my discussion of the opening chapter. But were he to hitch a ride on what I say, he would, for accepting the difference between Genesis 1 and Genesis 2, owe an explanation of the meaning of God's breath of life. Schwarzschild may think that what he says about image and likeness discharges the debt. But it doesn't. He also fails to appreciate that the Bible's basic principle, connected with the deity of Genesis 2, is an ontological principle applicable *within* the physical realm.

Here, in syllogistic terms, is the real sense in which, according to the Bible, nature is never in any way identical with God. (1) Nature is a system of interconnected parts. (2) The Bible's deity is autonomous and self-contained. (3) Therefore, the Bible's deity is extra-natural.

The biblical representation of God's appearance to Abraham dramatizes Abraham's appreciation that the ontology of his father's house/native culture is inadequate to *his* reality, *qua* enlivened by God's breath, in the world.

The Bible has to be understood from the standpoint of its self-contrast with paganism/naturalism. The latter cannot be criticized from the standpoint of an autonomous and self-contained understanding of the former.

I have no problem with a linkage of volition and particularity. What could a part of a functional entity do with choice? Would an automobile's tire head to the bridge club for a rubber while the rest of the vehicle grinds to work? But volition requires an ontology richer than Genesis 1's. So you can't explain the Bible's opposition to paganism by speaking of the ethical and the rational. As if Plato had nothing to say about ethics! As if Aristotle was deficient in rationality! To discharge your explanatory duty, you must promote the ontological difference. How are people like you and me separate from nature? It is because it has an answer that there is a Bible. The position is not that we men and women are *absolutely* separate from nature. Rather, our basic character requires, for its effective explanation, a principle that is not among the principles adequate for analysing the (purely) physical world. That world is of *individuals*, not of particulars.[17]

The presence of God's breath of life in each of us can be made sense of, also, by appeal to the idea of incarnation. God is, in the Bible's view, immanent. Christian thinkers are in a way more consequent here than Jewish ones. Pascal said: "It is unworthy of God to unite Himself to wretched man; but it is not unworthy of God to pull him out of his misery" (*Pensées* 510). Is Schwarzschild really saying anything different when he says that God is absolutely transcendent?

Pascal's "associate" is evasive. Doesn't the ordeal on the cross imply that God suffers? Orthodox Trinitarians have the resources to block the implication. But they don't take the stubbing of a toe as the model of human adversity. If Schwarzschild thinks that in asserting God's absolute separateness from nature he is only being true to what is written, his thinking is faulty. The biblical account ties our mortality to the breath of life. What could implicate God more in happenings down here than the link between his respiration and our expiration? Certainly, our mortality is a source of suffering. The reality of it causes pain; the thought of it, anguish. Non-human nature, by contrast, does not involve death, only exchanges of matter and energy. "[T]here is nothing new under the sun" (Ecclesiastes 1:9). Or, for that matter, in the sun. To say that God is from the biblical point of view absolutely separate from nature is to say that God is, or stands for, a non-natural principle. Schwarzschild misdescribes the non-identity. He applies spatial language ("outside of") to principles, where the idioms of logic ("inconsistent with," "irreducible to") are appropriate.

Grey Zone

At the Bible's core as a revolutionary document is the category of the particular. But the Bible plays up this category in a potentially misleading form, misleading both because of the theological content of the story of Genesis 2 and because of the story's genetic character. God's breathing *his* breath of life into the first man, the original of all men and women, carries the non-theological and non-genetic message that the character of each person, the particularity of each man and of each woman, cannot be captured by naturalist resources of ontological analysis.

Schwarzschild, following the precedent of the greatest Jewish thinkers whose interest in the Bible has a philosophical character, looks to the canon of philosophy for materials to develop his view. When he catches a whiff of paganism in a philosophical reading of Scripture, he attacks. If in the Bible's name a reflective thinker distinguishes nature from human reality, he says Amen.

True, the heart of the Bible is anti-pagan. But the opposition isn't black and white. The incapacity of paganism to account for human reality draws biblical fire, not its conceptualization of (extra-human) nature. If one wants to express this by saying that the Bible's view is anti-natural, well and good. The Bible does however render unto naturalists. Appearances to the contrary in the core of the Tanakh are due to this, that all the energy is applied to securing the point of opposition.

God, Schwarzschild says, is absolutely transcendent of nature. It follows that nature is absolutely separate from God. It follows in turn that if nature has principles, they are unavailable to the worshippers of God, to the theists.

The world of Genesis 1, humankind included, is a well-ordered system. The biblical position in Genesis 1 is in this respect Platonic. Plato, like the Bibleists, appreciates that men and women are unusual elements of the system. But the Bible has two accounts of their oddity. Niche-freedom, dominion, is central to the one; particularity, to the other. Plato runs them together, though in the opposite direction to biblical scholars like Schwarzschild. Plato denies the will. In Plato's view, men and women go astray not because they are contrary, but (only) because they are ignorant. "To know the good is to do the good." Nor does he ever reintroduce the will. The world according to Plato is the world of Genesis 1.

Philo draws on Plato to "philosophize" the Bible. Genesis 1 *is* receptive to the Academy. But the world of Genesis 2 is not. *God* is present in the world of Genesis 2. His presence is one side of the coin whose other side is the particularity of each one of us. The Bible thus contains what is missing in Plato's world: theologically, God; ontologically, the category of the particular.

Schwarzschild doesn't spare the whip from pagan thinkers among Jews: Philo; Spinoza; the neo-pagans of the early Zionist movement. Although the criticism is not idle, the error of interpretation that I have underscored affects it. To deny that pagan thinking has any purchase in the Bible is to throw out Genesis 1 or, in a reverse of Kirk and Raven, it is to read Genesis 1 as a version of Genesis 2. Underlying the error is Schwarzschild's failure to see that the Bible is the book that it is because it has a philosophy of its own *on the Genesis 2 side.*

Schwarzschild quotes Avoth 3:9 – his favourite Talmudic text. "Rabbi Jacob said: 'One who walks by the road, studying, and interrupts his study and says "How lovely is that tree!" or "How lovely is that furrow!" – Scripture imputes it to him as if he had forfeited his soul!'" To admire nature is to lose one's soul? Schwarzschild reads the point thus. If you want to understand yourself, nature is not the place to look. The truth is different. It's not the only place to look.

The Bible does not subordinate specifically human interest to the integrity of the natural world; nor does it take the view that nature is nothing more than supermarket and dumping ground. Consistently with its view of the world, the Bible's position is two-sided. In addition to the system story of Genesis 1, there is the story of the particular in Genesis 2. The normative position that can be read out of the text is that accommodation has to be sought between the integrity of the system, nature, of which humanity is a part, and the flourishing of the particulars, each man and each woman, who stand apart. That it has to be sought does not guarantee that it will be found once and for all. In our activities in and dealings with the world, we are therefore required, if we follow the Bible, to perform a juggling act, to mix white and black.

HFM Revisited

In the presentation of the commandments, sabbath observance, OS, is motivated by appeal to God and his doings. Doesn't HFM more than just lack a basis in God? With regard to the closest thing to progenitors that God has, namely the "other gods" of paganism, isn't the attitude hostile? Doesn't this change the "H"? Albeit with a pinch of speculation, we now have wherewithal for upholding the parallelism. One: In fact, Genesis treats the pagan gods respectfully. It's what they *don't* do that draws criticism. Two: The Bible does maintain that not to respect the other gods will in fact stunt our lives. The disrespect, which will come from the actions of the men and the women of Genesis 2, will upset the equilibrium in which we, in our complex way, flourish as a species.

7
Political Philosophy: The City and the Tower

State of Confusion?

"Babel," a transliteration of the name that the inhabitants of (as *we* know it) Babylon applied to their several *iku* of the world, means "gate (bab) of god (el)."[1] Picking a verb from their branch of the Semitic language tree, the writers of the Bible concoct an insulting pun. "Come," says the Lord, "let us go down, and confuse their language there, so that they will not understand one another's speech" (11:7). "Therefore it was called Babel, because there the Lord confused the language of all the earth" (9).

Could it be that the Bible's application of "State of Confusion" to it does Babel a disservice?[2]

As with Thebes of classical Greek tragedy, Babel is the *topos* for exploring political existence. Indisputably, the Bible takes a dim view of the place. Yet the wider narrative tells a parallel story whose protagonist, Cain, is spared the criticism, even though *his* city-building stems from a transgression that seems a lot graver. "Cain rose up against his brother Abel, and killed him" (4:8). The fratricide starts a chain of events. "Cain knew his wife, and she conceived and bore Enoch; and he built a city, and named it Enoch after his son Enoch" (17). The implication? In some sense that distinguishes it from natural offspring, the city is the offspring of man. The Babelites also link their baby, which like Cain's is self-conceived, to name-giving. They undertake *their* project desirous to "make a name for ourselves" (11:4). Yet although those who congregate "on a plain in the land of Shinar" (11:2) proceed in a spirit of brotherhood never before seen, God disperses them like keeperless sheep. Cain is by contrast permitted the home-and-garden setting over

Abel's more diffuse way. Isn't the Bible condoning conflict and condemning cooperation? To resolve the puzzlement here, we need to factor in the Bible's ontology.

Cain is of Genesis 2's world, a world of particulars. The Babelites have *their* roots in the world of Genesis 1, a system of mutually dependent parts. Equipped with the distinction, not only are we in a position to understand the Bible's moral preference for Enochville over the construction that (therefore) got Berlitzed before it was named. We will also, I think, endorse the preference.

Death by Water?

The biblical story is lodged in the cultural consciousness as the story of *the tower of Babel*. The contents of Genesis 11:1–9 do not justify that title. The *dramatis personae* propose a two-part plan: "let us build … a city, and a tower with its top in the heavens" (11:4). In the sequel, vertical never dominates horizontal. The last verse to speak of the tower, verse 5, embeds it in the conjunction "city and tower." When the enterprise is finally terminated, the builders, we are informed, "left off building the city" (8).

For being just one element of a pair, "a city … and a tower," the skyscraper of Babel corresponds less to the Eiffel Tower of the 1889 World's Fair than to the Trylon of the Trylon-and-Perisphere duo that themed the 1939 event. This points up a difficulty in what is bound to suggest itself to readers as the motive for the construction.

You live along the San Andreas Fault. Eventually, anxiety triumphs. You load the U-Haul and head for stable terrain. Wouldn't fear of a second watery cataclysm fix mankind's mind wonderfully? Boarding a super-buoyant vessel will recommend itself, as will taking up residence atop a skyscraper.

Netherlanders of their age, the tower builders made common cause to protect against a watery repeat. That, on a first pass, is the unavoidable explanation of the collective goings on.

"The extensive Noahic family-tree of Genesis 10 puts thirty-two verses and several generations between the end of the flood in Genesis 9 and the tower in Genesis 11. Isn't the explanation unavoidable only if a considerable swath of text is avoided?" Consider: when the waters subside, the human population numbers in the tens. Needed for narrative plausibility are a few generations of multiplying. So Genesis 10 is as it should be and where it should be. Since the genealogy of Noah in this chapter follows a branch that extends from Ham, close to the trunk, out to Nimrod, "the beginning of [whose] kingdom was Babel, Erech and Accad" (10), a link is forged with what follows.

Massive construction requires muscle to match. Although the presence of a chapter separating 9 from 11 is thereby rationalized, textual presences and absences like the following ones eventually swamp such interpretive dikes. After the spillways of the heavens are closed and the hydrants of the deep are shut, the ark comes to rest on a mountaintop (8:4). In God's world, high places are never far off. The construction site, Scripture reports, is "a plain in the land of Shinar" (11:2).[3] As for what the chapters and the verses do *not* contain: worry about rising waters would place a premium on the topmost stories of the tower; none of the concerned express reservations about a *pied-à-terre.*

The project doesn't appear to be swept forward from its narrative starting point, the flood. Could the tower be a painterly flourish?

The question directs our attention to the story's other element. It is however no easier in regard to the city to make out the point.

City Lights

Those who front the project want to live in the city. "Let us make a name for ourselves; otherwise, we shall be scattered abroad upon the face of the whole earth" (11:4). Why work so hard to make a name? Most readers and interpreters say that the speakers of the quoted words crave fame. True, a non-negligible number of men and women seek celebrity and work overtime to keep it. Still, obscurity doesn't trouble the sleep of the majority; indeed, not a few of the celebrated would give a lot to regain anonymity lost. This reading of "make a name" leaves us baffled about the idea's gripping mankind as a whole. Similar remarks apply to "otherwise, we shall be scattered." Reflexively, readers say that the builders *value* making a name, understood as achieving renown. Typically, they think that the builders *fear* the scattering. But where does the text identify the emotion? The bricklayers could be coolly expressing the near-analytic claim that avoiding diffusion requires residing together in numbers, as was first done in post-nomadic proto-urban environments.[4] Obviously, God's intervention, which generates the diffusion, is meant to prevent that dwelling place from being completed. But lack of clarity about what it is that God takes exception to – the dwelling place? the desire to make a name? – matches murkiness about what it is the builders are up to. God says that unless he steps in "nothing that they propose to do will ... be impossible for them" (11:6). "Nothing" cannot be meant literally. We today, agnostic about the extra-natural, work together to build the cities in whose high-rises many pass their lives. Should we be in the least forgetful about the limits of our powers, each return of the sun illuminates them afresh: snarled traffic, fetid air, boil-water advisories. What does God think the masons will do? It is also worth asking whether the scattering that ends the episode is a punishment. Couldn't it be a return to a condition that in the Bible's estimation better fits men and women?

The builders' motivating claims about nomination and scattering are opaque. Since God's attitude signals what by the Bible's lights is normative, God's reaction will stay a puzzle until we figure out why the builders swarm onto the site.

One point of stability can be found in all this: the scattering is a reversion to a more chaotic state – a move back in the direction of the flood. The condition the flood precipitated was also more chaotic than the condition of greater order that God found obnoxious.[5] It's worth adding that Abraham's departure for Canaan is also entropic. Since the chaos/order spectrum preoccupies the Bible from the beginning, the suggestion that the problem at Babel has to do with order is a credible one.

God is dead set against the enterprise. Grave reservations are acted on in the case of Sodom and Gomorrah too. Nevertheless, the Bible reconciles to city life. (God speaks of the "sin" of those who dwell in Sodom and Gomorrah [18:20]. Who are the unclean of hands among the Babelites?) Despite high regard for the shepherd's crook, the text is aware that the nomadic form of existence is a way station. The problems that settling down raises have therefore to be confronted on their own terms. Since the Bible has no final objection to societies of unrelated men and women, why does God multiply the tongues *here*? One expects some pertinent difference between the city at Babel and a place even so disreputable as Sodom. The expectation is met. Thematically speaking, "Collective World" is a more appropriate sign at Babel's limits than "City."

A Discontinuity and the Possibility of Interpreting the Bible

Is the tower, the element of the construction that associates with rising water, more than narrative trimming? Appreciating as we now do that flood and Babel are not thematically linked in any straightforward way, we might begin to wonder whether they are thematically linked at all.

The hypothesis of a link runs up against a narrative discontinuity. The genealogy of Noah gives us a world that through population increase and migration has become multi-national. Thus the final verse of chapter 10: "These are the families of Noah's sons, according to their genealogies, in their nations; and from these the nations spread on the earth after the flood." Genesis 11 starts with "Now the whole earth had one language and the same words." How could this condition have arisen from "the nations spread abroad … after the flood"?

Many scholars appeal here to the Documentary Hypothesis. By the usual tests, chapters 10 and 11 have different origins. That being so, many DH-ers rate as snark-like a reading that makes thematic sense of the whole.

It cannot justifiably be assumed that the Bible is interpretable. Still, accepting DH is consistent with resisting the inference from it to the conclusion that the whole lacks thematic unity.

The pressure to accommodate the elements might well constrain the redactors. Despite that, the redaction might yet produce a product with a single message. Moreover, the presumption will be that the redactors are trying for a coherent whole. (If it's dogmatic to rank readings on which all the elements cooperate higher than readings on which they do not, then we're wired dogmatic.) Oddly enough, crediting DH is even a fillip to interpretation. A reader alive to the certainty that coarse ligatures feature throughout the text will tend to give up less quickly.[6]

The flood doesn't motivate the construction at Babel. Nonetheless, flood and Babel are adjacent on more than just a parchment scroll. The Babel episode follows the story of the flood because those who fashioned the text have a reason for the positioning, not because the builders at Babel looked over their shoulders at the flood and were afeared. The link has proven elusive because we've been scouring the tale rather than interrogating the tellers.[7] The flood doesn't bear on the construction. Short of a massive rewrite, the flood's occurrence nevertheless supplies the optimal narrative spot for the story. The flood is an instrument of reversion to an earlier condition, and the enterprise is a reprise of the original creation. Note the echo between God's "nothing that they will propose to do will now be impossible for them" (11:6) and the claim that having eaten of the fruit of the tree of knowledge the first man and the first woman will "become like one of us" (3:22) unless the other tree is placed off limits. In both cases intervention is called for because of what is represented as a going too far. But while the account of the flood supplies an apt location for the story of the project at Babel, the tower could from *this* perspective have remained on the drawing board.

Here, schematically, is how we got to where we're at.[8]

FLOOD OF NOAH	TOWER + CITY	SCATTERING

This diagrams the position first taken. The flood explains the tower: the builders are seeking security from a repeat. Thematically, the city is an indivisible part of the unitary project: tower + city. Those involved in the project get scattered, possibly because they show distrust in God's solemn promise: "nor will I ever again destroy every living creature as I have done" (8:21).

Once the flood of Noah is disconnected from the construction, the cataclysm is cut off thematically from the rest.

FLOOD OF NOAH		TOWER + CITY	SCATTERING

But while, as the shaded divider symbolizes, the flood *qua flood of Noah* is not linked to the construction, the flood *qua flood* is. With the divider removed, here is a more articulate graphing.

FLOOD	CITY	SCATTERING-1
	TOWER	SCATTERING-2

The city is the upshot of the flood, albeit the flood considered as a return to disorder rather than as the destruction of Noah's world. The featureless plain, an endless desolation, is the dry version of the flood. Although linked on the construction site to the city, the tower has thematic affiliations unrelated to the deluge. The scattering as concerns the tower differs from the scattering as concerns the city.

God: A Biography

The location of the construction is named from the real world. Could some other location have been used, albeit at the cost of the Bible's pun? I said that the site's being level has a thematic bearing. The Sumerian plain, I will now show, is relevant. This will rationalize the story's being of a city *and* a tower.

The enterprise at Babel seems to be drawn forward from its destination, the city and (whatever this means) the desire not to be scattered. Looking farther ahead still, to the next biblical phase, will enable us to make thematic hay with the second conjunct of "city and tower."

The story of Babel immediately precedes the national story. That too is a creation story: of the chosen people. Abraham hails from the lower reaches of the Euphrates. "Go from your country" (12:1) is a call to put Sumer in the rear-view. Is it significant that the call concerns a place adjacent to the location selected for the tower? Unlike the Eden phase of the narrative, this phase is proto-historical.[9] Since people thought of as real can't be represented as growing on trees, perhaps a point of origin in the environs of Babylon is specified for reasons of verisimilitude. "To understand what Abraham stands for, what moves him from the inside needs to be understood." There is however a basis for a reading that connects inside and outside. That Abraham's idea of a destination will be informed by his dissatisfaction with the status quo is only to be expected. He does not set out *ex nihilo*. This basis makes interpretive use of both facts: Babel is the site; a tower is a component.

A tower figures at Babel because – relevantly to Abraham's story – towers were prominent in the land that he left. Although the ziggurats of ancient Babylon come after plausible dates for Abraham,[10] vertically oriented items of architecture did punctuate the Sumerian sky at an appropriate time. The pre-biblical Mesopotamian creation myth, the *Enuma Elish*, echoed in several phases of Genesis, tells of a skywards construction.[11]

In the land of towers, Abraham, a native son, receives God's call to depart. He has a flash of insight regarding the culture – the philosophy – of this land. What he comes to understand has to do with Babylon's being by name a gate to heaven. What might that be?

The tower project could not be a *repudiation* of God. The world is as yet ignorant of Abraham's inspiration. Many interpreters, viewing the project as idolatrous, see Abraham's departure as a repudiation of idolatry. True, the building of the city has a non-religious flavour. Without appealing to the extra-natural, the enterprisers try to implement a plan of living. A city of man, then, as opposed to a city of God. Doesn't the same go for the tower? That isn't obvious. In any case, Abraham's enterprise is also a back-turning on a form of religious thinking.

The tower builders know nothing of God. I'll amplify this by answering a few questions – biographical ones. Who is God? Where does God come from? Although the Bible does not respond explicitly, lateral thinking unearths pertinent data.

Abraham puts distance between himself and the Lower Euphrates. God promises national success and greatness. Abraham believes the promise. He starts the engine and heads off. God and Abraham march in step.

The creation of the nation, like the (biblical) creation of the world, is an attempt to enlighten. In the one case, a literal darkness of being is confronted: light is created. Tackled in the other case is a figurative darkness about a way of being: one group, through its trailblazing, is made a light unto the nations. Immediately this is noted, supplying God with a real-world biography becomes attractive.

God is signposting a new way. "[A new] land ... I will show you" (12:1) he says to Abraham. The old land – dark, benighted – is Babylon. In separating himself from the old ways and the old gods, God is kin to Prometheus. Albeit on a larger scale, he creates the world with men and women in mind.

Who, then, could God be? Why not, like Prometheus, a minor and dissident member of the Babylonian pantheon who forswears the "other gods," as Abraham is a marginal Babylonian who takes matters into his own hands?

Abraham's departure mirrors God's. Better: God's heavenly trailblazing is a projection of Abraham's more terrestrial pioneering. Why would Abraham listen unless he bought into the idea? God calls to Abraham: "Go from your land." His land is, nearly enough, Babylon. So too does God depart the place. God steals out of *his* family's house.

Is the reader receptive to my *God: A Biography*? The main thrust ultimately hits (or misses) the target on its own. What the builders at Babel are up to overlaps with what Abraham, conceived and raised on the lower reaches of the Euphrates, stands for.

Why at Babel? Why a Tower?

"Babel" means "gate of god." The tower reaches up towards heaven's gate. That is a clue. What was (felt to be) wrong with the extant arrangement on high? Hear the Editor of the Anchor Bible Genesis:[12]

> In Mesopotamia, the very tenets that stimulated the social growth of the country proved to be a source of weakness in its spiritual progress. The terrestrial state was non-autocratic because man took his cue from the gods; and in the celestial state no one god was a law unto himself, not even the head of the pantheon. All major decisions in heaven required approval by the corporate body of the gods. And since nothing was valid for all time, the upshot was chronic indecision in heaven and consequent insecurity on earth.

Speiser is aiming to explain monotheism's significance as one theological position from a range and also to explain its significance to the Bible. Having described the social effects of "Mesopotamian polytheism," he proceeds:[13]

> Because the cosmos was viewed as a state in which ultimate authority was vested in the collective assembly of the gods … mankind … lacked the assurance of absolute and universal principles.
>
> Monotheism, on the other hand …

"[T]he genesis of the biblical way is bound up with the beginnings of the monotheistic concept; both converge in the age, and presumably also the person, of Abraham." If the tower builders were associated with such beginnings, to make sense of God's objection we would have to liken God to an inventor who sabotages a competitor's workshop. Had the redactors left such a story in the product, they would have blown their subversive cover.

The tower builders' blueprint looks proto-monotheistic. On Speiser's reading, the believers in Babylon wish to *overcome* the discord in heaven which, since they look aloft for guidance, makes them less effective in life.[14] The reform is predicated on abandoning the belief system that obstructs their flourishing.[15]

Shouldn't an enterprise animated by the idea of *reducing discord on high* seem meritorious from the standpoint of monotheism? Two quotations back, I interrupted Speiser. Here's the completion of his thought.

"Monotheism, on the other hand, is predicated on the concept of a God who has no rivals, and is therefore omnipotent."[16] God, monotheism's theological face, scuttles the enterprise; does so, moreover, by *increasing discord down low*. Were that the sum total of it, the court would judge Abraham's departure from his native land a pusillanimous response to an internal challenge.

The tower and the city must be separated. Doing this puts us in a position to tackle the problem. What I wrote in the preceding paragraphs assumes, as Speiser does, that the multiplying of tongues is a critical response to the tower.[17] Why assume that? The response to the tower is monotheism. Monotheism is the topic of chapter 12, not of chapter 11.

God has declared independence of the Babylonian pantheon. He has left *his* native land and *his* father's house. The reform is in train. The tower to the heavens is not needed. Abraham's departure is the earthly version of God's. Abraham has initiated the Bible's reform. We can therefore add to the bottom right cell of the preceding schema.

FLOOD	CITY	SCATTERING–1
	TOWER	SCATTERING–2 ABRAHAM ≈ MONOTHEISM

The construction at Babel, the tower particularly, connects with the monotheistic démarche. The city + tower whole is however subjected to criticism. Here's what's happened. The positive point the tower makes, the point about revolution and/or reform, is picked up in Genesis 12. God has descended, or departed, and is now moving onwards. *We*, however, are still with the city builders.

Making a Name

In many respects, the building of the city seems meritorious. Harmful as far as one can see to no one, it is pursued in a spirit of cooperation that is already fraying in the first couple's relations and that has enmified in the interactions between the first siblings. No slavery is involved – a nonsense in the contemporary world for an undertaking that large. To pinpoint the fault that is found, let's look at the details.

The city builders' motivating words were quoted: "let us make a name for ourselves" (11:4). Under the influence of English phraseology, the reader will see fame as the goal. Why the city builders would want celebrity is unclear, though.

Let's try another road. The city builders speak of "making a name." Genesis in its early parts is chock-a-block with namings. To much of the activity, renown is irrelevant. The issue is identity and ontology. Names, which we go by, are windows on who we are and on what we are.

The giving of names begins no later than five verses into Genesis. "God called the light Day, and the dark … he called Night." After the tower story, God (17:5) gives Abraham a name. Whatever (else) the builders are attempting, their activity exercises a function that is closely associated with God.

God's name-calling in Genesis 1 links to his world-creating. Albeit on a lesser scale, men and women create worlds too. Planting fence posts and stringing wire, Cain makes the world that he inhabits. The first farmer is also the first city builder. In this capacity, Cain gives a name, an action the text does not inflect negatively. Nor should we forget that God enlists the man to name the animals. From the biblical perspective, a mortal's assuming the name-giving function isn't necessarily presumptuous. Made in God's image and likeness, we are *supposed* to perform the *imitatio Dei.*

What then is wrong with *this* effort? The effort starts too far back; back behind Genesis 2.

Deliberately or not, the builders are attempting what God had done. "Attempting what God had done" sounds prideful. Again, however, the text doesn't turn an unequivocal thumbs-down. Despite initial misgivings, many parents are *delighted* when children strike out on their own. It's possible to see God to be offering encouragement (albeit mingled with concern about the implications) to the first man and the first woman. We are still at sea, therefore, as to why *this* effort is objectionable. In what sense does God's accomplishment fall beneath the result the city builders envisage? What's the sense in which God's (as it may seem) less ambitious activity is normative? Whatever the sense, what's to fault?

"The builders are unhappy with God's world." Many readers and interpreters assert this. Where's the textual basis? As the narrative presents the builders, they have devised a project and are moving to implement. It accords better with the text to reverse the direction of unhappiness, does it not?[18] But why the dissatisfaction?

The builders set to work "upon a [featureless] plain" (11:2). The construction materials they manufacture themselves. "[T]hey had brick for stone" (11:3). Evidently, the idea is to start from scratch. Their activity thus echoes God's. The builders are making a world *by* themselves ("let us" [3, 5]) and *for* themselves ("ourselves" [4, twice]).

Alterations to God's world the Bible is willing to accept. On one occasion God dismantles his own handiwork. If we were driven to the conclusion that God spites the Babelites, we would suspect some printer's devil of having snuck the episode in while Ezra was on a break.

The repeated use of the first person pronouns ("us," "ourselves," "we") suggests that the builders, utterly self-absorbed, will forget God. Since no awareness of God is ever evinced by them,[19] the charge of forgetfulness lacks a basis in the text. The self-contained character of their activity does however provoke a set of questions that leads forward.

Didn't God indicate that Cain's way of life will be accepted if its solution to the problems of human flourishing posed by Abel's way doesn't worsen matters overall? If the envisioned world is a better one, why not close the book on the past? If we insist on looking over the city builders' shoulders, don't we *by the Bible's own reckoning* deserve to be turned into pillars of salt? Where in the text is a substantive criticism of the project entered?

Answers to the questions are present in a so far unremarked element of the story. What, we ask, is wrong with attempting to make a name for oneself? The text does not however speak of *making a name for oneself*. The builders express the aim of *making a name for themselves*. The project is collective. All the personal pronouns are plural. The text always refers to the builders as "they," and several times employs "themselves."[20] The fact that in interpreting we do not usually focus on the plurals indicates how easily the key feature is passed over.

The implicit contrast with the Bible's normative position is that where God creates alone, the city builders act *en masse*. This makes all the difference. Also, it tells us a lot about monotheism.

Our topic is the story of the city and the tower. The key to the story is understanding the conceptual underpinnings of the mentioned contrast.

Conceptual Underpinnings

The story of the city at Babel is linked to the story of the original creation. The language of Genesis 1's anthropogenic part regarding men and women is plural too. "Humankind." "Make them." "He made them." This language differs in its number from the language of Genesis 2. In Genesis 2 God fashions a particular man, and (then) a particular woman, each very much a separate individual. That is how we think of our coming into the world: one person is born; then another; then another. Of animals, our thinking is (more) along the lines of Genesis 1. "The dinosaur walked the earth eighty million years ago."

In Genesis 2, God forms *the man* and breathes him into life. *Humankind* comes into being in Genesis 1. Although the species is already recognized as distinctive, *no member is inspired with life by God*. Made in God's image and likeness (there are no non-human tower-and-city builders), the humans of Genesis 1 do not have God's breath in them.

A driver of the biblical narrative is the indisputable truth that the organization of the human world must be sensitive to what human beings are. Disputation begins with the specifics. In Genesis 2, human beings are said to be essentially sociable. "It is not good that the man should be alone" (18).[21] The family is advanced as a basic unit. "Therefore a man leaves his father and his mother and clings to his wife" (24). Starting in Genesis 2 the Bible explores the ways in which men and women, so conceived, live their lives – lives of particulars. The particularity is crucial to what the Bible, in its normative mode, says about men and women. In the origin story relevant here, the story of Genesis 2, men and women receive what no (mere) animal possesses – the particularity of the monotheistic deity.[22] The city builders are visitors/atavists from the world of Genesis 1 – Paleoanderthals, so to speak. In initiating their enterprise, they, like water seeking its level, are doing what comes naturally to them.

And "making a name for ourselves"? The builders at Babel do not regard themselves as God does (and hence, normatively, as the text does). One language they have; few words. Those not enamoured of the idea of painting the earth one colour might detect in the Bible a kindred distaste. The Bible's view is more articulate. The Bible is pluralistic because it is particularistic. Attributing "one language and the same words" (11:1) to the builders is tantamount to attributing to them, as to a herd of animals or to a flock of birds, a group mind.[23] As the climate problem hammers home, we *are* in it together. But God is one. And so, since each of us is inspired with God's breath of life, there are many people; many tastes in colour too.

Why is the city enterprise placed after the flood? The text is dealing with material in the conceptual field of Genesis 1. It is necessary to go back behind the world of Genesis 2 – the world in which Noah lives.

The obliteration of this world supplies the best narrative occasion. But although the city builders' doings at Babel belong to the field of Genesis 1,[24] the contents of the opening chapter are too elemental to sustain the story.[25] As to why the project is metropolitan: a detail in the story of Cain determines the choice. There, the city is identified as the (non-biological) issue of man. "[H]e built a city, and named it Enoch after his son Enoch." How then do Cain and the Babelites differ? In Cain's case, it was (singular) *he* who built.[26] Here, the city is the issue of *us* (plural). It may be inferred that the collective character of the project at Babel (note that the streaming to Babel is like the pooling of water in a larger body) is thematically essential. While the city does offer us numbers of (non-related) individuals acting in concert, the association with Cain gets in the way of appreciating that the story goes back to Genesis 1. A kibbutz, commune, or *kolkhoz* would have done the job better. Why "make a name for ourselves"? The Bible's logic entitles humankind of Genesis 1 to do that. In Genesis 2, God calls upon the man to name the animals. The man doesn't name himself. But since God has not breathed life into Genesis 1's human sector, the self-naming is appropriate to *its* constituents. Why scattering? Dispersion in a figurative sense, the scattering is reversion to particularity. By the normative lights of the Bible, the order of Genesis 1 is too tight. God claims that if they succeed, nothing will be impossible for them. This means that their natures, being in their own hands, won't be subject to the ethical constraints and the moral limits that otherwise attach. If we were our own parents, parental curfews would not bind us.[27]

Cain deviated from God. Cain built a city. Doesn't the same occur at Babel? Cain's activity takes place along the Genesis 2 path. From Cain God is therefore prepared to learn. "If you do well, will you not be accepted?" (4:7) Cain might easily be conceived to pose the question. "If I do well, will you not accept me?" *We* ask the question all the time, of our elders, of our betters, of the world. Cain's wandering is not literal. His departure from the gathering way of his parents and from the shepherding way of his brother demagnetizes his ethical compass. Possibly, he's gone farther than is good for him. From the start, the city builders at Babel are (by contrast) out of God's range. So the antecedent of God's question to Cain doesn't apply. The Cain-side *and* the Babel-side are discernible in the story of Lot. Zoar, the small city[28] in which God permits Lot to settle after the acid rain wastes and voids Sodom, is like the world after the flood. God is starting again with a few seeds. But Lot decamps Zoar for a cave. When he enters the lair, the Bible is quit of him.[29] Taking up residence there, he exhales the divine breath of life. Never having been inspired, the Babelites haven't it to lose.

This reading accords with the writing. The man fashioned in Genesis 2 names the animals. Auto-baptism? No. The men and women of Genesis 11 set out to "make a name" for themselves. The logic of the story entitles them to such an initiative. Once men and women are particularized, the liberties with respect to nature (*their* nature, I mean) are removed. The integrity of each man and of each woman is now ratified.

"[Y]ou shall have no other gods before me" (Exodus 20:3; Deuteronomy 5:6). Our interpretive efforts give a fresh perspective. The plural "gods" can be made sense of, and "before" can be construed in temporal terms. "Men and women," God can be understood as saying, "must not revert to the deity of Genesis 1 from the deity of Genesis 2." This is revealing about the core meaning of biblical monotheism. Monotheism is the theological face of the view of human particularity as basic.

Our final schema is this:

FLOOD ≈ CHAOS	CITY	SCATTERING–1
		PARTICULAR MEN & WOMEN
FLOOD OF NOAH	TOWER	SCATTERING–2
		ABRAHAM ≈ MONOTHEISM

Scattering–1 is ontological. It stands opposed to the idea of a non-voluntary collective of men and women: humankind as a herd. Scattering–1 is thus the narrative expression of particularism. Scattering–2 takes a more specific line against an excess of voluntary or distributive unity. Scattering–2 is the dramatic expression of (particularistic) pluralism. From a distance the two can seem identical – which may explain the story's being told so as to oblige us to ask: Why a city *and* a tower?

The Bible objects to unity of a tight, organic character. The story of the city at Babel (Scattering–1) is the story of non-distributive unity. Why should the Bible combine this with a criticism of distributive unity (Scattering–2)? As is usual with Holy Writ, the position is nuanced. Consider the conquest of the Promised Land. When the Reubenites and the Gadites seek leave to remain east of the Jordan, Moses explodes. "Shall your brothers go to war while you sit here?" (Numbers

32:6) *Some* projects admit of no exceptions. Could the war against global warming be the war from conscription into which no man or woman can get a waiver? Cases of *force majeure* aside, the Bible's view is particularistic. The particularism is evident in Jacob's laying of hands on his sons. The blessings play up their differences. The position is that non-distributive unity should be the exception. Its being the rule is likely to challenge the flourishing that counts – that of particular people. Reuben and Gad can, *ceteris paribus*, be allowed to settle east of the Jordan. God won't stand in their way, despite that making the Israelites a great nation *in* the Promised Land was covenanted.

It's no accident that the first murderer is the first city father. Institutions of justice manage conflict. The city is their natural location. More deeply, in having the third human mentioned being the first taker of a life, the Bible brings out that the human beings of Genesis 2 are particulars and that their being beings whose existences terminate has implications for how they live their individual lives and for how they conduct themselves communally. Not so the constituents of Genesis 1. The point lights up the contrast between the fraternity of the Babelites and the antagonism of the sons of Adam. When we think of the world as an organic system, change is processed as exchange. Night does not kill day, nor does day have the duty to be night's keeper. Night has no grievance when day dawns, nor does day feel resentful at dusk. The same goes for antelope and lion. Judgments are made from the standpoint of the system. In Genesis 1, this comes out in God's judging "good" everything that is created. "Bad" is first heard in Genesis 2. When everything is good, adjudication is unnecessary.

My talk of fraternity at Babel was hasty. The harmony of the Babelites isn't that of a Cain and an Abel after they settle their differences, or of a Jacob and an Esau who let bygones be bygones. It's the meshing of the parts of a well-constructed machine. In this world, the world of Genesis 1, death has no dominion. The whole rolls on through changes to the parts. Politics presupposes particulars with competing interests and a stopwatch on their satisfaction. So here there are no politicians, only mechanics to grease the wheels if they squeal and to repair the gears should their teeth chip. Yet although politics proper therefore begins in the Bible only in a world of scarcity, it remains that the inhabitants of Eden are potential *zooi politikoi*. This is not true of the constituents of Genesis 1's humankind. In scarcity as in plenty, *their* ballots would specify only one party.[30]

Polytheism: Guilt by Association?

The account of the city, the first element of the Babelite project, is complete. We men and women are particulars. Arrangements of an organic kind suck out the breath of life that God breathes into the first person and that is transferred over time to each of us. As a description of how we think, the Bible's normative position is compelling.

And the second element? The Bible's attack on the tower undeservedly benefits from association with the other. Although the Bible advocates strongly for the view that there is one and only one deity, its position in this case is ultimately difficult to distinguish, functionally, from, in the strict sense, polytheism.

The Bible contains another double of the story of Babel: the episode of Jacob's dream in Genesis 28. In a dream, Jacob has a theophany. God repeats the promise of national greatness made to his grandfather. Jacob awakens, and says:

> "Surely the Lord is in this place – and I did not know it!" And he was afraid, and said, "How awesome is this place! This is none other than the house of God [in Hebrew: *beth-el*], and this is the gate of heaven [*shaar hashamayim*]." (16–17)

"Shaar hashamayim" sounds nothing like "Babel," although it means roughly the same. "Bethel," the name that Jacob gives to the place (19), resembles "Babel" on both counts.

As the case may be linguistically, Jacob's is a story of a single individual and of reciprocity between that individual and the single deity who sponsors him. It's also a story of a man who dreams of God and who, because of the medium, has doubts. However rich God's promise, Jacob's asks are modest: food, clothing, passage home. The modesty makes sense: under conditions of uncertainty, asking a lot is asking disappointment.

We have here, then, a monotheistic version of the same problem that the tower builders' story embodies. Adherents to polytheism, Speiser was quoted to say, got no clear directives from on high. But Jacob's story too tells of one not untypical monotheist who is floundering. Jacob's heaven's gate is functionally like the gate of god.

The functional equivalence between (1) clashing messages from different sources and (2) ambiguous intelligence from a single source again confirms that the national narrative strain beginning with Abraham continues the tower part of Babel. It is as it should be that Abraham's message was more direct and clearer than Jacob's.

Adherents to a religion that is in the strict sense polytheistic would worship a multiplicity of gods each of whom, like God, is a one. Anyone who agrees that the class of particulars in the human realm is coextensive with the set comprising each and every person must budget for such a thing. It follows the construction of the city in Shinar would not have been disrupted had the Babelites adhered to a theistic system with more than one deity. Moreover, because of *their* Commandment One – "Have no other non-theistic god or gods before us" – the several deities of such a system would together have done what God did.

The Goldilocks Zone

"In the compendium of foundational myths that open to the Hebrew Bible, one tale seems to be oddly out of place."[31] The reference is to the Tower of Babel episode. Gordis continues: "Adding to the story's enigmatic character is its unique context, situated as it is between the tale of the flood, which concerns humanity as a whole, and the election of Abraham, which deals with one nation." The tale of the Flood is part of the Genesis 2 narrative. Gordis misses that the myth of Babel connects, specifically, to Genesis 1. The Bible he sees as taking a stand against the wisdom of a single-nation arrangement. But the biblical concern is deeper. It's whether nations are collective (humanity of Genesis 1), or collections of particulars (the man and the woman of Genesis 2). The defence of Israelite nationhood is a different matter. This brings us to the issue of chosenness.

Each person is, on the Bible's view, holy. The Bible also represents Israel, the nation, as holy. The extension must be resisted. It is a retreat to Genesis 1 from Genesis 2.

The Goldilocks Zone is the region in the field of a star where the temperature range doesn't rule out life as we know it. In these terms, the thesis is that the natural is too cold for biblical life, the national, too hot. The thematic centre of the Bible is the character of the individual man and of the individual woman. Men and women are the only God-like things in the creation. The Bible's Goldilocks Zone is the God-like Zone. But each individual Ammonite, each individual Midianite, is as God-like are Reuben, Simeon, Levi, and Judah. Nations, if God-like, are not so in the same sense.

Eager Covenanter, Balky Patriarch (1)

Abraham is a willing covenanter. So strongly does he feel about the rightness of the new view that he is prepared to break with the culture of his nativity. In return for leaving, Abraham will, God says, become "a great nation." Is it, as the phrasing seems to imply, a prophecy about Abraham's bloodline? Is national existence in the Goldilocks Zone?

Abraham's career explores the issue. The various stages in his coming to understand the covenant resolve a tension between his (as I see it *accurate*) understanding of what it is to be God's man, and the (as I see it *problematic*) issue of chosenness.

In Genesis 11 we are told that Abraham's father, Terah, departed Ur, trekking as far as Haran. "Terah took his son Abram and his grandson Lot, son of [Terah's deceased son] Haran, and his daughter-in-law Sarai, his son Abram's wife" (31). In Genesis 12, God is said to have appeared to Abram, and to have made the offer of greatness. Then (verse 5) "Abram took his wife Sarai and his brother's son Lot, ... and they set forth [from Haran] to go to the land of Canaan." What's Lot's part in all this?

Lot is from one perspective a competitor to Abraham. While signalling that the uncle will come out ahead, the text nevertheless shines the light of promise on the nephew. Relevantly to the rivalry, their living arrangements differ. Abraham dwells throughout in a tent. During the most significant part of *his* career, Lot's locale is urban. "Lot settled among the cities of the Plain and moved his tent as far as Sodom" (13:12), where, obviously, he folded it and moved into a house. Through Lot the Bible thus gauges the potential of urban existence. It does this as a sequel to the examination of shepherding and farming as post-gathering *modi vivendi*.

Their visit to Abraham in "his tent" (18:1) concluded, the angels "went towards Sodom" (22), encountering Lot "in the [city's] gateway" (19:1). What they find in Sodom is the inflammatory last straw, at least for this phase of the anthropological exploration.

Why is the issue of the city tackled *after* God's new way is announced? Why not as a follow-on to the life of Cain, through which the pre-urban, agrarian, *modus vivendi* is explored? Pertinent is the difference between what the wayfarers find in Abraham's tent and their experience in Lot's "house" (2).

Sarah participates in the hosting. *Chez* Lot, the wife is nowhere to be seen. The suggestion is that something's wrong with *Lot's* family. Since

Lot's father died when he was young, interpreters might think to read the text as ascribing to him a defective sense of the hearth, and by doing that contrasting him unfavourably with (the psychologically healthy) Abraham. But although the narrative does systematically approve Abraham over Lot, this construal is fanciful. The point being made by contrasting the family dynamics is proto-national.

The Bible thinks of nationhood in natural terms. The nation is an extension of the family – a natural unit. The city of Sodom, where Lot took up residence *after separating from his kin*, is by contrast an artificial grouping. When the Sodomites demand that the visitors be handed over, Lot, in a futile effort to avert the abomination,[32] addresses them as "my brothers" (7). But they are no more his brethren than the Smiths across the back lane are mine.

The Bible's disapproval of the sort of supra-family grouping that Sodom is is in the first instance dramatized through the loosened ties within Lot's family. Lot's wife doesn't assist in hosting the messengers because she isn't present.[33] That she is elsewhere is made plain by her looking back at the city as the family flees. Her allegiances are not familial, not proto-national. Abraham, although no recluse, keeps himself apart and his family together.

Through the narrative the Bible is exploring, in an emotionally heated and moralized fashion, the character of and interrelations between several sorts of groupings: family, nation, city. Of the city the Bible does not disapprove, as long as the family isn't corroded and the larger units that grow from the family (e.g., tribes) are denationalized.[34] But although the city *per se* is not disapproved, the Bible's case is slanted. Would anyone who thinking of the city thinks of Sodom not shake his or her head? But to object (as I would) to political arrangements that are hostile to the family is not the same as to hold that acceptable political arrangements must have a family-like unity.

As I'll show in the next section, there's a (recessive) side to the Bible's story that resists equating political cohesion with the tie that binds family members.

First, though, here's the explanation of why the Bible doesn't deal more fully with the issue of the city in its discussion of Cain. At that stage two needed elements, now available, are missing. The effects of the city on the family can only be explored once the city is a going concern. The national element, a key part of the Bible's conceptual mix, is missing too.

Eager Covenanter, Balky Patriarch (2)

When he departs Haran, Abraham is "seventy-five" (12:4). Why isn't Lot left in the care of the other relatives? Despite having been told that God will make him a great nation, Abraham is nagged by a doubt. His wife, sixty-five years of age, is past childbearing. What view does God take? God, we know, will arrange for Abraham a "proper" son.

Observe now Abraham's redemption of Lot in the war of "four kings against five" (Genesis 14:9). Apprised of the nephew's plight, Abraham rides forth with little more than a company – "three hundred and eighteen" (14). "[D]ivid[ing] his forces ... by night" (15), he frees the captive. During the mission, Abraham displays bravery in abundance. Also, he proves himself a wily tactician. But observe, too, that the exemplar proceeds on his own initiative, mustering his own forces, calculating without higher arithmetic. Lot is of course kin. So Abraham cannot stand idly by. Isn't it on the same ground reasonable however to attribute to Abraham in regard to Lot the thought that Sarah voices about Hagar? "[I]t may be that I shall obtain children [in him]" (16:2).

How can so Odysseus-like a man have shown such spinelessness when *his* Penelope was under threat? "[T]hey will kill me" (12:12) – Abraham whispers to Sarah in the court of the Pharaoh. "Say you are my sister," he pleads, "so that it may go well with me" (13).[35]

A literal reading of what happens in Egypt seems at odds with what we know of Abraham. The telltale parallels with the case of Lot even up the odds.

Contrary to God's literal view of the pronoun in the promise to "make of you a great nation," Abraham is prepared to misrepresent nephew as son. Here he is prepared to pass wife off as sister. How do wife and sister relevantly differ? Of the two, only sister is available to another. The message is obvious. Being God's man requires no such rigid observance of bloodlines.

The story of spousal misrepresentation is told twice more. In Genesis 20, Abraham and Sarah again do the honours. In Genesis 26, it's Isaac and Rebekah. In both instances, God steps in, as he did in Egypt, "afflict[ing] Pharaoh and his house with great plagues" (17). Should they veer, God will see to it that the patriarchs return to the national path. It's revealing that the examination of patriarchy and nationhood, a genuine issue, should be slanted by portrayals of the patriarchs as cowards, not to say panders, whenever their resolve as nation-founders slackens.[36]

Observe how the misrepresentations take on a positive inflection when viewed from the perspective of Genesis 2. The matter reaches a pitch of intensity in the episode called "The Akedah." It is productive to combine this episode – the sacrifice of Isaac – with an earlier one in which Abraham and God interact over a son.

In the case of the banishment of Ishmael, the national agenda clashes with the broader enterprise of spreading God's word. Once more, Abraham is torn. Issueless by Sarah, he pleads for Ishmael. "Can Sarah, who is ninety years old, bear a child?" (17:17) "O that Ishmael might live in your sight!" (18) God stands fast. "No" (19). Does Abraham believe that no more sons will be born to him? That's not the point. The point, that Ishmael is acceptable to him, comes out in the Akedah.

God, it is written, "tested [Abraham]" (22:1). "Take your son, your only son Isaac, whom you love, and go to the land of Moriah, and offer him there as a burnt offering" (2). "[Y]our only son Isaac"? Genesis 25:12: "[Abraham's] sons Isaac and Ishmael buried him in the cave of Machpelah." Nor has Abraham shown towards Isaac the fatherly feeling that he exhibited towards the other. Isaac is Abraham's only son, the beloved son, from *God's* point of view, a point of view displaced from Abraham's. Is the sacrifice made easier if a father is remote? But once we appreciate the gap between the two viewpoints, the story's complexion changes. Abraham was prepared to sacrifice Sarah. Why not read the Akedah with that in mind? Is Abraham, the national patriarch, willing to give up God's designated Abrahamic offspring? Is he willing to sacrifice the national enterprise? When approached stereoscopically, the story answers thus: *Abraham* does not see the revolutionary change in human self-understanding as requiring a national agenda. *God* steps in and stays the knife.

Someone behind the text is firmly anti-catholic.[37] This comes to a head in Genesis 34: the shocking episode of Shechem son of Hamor the Hivite.

Having raped Jacob's daughter Dinah, Shechem falls in love with the girl. He asks his father to arrange a marriage. Hamor proposes for the two groups to connect through multiple bonds of marriage. Feigning acceptance, the sons of Jacob request that the Hivites first get circumcised. "[W]hen they were still in pain, two of the sons of Jacob, Simeon and Levi, Dinah's brothers, took their swords ... and killed all the males" (25). Told of the massacre, Jacob complains: "You have brought trouble on me by making me odious to the inhabitants of the land, the Canaanites and the Perizites; my numbers are few, and if they gather themselves against me and attack me, I shall be destroyed, both I and my household" (30).

The story presents a sister and a potential wife; a deception; a betrayal; a patriarch bowing to outside pressure. This is a national version of Abraham's "they will kill me." The message? The patriarch who does not defend the nation needs God's help, or the help of better-resolved minds. Also, the nation has here to be interpreted narrowly, as the family, the bloodline.

Somehow, the idea of Godliness comes to be Super-Glued to the nation, narrowly considered. Abraham is craven in the court of the Pharaoh. But isn't the idea of Godliness, the idea that breathes life into the creation story of Genesis 2, *Abraham's* idea?

God is the principle of particularity, the principle called "I AM." God imparts this mode of existence to the items in one sector of creation. For God to prefer (sc. to be represented as preferring) one group of humans violates that principle. Such preference, unless it is temporary, implies that only one nation's members see God's image and likeness in the mirror.

The screw is turned in Exodus. God again imparts his word – to the newly liberated Israelites. Excellent propaganda, this, gluing the word to the group.[38] Abraham was one man. Receiving the word, he left his native land. Was he pressured? There is no "Let my people go." The Israelites have been through generations of bondage. Group resolve is essential to survival. Is Abraham's departure from the culture in which he grew up emblematic of the Bible's core message, or is the Israelites' flight a flight from a culture that enslaved them? The Ten Commandments are handed down to the Israelites at Sinai. The ordinances are obligatory on each and every man and woman.

I return to Rashi's response to Rabbi Isaac. God creates the world. God can dispose of it *ad libitum*. God chooses the Israelites and deeds them the land. But in Genesis 2, God creates a man and a woman. From the original pair all of us derive. Let's try to say about Genesis 2 what Rashi says about Genesis 1. "Because God created you and me, he can … ." He can give all of us dominion over the (other) animals. He can command all of us to restrict our diet to greens. But distinctions *within* the set of particular men and women lack a principled basis. Agreed, as long as nations exist, an individual's flourishing will depend on national cohesion and strength. Chosenness in the Bible transcends secular politics, however. In the absence of a basis in ontology (a basis that would undermine Genesis 2), only sentiment, of whose instability the Bible is well aware, is available.

God says to the children of Israel (Deuteronomy 7:7–8): "It was not because you were more numerous than any other people that the Lord set his heart on you and chose you … It was because the Lord loved you." Yet God disapproved of Jacob's love-based preference for Rachel. How to reconcile these things? Love binds in a way that also blinkers. That is one reason why, ethically, an officer of a public company steps aside when a job applicant is family. But love of the sort that the above passage refers to has another aspect, unique in the human sphere: it goes directly to the particular. That is why one cannot reason a person out of love. A condition doesn't mediate the attachment. Reason has no fulcrum to use to lever lover from beloved.[39] Consider parents whose child is smitten with a person whom they deem unsuitable. "Think carefully before saying 'I do' to a bond that is hard to sunder" is sensible advice. "Don't love that person" is silly. "The heart," as Woody Allen puts it, "does not know from logic." The problem is that God is *acting* on the basis of the unreasoned love.

The passage from Deuteronomy continues curiously. Here are verses 8 and 9:

> It was because the Lord loved you and kept the oath that he swore to your ancestors, that the Lord has brought you out with a mighty hand, and redeemed you from the house of slavery, from the hand of Pharaoh king of Egypt. Know therefore that the Lord your God is God, the faithful God who maintains covenant loyalty with those who love him and keep his commandments, to a thousand generations.

How does "The Lord loves you" turn into "You love the Lord"? Doesn't the unconditional lover love with no assurance of requital? The continuation of the Shema contains the key to the interchange. "Hear, O Israel: The Lord is our God, the Lord [is one]. You shall love the Lord your God with all your heart, and with all your soul, and with all your might" (6:4–5). Love goes to the particular. Those whose creed is the Shema accept the particularity to which love especially among human emotional attachments goes. The emotion of love; the particularity of people: the two are heads and tails. And so: "you shall love your neighbour as yourself: I am the Lord" (Leviticus 19:18). It's an implication of God's "I AM."

Which again shows how problematic the notion of Israelite exceptionalism is from the philosophical standpoint that, first and foremost, is the Bible's standpoint.

8
Epistemology and Metaphysics: Naming and Being

Acts and Facts

"In the beginning was the act."[1] Thus (Goethe's) Faust's revision of John 1:1 – "In the beginning was the word" – itself a gloss on the all-time No. 1 1:1. An identically numbered proposition well-known in philosophical circles, the 1:1 of Ludwig Wittgenstein's *Tractatus Logico-Philosophicus*, echoes Faust. "The world is the totality of facts."[2] Are Wittgenstein's words, like Goethe's and John's, chosen with an eye on Holy Writ? By tacking the assertion that the world is "not [the totality] of things"[3] onto the quoted part of *Tractatus* 1:1, Wittgenstein *might* be poking fun at Genesis 1:1. But a criticism of the Bible for raising things up over facts packs little force. Suppose that to 1.1 Wittgenstein had added this 1.101: "So, am Anfang bildete Gott Tatsachen, nicht Sachen." If the position is that thing-making supervenes on fact-making (and we do speak in English of "creating facts"), what prevents philosophical defenders of the biblical creation account from helping themselves to the analysis and saying that God creates things by creating facts?

Although an irony relevant to the objective of this discussion – which is to clarify the anti-realist position that its propounder, Immanuel Kant, baptizes "transcendental idealism" – arises from the contact between *Tractatus* 1:1 and Goethe's version of (ultimately) Genesis 1:1, I mention Wittgenstein's work here only to supply an instance of metaphysical realism.

The *Tractatus* is put forward in the frame of what its creator conceives as realism, yet its formulations echo a text redolent of the contrary. In replacing John's Greek *logos* with the German *Tat*, Goethe (or, if you prefer, his Faust) is playing up a primordial *doing* at the root of *being*. *Tat* nominalizes the verb meaning "to do"; clearly then, Goethe is going with the Teutonic flow.[4] English "fact" has a similar process-based etymology, although the lack of a *tuen* to *its Tat* obscures this from the sight of those not fitted out with scholarly spectacles.[5] Because the connection with the verb *faire* is plain, *fait*, the French word meaning "fact," displays the derivation to the naked Gallic eye. In Latin, from which the English and French words come, facts and acts are transparently linked. The exculpatory principle of law *non est factum* means "the accused didn't do the deed."

Who could miss the irony? The ontological language of the *Tractatus* goes against the position of the author of the *Tractatus* that the world itself resolves into (atomic) facts – *Tatsachen* in Wittgenstein's German.[6] Obviously, Wittgenstein's fastidiousness regarding language only heats up the irony.

With the idea that but for the activities of those who come to factual awareness there would be no facts, we arrive at Kant's door. "[A]ll combination – be we conscious of it or not, be it a combination of the manifold of intuition, empirical or non-empirical, or of various concepts – is an act of the understanding" (B130).[7] The words call Goethe's to mind. The objects of cognition, Kant is saying, are the products of an activity. *Sachen*, to convert what Kant says into Wittgensteinian coin, are the products of *tuen*. Goethe *was* active in philosophy. It is not however to Goethe's writings that I will here appeal. The shoulder of the more venerable of the other two exotic texts will be put to the wheel. A view about the nature and structure of being, a view with Kantian affinities, informs the story of the beginning in the Bible. Through a recovery of the ontology in the biblical narrative of ultimate beginnings the objective will be reached.

To adjust his Christian name to the Messiah's nickname as Luther rendered it, Kant, in adulthood, changed "Emanuel" to "Immanuel." Since the "critical" writings target the cognitive bona fides of traditional religious tenets, the change comes across as impious. In the Preface of the *Prolegomena*, the auto-baptized Immanuel trumpets that he is giving to the world "a perfectly new science, of which no one has ever even thought, the very idea of which [is] unknown, and for which nothing hitherto accomplished can be of the smallest use" (7). One half expects him to make the point that his surname is a tetragrammaton! If, as I say, Holy Writ can be enlisted to illuminate the central tenet of Kant's redemptive metaphysical Bible, a second irony comes to light. Kant fits perfectly into the "New" slot of Augustine's epigram about the

Testaments: "In the Old the New is latent; in the New the Old is patent." Far from "the very idea" being unknown, Moses anticipates Kant by over three millennia.

In a manner that cools *this* irony, light shines both ways. Attention to the interplay between the *Critique of Pure Reason* and the Bible firms up our grip on Kant's denial that experience is of unvarnished reality. A better sense is gained of the claim that apperception grounds all unity found in experience. Also, we see that in its own terms the Bible's account of creation could have been less oblique. The postulation of a transcendent God is misleading vis-à-vis its view of reality. Had the Bible rejected Kant, we could then have spoken of an irony in *its* regard. As will emerge, the Bible's central thrust is genuinely Kantian.

Antecedent Doubts Allayed

The announced enterprise beds together unlikely fellows. Let me quell a few doubts about the need to place them on the same sheets and/or about the wisdom of doing so.

"To interpret transcendental idealism, why, except to smooth out the wrinkles in a construal thrown hastily together, consult extra-Kantian writings?" Kant's expositions *are* the primary data. Still, more than two centuries of dissecting the "critical" corpus (which some decry as vivisection) have generated little convergence about the body.

Regularly, interpreters who tackle transcendental idealism factor in Descartes, Hume, Locke, Leibniz, and so forth. This displays no initiative on their part. Who among the beginners doesn't know Kant's "dogmatic slumber" remark about Hume? Who among the more experienced doesn't have by heart Kant's description of positions of Cartesian stripe as amalgams of transcendental realism and empirical idealism? *Internal* reasons exist, however, for scepticism about this route to the Promised Land. Since *Kant*'s retrospective descriptions are the spark,[8] interpreters who travel the route do not really *exit* Königsberg when they visit Ulm, London, Leipzig, and Edinburgh. They are rather like the sea captains who, dining at Kant's table, found themselves corrected about details of their home ports by a man who, famously, never ventured beyond his city's limits. Indeed, scholars who deal independently with Descartes, Locke, Leibniz, Hume, and the others, often disparage Kant's portrayals. Also, doesn't Kant's claim of epochal originality clash with the idea that he is offering an untried permutation of counters in play?

Transcendental idealism is a tough nut. Why is it that those who wield the nutcrackers so often disagree over the doctrine's identity? As I see it, the textual husk is poorly synchronized with the doctrinal kernel.

The quality of the harvest gleaned by using the Bible to thresh Kant's position will ultimately decide whether the effort is worthwhile. Still, interpreters of Kant who are looking outside Kant's corpus for help can find within the "critical" texts a ground for consulting a book that does what the Bible does "in the beginning." I will identify the ground after I conclude the Q & A session.

"No one would say that the biblical position itself is clear. Isn't it quixotic to appeal to an enigma to clarify a mystery?" It is. But appealing to a mystery to clarify an enigma can be clarifying. Indeed, especially *faute de mieux*, it's a reasonable thing to do.

The main reason why the Bible's teachings about the character of being are less clear than they might be is that the accounts of Genesis 1 and Genesis 2 aren't kept as separate as they should be.[9] Kant himself tells us only what things-in-themselves are *not*. That's what causes the interpretive difficulty in regard to *his* position. Only set the relations between Genesis 1 and Genesis 2 straight, and we will have the wherewithal for describing both sides of the appearances/things-in-themselves contrast.

Kant on Experience: The Problem

Interpreters of Kant who look for parallels might look to the Bible because of an *anthropological* slant in Kant's writings.[10] That Kant employs the language of anthropology in the texts of his maturity attests that an interest in men and women of flesh and blood informs his core activity, not an abstract interest in cognition and reality. The evidence is circumstantial. If pressed, most interpreters would I am sure deny that the frequency with which the qualifier "human" and the noun "man" are used in the *Critique of Pure Reason* signals something of interpretive significance. "Kant has no other possessors of cognitive experience to reflect upon. Claims to the effect that he is dealing with *human* cognition are therefore unlikely to mislead."

The anthropological vocabulary of Kant's mature period could be a carry-over from his early lecturing. It could be. But is it? Although the structures of reasoning aren't to be found outside the human realm, no logician would characterize his or her subject matter as *human* logic.

Would Archimedes have said that he discovered the principle of the human body's displacement of water?

The two cases aren't really parallel. A logician who in a casual moment characterizes logic as concerning itself with the structures of human reasoning would never say that (other) beings exist or can be conceived whose (valid) reasoning violates those structures. Yet Kant enunciates a contrast for our modes of cognition *at the very start* of the main body of the *Critique*.

Here are the first three sentences of §1 of the *Critique*, the opening of the Transcendental Aesthetic, the "First Part" of the Transcendental Doctrine of Elements:

> In whatever manner and by whatever means a mode of knowledge may relate to an object, *intuition* is that through which it is in immediate relation to them, and to which all thought as a means is directed. But intuition takes place only in so far as the object is given to us. This again is possible, to man at least, in so far as the mind is affected in a certain way. (A19/B34)

Kant in these sentences is addressing himself analytically to the cognitive grasp of an object. He is not making what he regards as novel claims, only anatomizing the taking up of an object into experience.

Kant explains that he will apply "intuition" when the cognitive grasp of the object is im-mediate.[11] Evidently, he holds that a different kind of grasp of an object exists – a mediate one. When Kant's language is translated into ours, what he is saying turns out to be uncontroversial. His im-mediate/mediate contrast is between picking an object out via a condition that, in context, it (alone) satisfies ("heavy-set red-headed person"), and picking it out referentially ("Albert"). The intuitional or im-mediate form of cognition is the form whose logico-linguistic expression involves singular terms. The non-intuitional or mediate form involves general terms and bound variables.

So far, smooth sailing. Beyond the analytic accounting, the waters turn rough, both from an interpretive viewpoint and philosophically.

The first sentence is formulated impersonally: a general reference is made – "in whatever manner and by whatever means" – to modes of knowledge involving objects. No mention of who or what might know objects in those ways. [Annotation: Nothing remarkable here. It's just an articulate description. It isn't intended to get down to cases.] The second sentence employs the first person plural pronoun. [Annotation: One might have thought that that to which the pronoun is in apposition would be specified before the pronoun is used. In any case, could "to us" not have been suppressed without affecting the analytic meaning?] In the third sentence a common noun, "man," appears. [Annotation: shouldn't "man" have been used in place of "us" in the second sentence? Shouldn't "us" have been used in place of "man" in the third?]

The progression is from the fully general to the indefinitely specific to the fully specific.

Does the indefinitely specific, the hinge, go with the fully general, or does it go with the fully specific? Is the move in the direction of increased specificity, as per the order of sentences, or is it the reverse, an abstraction from the fully specific?

Kant could be saying that while when we grasp an object intuitionally, the object is given to us, an object can otherwise be taken up immediately into cognitive awareness. Given-ness, in other words, is not a necessary condition for im-mediacy. Kant could be taking the line that while in all cases of im-mediate cognition the object must be given, men and women only get the given by being affected. Passivity, in other words, is not a necessary condition for im-mediacy. I believe that Kant is, objectionably, doing both. He has a question-begging motive for formulating indeterminately: the defence of transcendental idealism.

For his theoretical purposes, Kant wants a mode of object-cognition that contrasts with factual experience as we know it. The only mode available to him is the one that philosophers of the Cartesian tradition ascribe to God: the object is given actively.[12] Since the *Critique*'s Dialectic argues across a wide front that the idea of God is a *façon de parler*, Kant can't feel comfortable with this. If the idea of a (superior) alternative is merely regulative, it would constitute a problem for transcendental idealism's defence to be routed through the contrast. Conscious of the problem, Kant (I conjecture) proceeds to speak in the second sentence of cognition "for us," but without going right to the passivity that features our *de facto* mode of basic factual experience. He splits the difference between active given-ness (a divine prerogative, problematic for him) and passive given-ness (the lot of men and women, not enough for his purposes).

"How does the active differ from the non-passive?" As I see it, "active" and "non-passive" *are* synonymous. This strands Kant in a distinction without a difference. Active given-ness, although active, is given-ness only by courtesy. God makes, he does not get. The world is in no intelligible sense *given* to God.[13] Kant therefore needs non-passive given-ness – objects not of our making entering consciousness otherwise than through a receptive faculty – in order to cash the claim that our (sense-based) style of grasping objects, passive givenness, isn't unique. In short: Kant can make some sense of active given-ness and of passive given-ness, but not of non-passive given-ness. The first cannot however serve as a contrast for the third. Kant *needs* the second.

If we assume that Kant does not want to treat the content of the first sentence in the excerpt as a product of abstraction from the content of the third, we get a non-literary explanation of why the general "to us" precedes the specific "to man." Its precedence makes it seem as if our case is a specification of a more general structure, rather than just a fuzzier articulation. The second comes however from nothing.

The analysis of cognition *looks* non-anthropological. It seems that the cognitive structures, like logical ones, are not inextricably bound up with men and women. This is important to Kant. He thinks that to make sense of things-in-themselves he has to offer a mode of cognition adequate to them.[14] This is how things look; but it is not how they are.

Theory of Being, Not Epistemology

Taken as it comes, Kant's account is, theoretically speaking, overdrawn. The generality for which Kant strives in his anatomy of cognition is abstractive. He does not have any serviceable idea of cognitive im-mediacy common to different sorts of object-experience, that is, sorts exemplified by beings not all of whom are of the human variety. The classificatory scheme would however be non-abstractive only if such an idea were in his possession. As things stand, what Kant says about im-mediacy outside the human case is like someone's saying that not only geometrical figures can be square, deals can be too.

Examination of the square deal cannot enlarge the geometer's understanding. In the same way, the case of God, if reached by abstraction, can't be recruited to illuminate transcendental idealism. "God's grasp is not mediate." That's correct. But "God's grasp is im-mediate" is wordplay. The world is not in any intelligible sense given to God. Realism makes synchronization with the facts a requisite for knowledge. Where the facts have all the independence that a rabbit materialized out of a hat has of the conjurer's incantation, talk of synchronization is idle.

To make sense in conceptual terms of the thinking behind transcendental idealism, it's necessary therefore to proceed in an ontological vein. True, the proposition that the world as it is in itself, X, differs from the world as we grasp it, Y, is uninformative about X. Since the negation of a something might be a nothing, it may yet turn out that $X = 0$. But having said that Y is the world of human beings, I am, albeit unspecifically, giving distinctive ontological content to X. X = the world of non-human things; the constituents of the Bible's first five and a half days of creation. So "$X \neq Y$" is not stated as an axiom. The task is to defend the inequality consistently with $X \neq 0$.[15]

Dispensing with the cognition-theoretic approach to the world as it is in itself necessitates two substantial shifts. *Human* cognition must be understood to be the basic *analysandum*. Despite how Kant formulates the case, what he presents must not be taken as an investigation of experiential structures that, in modified form, men and women happen to exemplify. That is one shift. It follows that the anthropological colouring of Kant's analysis isn't ornamental. He isn't dealing with men and women *at least*. He isn't dealing with men and women *at most*. His subject is men and women *full stop*. Not that an interpretively pertinent (as opposed to a notional) contrast for the human case is lacking. The contrast is however located among real things. "To man at least" is misleading in this connection too. It suggests a limitation. That is the other shift. Again, Kant's core thinking turns out to be anthropological. Focused on men and women, it begins with an account of the beings that we are – so much so that it would sow confusion to say "beings *of our sort*." Kant's core thinking does not treat men and women as ontologically degenerate. The thinking therefore dispenses with science fiction and/or theology. The only extra-human is the (quite real) non-human. Idealism is a position, then, about what our cognition is, not about what it's not, namely God-like. The key phrase is "to man at least." Although the thought of better plays into Kant's use of the phrase, the thought is theoretically inessential.

Kant's idealism places human-sized consciousness (as opposed to supra-human-sized consciousness, as in Berkeley) at the centre. Given that consciousness of human size is the measure, students of Kant expect a pure anthropology. The *Critique* seems to disappoint. But analysis brings out problems in the exposition, and Kant's language points towards a treatment of invariant characteristics of creatures such as us (men and women, persons). Kant says on one occasion that three core philosophical questions – the *moral* question "What ought I to do?"; the *epistemological* question "What can I know?"; and the *eschatological* question "What may I hope?" – "relate ... to" a fourth question: "What is Man?"[16] Which is precisely the question that those interested in the *logos* of *anthropoi* would ask. Which is what Kant himself adds. "[A]ll this could be reckoned to be anthropology."

Here, from outside philosophy, is a parallel of the lie of the land. The Oedipus complex is central to the Freudian story of human psychic development. Freud is also however a naturalist. Men and women are parts of nature. Do non-human things, parts of nature too, exemplify the complex? "No," says Freud. This indicates that his thinking is less natural than Darwin's. For Freud it is not true that the human case is more of the same. Freud's position is a kind of *empirical metaphysics*. He is singling the human case out at the start. This is no accident. Had he reached the Oedipal structure by forward stages from a more general account of psychology, some sharp break would have had to occur en route. Which would have challenged his naturalism.

An extension of the parallel reverberates with Genesis. The social world (individuals living together at peace) is different for humans than for non-humans.[17] Roughly and readily, the difference is parallel to the difference between how things are in themselves, and how they are to us. Animals are not criticized for licking their privates in public.

The Bible's Philosophical Anthropology

The character of the world as we experience it is, Kant says, bound up with the experience of it. This isn't the triviality that the world as we experience it is a world experienced. It's the substantial claim that the world as it is in itself differs in structure and in constitution from the world as we experience it. In Genesis's story of the world's creation, for the first five and a half days of its existence the world is without men and women. If their advent introduces something unprecedented, then the world prior to the afternoon of Day 6 is clear of it. What can we mine from the text to cash these general formulations? The first place to look is at how the biblical narrative distinguishes men and women from the rest.

In its best-known distinction between them and the other creatures, the Bible asserts that persons are made "in [God's] image, according to [God's] likeness" (1:26). Current attitudes towards the Bible being what they are, it's not surprising that secular readers close the book. The reaction is hasty. The theological form of 1:26 is conceptually otiose.

Immediately after asserting God-likeness, the text makes a point whose truth needs no eschatological backing. Men and women have "dominion over ... all the ... animals of the earth" (ibid.). Obviously, the proposition that men and women stand to the rest in a relation of domination is comprehensible independently of the assertion that for that position men and women are beholden to God.[18]

"If our dominator status is understood in secular conceptual terms, why the reference to God?" One part of the answer to this apt question is that the capacity to dominate is felt to distinguish men and women *more strongly* from all else that inhabits the earth.[19] In representing *God* as bestowing it, the writers aren't sourcing the capacity – they're giving voice to the feeling. The claim is that the capacity is only more of what other creatures possess or what consistently with their natures the other creatures might have possessed. Another part of the answer is that higher beings figure prominently in books with which the Bible competed.[20]

The Bible's assertion of God-likeness is not *a priori* problematic. One may quarrel about the extent of the difference between men and women and the rest. But it's indisputable that it outdoes the difference between any two non-human (physical) things. The idea of an asymmetrical sort of domination is (simply) part of the assertion's basis. More important is the other biblical manner of setting men and women apart, to which I turn in a moment. Although the theological-sounding language puts many off the scent, the Bible, then, is engaging in reflective (sc. philosophical) anthropology.

"Men and women alone are made in God's image and likeness." That's how the Bible says that we are unlike the rest of nature. To the claim of difference most of us would assent whether or not we "kiss the book."[21] The biblical assertion can in fact be freed of reference to the transcendent. In the biblical story, God creates and controls the world. To say that we are God-like is to say that that kind of creative control is ours.[22] And certainly, it is. We build houses. We build cities. We raze and demolish them too.

Once preconceptions about an eschatological agenda are set aside, the part of the Bible at which I have been looking is seen to be anthropological, empirically so.[23] Correct or not, the Bible's account of the distinctiveness of men and women is deeper than Aristotle's. The characterization of men and women as *zooi politikoi* amply evidences his greater distance from bedrock.

The Garden contains the Bible's second way of distinguishing us. Again, only men and women disobey. They alone draw the curse. An innocent reader it would be who pinned a decoration on the non-human creatures for their dutifulness. The finger about eating of the fruit of the tree of knowledge wags only at the creatures fashioned in

God's image and likeness. The capacity of men and women to disobey is a presupposition of the story's making sense. If God had warned lions off the knowledge tree, or threatened to douse the sun should it take a walk among the more distant stars, the story would have been a bedtime story.

As in the case of domination, this distinction is conceptually independent of theology. It remains to pin down the biblical issue of knowledge. If the capacity to know of which the Bible speaks is, or requires, the capacity to process the world cognitively, most of us would say that more than their capacity to dominate *it* is a key distinguisher of human beings.

I begin to wind down with a more general point. The distinguishing of men and women in Genesis tracks the portrayal of God. Alone among creatures, we are said to have dominion. This characteristic God – when in Rome, even by name, "Dominus" – has. Men and women, uniquely among creatures, acquire knowledge of good and bad. This commodity God possesses – see Genesis 3:22 – from the start.[24] On the basis that the relation *being like* is reflexive, we could for neatness's sake say that God compares with the likeness-sharing men and women. Men and women, if so, do not lack any characteristic that God (distinctively) possesses. God, we may reasonably infer, is modelled on how we think of ourselves. The Bible's distinguishing of men and women is, that is to say, at base anthropological.

Enough content and structure is in hand for the final assault on transcendental idealism.

Once we understand what the Bible is doing, the Bible, we understand, is doing what our examination of the excerpt from the *Critique* indicates that Kant had better be doing, namely proceeding anthropologically. Men and women are what they are. No advance assumption is made that a wider class subsumes them. It's through appeal to God that the Bible highlights the distinctiveness of men and women. The contrast between men and women and something else is therefore lateral or downwards.

Can the content of the biblical account be used to illuminate the murk of transcendental idealism?

In the Beginning Were the Words: "Cow," "Bear," etc.

In Genesis 2, one of the earliest biblical acts of the man is to name the animals. God is at this juncture trying to determine which kind of thing would be suitable as a partner. Since what happens in Genesis 2 mirrors

Genesis 1, attentive readers can anticipate the story's direction. In Genesis 1, God had created something in God's likeness. The man will need something like the man. God's creation of something like himself had postdated the creation of non-human things. The same goes for the creation of the woman.[25]

God's invitation to the man to give names is not for the sake of building up vocabulary. It's in order for the man to overcome solitary status. The man's name-giving therefore means, at minimum, this: the incorporation of the things named into the man's world; the world in which he is at home. The giving of names is thus, in intellectual terms, the assimilation of the things named into the name-giver's world. To be nameable is to have a common denominator with the name-giver's capacities.[26]

What names does the man give? Not a single species name is mentioned. Through the absence, I come to the crucial issue of how Genesis 1 and Genesis 2 are related.

I am aligning Genesis 1 with Kant's things-in-themselves, Genesis 2 with Kant's appearances. In regard to things-in-themselves, Kant consigns us to inarticulateness. Genesis 1 says a lot about the (non-human) world. The simple reaction to this volubility is to say that the descriptions of Genesis 1 are chosen with an eye on Genesis 2. The principle I employed above applies here too. What is accounted true of God prefigures (and is in fact modelled on) what is thought to be true of men and women. God's name-giving in Genesis 1 (e.g., "God called the light Day, and the dark … he called Night" [1:5]; "God called the dome Sky" [1:8]) is a backwards use and upwards projection of the capacity for giving names that men and women recognize themselves to have – a capacity they exercise in Genesis 2.

A subtler reaction is possible. Species names like "cow," "bear," and "eagle" do not figure in Genesis 1. Mightn't the message be that our zoological vocabulary is inapplicable in that world?

More subtlety still. In Genesis 2 the man is said to have given names "to all cattle, and to the birds of the air, and to every animal of the field" (2:20). Yet not one of the names is sounded. Can it be that the names aren't from a set that includes "cow," "bear," "eagle," and so forth? That seems unlikely. Wouldn't it have been natural to specify a few? "Isn't the list obvious? Isn't that why no names are sounded?" I have another hypothesis. Had it been written in Genesis 2 that the man named this creature "bear," and that creature "eagle," the reader would have said that what God created during Day 5 and the morning of Day

6 in Genesis 1 were eagles and bears. Could it not therefore be that the names are withheld in Genesis 2 in order to counteract the tendency to assume that the same language applies in Genesis 1?[27]

Whichever reading is preferred, the datum remains. We do not have *different* vocabularies for the two chapters. This misaligns Genesis 1 with Kant's realm of things-in-themselves.

In fact, there *is* a difference. In speaking of living things, including human ones, Genesis 1 speaks of species. God, in Genesis 1, creates "humankind" (1:26, 27). All of the pronouns used to refer to men and women are plural. Genesis 2, by contrast, speaks of particulars. "[T]he Lord God formed man from the dust of the ground, and breathed into his nostrils the breath of life" (2:7). A particular man is fashioned, and (then) a particular woman, both over-and-against the rest of creation. What follows Genesis 2, which begins *our* story, is a veritable Domesday Book: an expanding cast of particular people.

Let me link up the difference to the earlier discussion of the distinctive features of men and women.

Men and women dominate. What (the sheer existence of men and women apart) is the basic precondition for this dominance, and what is the case when the basic precondition isn't satisfied?

The key is a further contrast between Genesis 1 and Genesis 2. In Genesis 1, "good" greets God's creative acts. "Bad" we do not hear until the mention, in Genesis 2, of the tree of knowledge. "Humankind is up and running in Genesis 1. Don't bad things happen to its members?" Most readers will answer with a modified affirmative. But "in some respects, yes" ignores the other contrast between the two stories – the contrast between humankind, the species, and particular men and women.

"Bad things do not feature the lives of men and women." In the biblical frame, the denial is ambiguous. Is bad unexemplified in the lives of members of *the species*, or of *the particulars*? The fashioners of the Bible know that Genesis 2 follows Genesis 1. Nevertheless, if our thinking is restricted to the species level, we won't think bad things to be present even germinally. Nor is it a matter of holding our breath until bad worms its way into the sector. Needed first is a breath of life into the constituents who already share God's image and likeness. In the human sphere, each person counts. This is what is sentimental when it comes to bison. The unit is the herd or, if one is thinking in global terms, the species. Thus the problem with species labels in Genesis 1 and Genesis 2.

The example of the bison does not mesh perfectly with Genesis 1. We can use the slippage further to clarify the position.

As expected, human voices were raised against the cull. Wood Buffalo National Park is *not* however a natural environment. Human meddling might have affected the herd. So perhaps the urge to dismiss the denouncers as sentimental ranters is misinformed. This signposts the position. Specifically human intervention apart, nothing in the natural world is objectionable. Should one species squeeze out another, that is perfectly "good." It's what happens through the evolutionary process. Should a comet smash into the earth, extinguishing life as we know it, that too would qualify as "good." It's what happens when the paths of such things cross.[28]

The Bible isn't reporting a congenial spot for happily-ever-aftering in when it describes the world of Genesis 1 as all good. The claim is conceptual: "good and bad" does not apply. The death of an antelope in the jaws of a lion benefits the antelope (i.e., the herd, or the species): a weaker member is eliminated. Isn't that good as opposed to bad? It isn't. For the same is true if the antelope escapes: a more robust member lives on to sow its genes.[29] In pitying the antelope, you are imagining *yourself* being run to ground. In commiserating with the lion, you are imagining *yourself* going hungry.

In fine: it is only when we think of antelopes and lions as particulars that good-and-bad comes into play.

The contrast between Genesis 1 and Genesis 2 is not arcane. Why is it overlooked? One reason is that it's a bit slippery.

It's natural to take species to be collections of individuals. The thought is therefore natural that Genesis 1 quantifies individuals, not that it speaks of a different unit of being. The Bible doesn't stop with the species, however. Related is the contrast between systems of interrelated parts and collections of separate elements. What I said about interactions between species applies more clearly still to intra-systemic changes.

Genesis 1 starts out with pairs: heavens and earth, dark and light, wet and dry. Sharp distinctions – dark apart from light, wet without reference to dry, up in isolation from down – are not natural. The heavens cannot be created unless what is under them is brought into being. Immediately the system-like character of the whole is remarked (in Genesis 1:1), interfaces are acknowledged (in Genesis 1:4). Swamp, marsh, fen, and bog: wet mixes and mingles with dry. Fog and mist shroud the intersect of upper and lower. Twilight is a blend of light and dark.

One familiar exception exists to our thinking of animals in species or system terms. But in regard to pets – to farm animals too if but a few dot the acreage – sentiment is at work, as it is in regard to a child and a doll. Onto the mentioned animals we superpose the arithmetic that we self-apply.[30] When Spot dies, the owners get another dog. Often enough to be revealing, one of the same breed is obtained. This is like parents of a deceased child having another because of the tragedy. As I say, the likeness is partial. The idea of the second child as a replacement is offensive.

In the case of pets, in short, the individuals are treated, albeit only up to a point, as particulars.

Examine the treatment of men and women at the start of Genesis 2. The descriptions are adjusted to the case of domestic animals. Like an ox and a horse on a small farm, the man and the woman, the two creatures on God's acreage, have jobs of work to do. For doing the tilling and the keeping assigned to them, they are fed and sheltered.

The Bible thus describes, step-by-step, the emergence of particulars: from the integrated system (Day 6, noon) to the asymmetrically placed species humankind (Day 6, afternoon) to the semi-particular (Garden, prior to disobedience) to the fully particular (disobedience and banishment). To its credit, the Bible withholds names until the last stage, the woman being the first to be named. The account, although story-like in character and genetic in mode, invites conceptual treatment.

The problem of the missing link predates upon the evolutionary explanation of human beings. The Bible, for its part, supplies, we see, a conceptual stepping stone from Genesis 1 to Genesis 2. Between nonhuman animals and particular men and women, it gives pets and petlike items.

That death enters in Genesis 2 makes perfect sense. In a system, all change is recycling. Night's passing into day, which gives no ground for mourning, typifies death in Genesis 1. In linking the eating of the tree of knowledge of good and bad to death, God isn't devising a torment. Once the particularity of the man and of the woman is in place, the angel of death is on the scene.

It's a tight conceptual network. "Bad" is absent from Genesis 1 because the world of Genesis 1 is a system. It's not possible therein to speak intelligibly of one thing's gaining at the expense of another. Good-and-bad has possible application only in a particular-containing world like the world of Genesis 2. Similarly, the relationship of domination requires particulars. Inside a system, talk of dominant status and subordinate status gets no grip. The day does not overpower the night at dawn, nor at nightfall does the night apply the sleeper hold. If we keep to species terms, we cannot take literally the claim that the lion dominates the antelope. The interaction benefits both species. Think of a system that is artefactual. Do the brake pads of an automobile, which abrade over time, suffer for the good of the frame?[31]

"What about the fact that nature frequently does damage to men and women? Doesn't that show that nature dominates them, and hence that they haven't an asymmetrical dominion over the rest?" This mistakes a conceptual point about domination for a generalization.

Vesuvius blows its top. Pompeii is engulfed. Triggered by an undersea quake, a tsunami decimates the population around the Indian Ocean. The philosophical point is that men and women alone are *of a type* that can dominate. The concept of domination is inapplicable to the devastation that a volcano visits on a region and to the destruction that a tsunami wreaks along a coastline. The truth of the claim that persons are dominators is not inconsistent with nature on occasion crushing them.[32] In "giving" dominion, God is not immunizing against a fast-mutating virus. Were that comet to collide with the earth, the survivors could not cite the cataclysm to challenge the description of us as non-dominated dominators.[33] The Bible's point is that men and women relate to nature as parts of nature do not interrelate. That's because only particulars can dominate (or be dominated). Within a system, assertions of domination can't literally be true. The bee takes pollen from the flower and makes honey. The flower transmits its genetic material via the bee to other flowers. Who or what is using whom or what? To make an asymmetrical judgment is to describe matters from an arbitrarily designated point. In the bee + flower + pollen + honey ensemble, no position is privileged.

Pre-Adamic Language

A different language than ours is needed for the world of Genesis 1. The language of Genesis 2 does not accurately represent that world. How is all this disposed where Kant is concerned?

The linchpin is the idea of particularity. *It* is absent from Genesis 1. The basic particular in the story is God. In breathing life into the first person, God is imparting to the portion of nature the life of a particular. Men and women, for being particulars, are not parts of a system, as is the humanity of Genesis 1. Men and women are in fact the basic particulars. This follows from the secularist reading of the early chapters. Let me switch lexical horses in midstream and refer to particulars as substances. Men and women are the basic substances. The implication is that the substantiality of all other substances is derivative from theirs. The story of naming in Genesis 2 carries the message. It's not that God has men and women participate the way a parent has a child help wash the car. It's that the decisions made are not available to God (*qua* presiding over the world of Genesis 1). It follows that "all combination – be we conscious of it or not, be it a combination of the manifold of intuition, empirical or non-empirical, or of various concepts – is an act of the understanding" (B130). The substantiality of the world of men and women is imposed on it by them. What happens is analogous to what men and women do when they make an animal into a pet.

Observe that Kant's talk of "combination" now has a contrast. It's not that without human cognitive activity there is a welter. Missing when the activity is absent is not structure *simpliciter*. Missing, rather, is the distinctive unity that particulars alone have; hence without which the unity cannot be spread about. The world as it is in itself – that is to say, the world as it is apart from human consciousness – differs from what we call the natural world.[34] Kant is at odds here with Berkeley. So is the Bible. The divine consciousness of Genesis 1 does not sustain the world of Genesis 2 in the absence of men and women. There is no tree in the quad in Genesis 1, and this is not because quads are human contrivances. A tree only exists in a cultivated place like a garden!

The rest follows. If the categories of causation and reciprocity are at the heart of our understanding, then they too are implicated, applying as they do to particulars. Genesis 2 doesn't speak in such terms. Nevertheless, the notion of the human particular in the Bible induces asymmetries: life and death; domination and subordination. These are missing from the world of Genesis 1.

The unity of apperception is, then, original. "This unity, which precedes *a priori* all concepts of combination, is not the category of unity" (B131). It is the source of all unity – meaning: unity of particulars. Aristotle characterized basic (non-general) things as substances. Both in Latin and in Aristotle's Greek, from which the Latin derives, the word "substance" means "that which stands under." By a near providential coincidence, "understanding" names a cognitive condition. If Kant is right, the homonymy turns out to be a metaphysical synonymy. Without (human) understanding, there is no substance. The Bible agrees. Without the man and the woman of Genesis 1, there are in the creation no particulars.

I offered two ironies at the outset. Here is a further ironic reversal regarding Wittgenstein.

In the section of the *Tractatus* governed by 5, Wittgenstein indicates that the subject does not enter into the cognitive nexus in a fashion that influences the word–world link. The subject mirrors the world but does not (any more than a mirror does) affect its nature:

> 5.542 But it is clear that "A believes that p," "A thinks p," and "A says p," are of the form "'p' says p": and here we have no co-ordination of a fact and an object, but a co-ordination of facts by means of a co-ordination of their objects.

This view is opposed to Kant's, and to Genesis 2's. If not for human cognitive intervention – if not for Adam's giving of names – the truths of experience would not be. The implication is that for lacking input from the subject, the world of the *Tractatus* is devoid of particulars. Since, for Wittgenstein, names are the basic links to the world, if there are facts, there is only one, a world fact, since the system as a whole is the only available nominatum.[35] This is the position of Genesis 1. The *Tractatus* is the theory of representation of the world of Genesis 1. Its language is pre-Adamic.

The biblical-sounding *Tractatus* 7 – "Whereof one cannot speak, thereof one must be silent" – boomerangs. For speakers of the Tractarian language, it is the world of Genesis 2, the Kantian realm of appearances, *our* world, of which we must be silent.

A Biblical–Kantian Novel

In *The Crossing*, the novelist Cormac McCarthy traverses a no-man's-land between (in effect) the nature of Genesis 1 and the world of particular men and women of Genesis 2. During his journey into homelessness, a journey that takes him across the border into Mexico, Billy Parham encounters various types who speak to him of the world at what through the biblical resonances we are to understand is a deeper level than is possible in New Mexico. They speak of it, as the writers of Genesis speak of it, and as Kant tries to, from both sides. Here is a report of what an old man says to the teenage protagonist:

> [M]en wish to be serious but they do not understand how to be so. Between their acts and their ceremonies lies the world and in this world the storms blow and the trees twist in the wind and all the animals that God made go to and fro yet this world men do not see. They see the acts of their own hands or they see that which they name and call out to one another but the world is invisible to them.[36]

Adjust for the zoological and botanical vocabulary, and the following words could have been lifted right out of Manuel Kant's *Critica de la Razon Pura*. The man is answering the boy's question about trapping a wolf. The question might equally be taken as an epistemological question about reducing *canis lupus* to *canis familiaris*: containing what is wild in our domestic conceptual enclosures:

> Lo que se tiene en la trampa no es mas que dientes y forro. El lobo propio no se puede conocer. Lobo o lo que sabe el lobo. Tan como preguntar lo que saben las piedras.[37]

I'll elaborate in terms of two panels of the Bible's narrative, the first from the Book of Job, the second from the Genesis 2 story.

Here are five verses of God's speech to Job from out the whirlwind:

> Can you draw out Leviathan with a fishhook,
> or press down its tongue with a cord?
> Can you put a rope in its nose,
> or pierce its jaw with a hook?
> Will it make many supplications to you?
> Will it speak soft words to you?
> Will it make a covenant with you
> to be taken as your servant forever?
> Will you play with it as with a bird,
> or will you put it on a leash for your girls? (41:1–5)

It's not a change of attitude, from domination (1–4) to playfulness (5) – as if the writers constitute an early Frankfurt School. The purpose of the claim that God plays with Leviathan isn't to play up God's power. It's to point to the fact that the cognitive interaction of men and women with the world puts on the world a human scale – "a leash" – alien to it "in itself." Job's book thus explains why from a different but non-fanciful perspective the catastrophes are nothing of the kind. This is not theodicy – that it's all for the best. The claim is that the world – the world, I mean, of Genesis 1 – isn't made for men and women. That's why Genesis 1:1 isn't the opener of Abraham's lecture at Beer-Sheba. The Kantian implication is that tinkering from on high could not overcome the problems that men and women encounter in the natural world. The idea of moderating disease (in the natural world) so as to obviate its effects (in the human world) makes no sense. The languages of the worlds differ. This bids to explain why Kant categorically rejects Leibniz's view that underpinning the phenomenal level is an ontological one; why, according to Kant, the world of space and time and cause is not a *phenomenon bene fundatum*.

Couldn't the episode of the serpent in the sequel to Genesis 2 be saying the same?[38] "Why," some might ask, "a snake?" The snake molts. In that regard, it is like a perennial, seeming not to age despite time's passage. Since the issue in this part of the story is the death connected with the fruit of the tree of knowledge, a snake is what the doctor ordered. Isn't a snake also a Genesis 2 emblem of Genesis 1 nature? Anatomically, end and beginning are not sharply distinguished. Just so, it is figuratively appropriate that God dispenses a copper snake, Nehushtan, as a cure for snakebite.[39]

Interpreting Transcendental Idealism

Here are four conditions that interpreters of the Kantian doctrine standardly verbalized thus – "the objects of experience are appearances, not things-in-themselves" – strive to meet. C1: Talk of things-in-themselves isn't a merely verbal variant of talk about the selfsame things spoken of when appearances are referred to. C2: It's in consequence of some essential feature that they possess that objects, as we experience them in sensory mode, are not things-in-themselves. C3: Space and time, substance and cause, are located on the appearance side of the inequality "appearances ≠ things-in-themselves." C4: Things-in-themselves somehow underpin the appearances; unlike the distinction between numbers and enumerated things, the distinction doesn't have abstractions on one side.

What we've learned from the Bible supplies the wherewithal for working out a reading that stands a chance. The shift of the centre of Kantian gravity from cognition-theory to anthropology also furnishes a basis for a more unified treatment of Kant's versatile *oeuvre*.

A lesson of the alignments – Genesis 1 with things-in-themselves, Genesis 2 with appearances – is that nature is less comprehensible than we tend to think. A paradox of transcendental idealism, in Kant's presentation, is that although our synthetic activities make (extra-human) nature, we know nature better than we know ourselves. From the standpoint of my account, this is a version of the claim that many religious thinkers about the Bible endorse. Although we are made in his likeness, although we are inspired with his breath of life, God is beyond our ken.

In a piece penned when Wittgenstein's later philosophy was in the ascendant, the writer and playwright Michael Frayn sends up the *Philosophical Investigations*. He offers "a previously unpublished fragment," sections 694–708. Here is the final entry:

> **708.** If a lion could speak, it would not understand itself.

The author of the *Investigations* might well have agreed. Our language would make no sense to whatever it is in the world that answers to the common noun "lion." The whole of the system that is nature speaks through the lion. There is no object in apposition to "itself." This, at any rate, is what I infer from the fact that the Bible mentions not a single name that Adam gives.

Here's a biblical version of Frayn's last entry:

> If a lion could speak, it would not be able meaningfully to intone the Shema.

9
Philosophy of Mind: Straddling Jordan

A Seminarian Manqué

"I AM." The Bible's distinctive philosophical teachings radiate from its philosophical anthropology, whose hub is this assertion of the principle of particular being. Not inextricably bound up with the system, each person, each man and each woman, is a locus of action. As such, each person is a locus of responsibility. This is why the high point of the story that begins in Genesis 2 is an act of *mis*behaviour. I quoted the opening of *Paradise Lost*. Here's the closing couplet:

> They hand in hand with wandring steps and slow,
> Through *Eden* took thir solitarie way.

The two set out on *their* way. This solitariness dramatizes their particularity.

In this chapter, I show, with respect to issues in the philosophy of mind and action, how a philosopher who needs what the Bible supplies flounders because of the distinctive thing's absence from the discipline as he or she practises it.

A student of the Bible like me is for a number of background reasons drawn to P.F. Strawson. One: Strawson's interest in Kant outstrips the interest of the historian of philosophy and/or the close interpreter. This attracts because among classic Western positions Kant's is the one that seems closest to the Bible's. Two: Strawson's "rehabilitation" of Kantian views (in *The Bounds of Sense*) does not accept Kant's idealism at face value. Having transposed Kant into an anthropological register, that's something that I also do not do. Three: Resonantly with my discussions of the use of "man" in Genesis 1 and in Genesis 2, Strawson objects to a certain formalism in the treatment of the distinction between singular terms and general terms. Four: In his work in metaphysics, Strawson assigns persons to an irreducibly distinct category of physical things. Five: Strawson links personhood to responsibility and agency, as, in explaining the Bible's position, I have.

Given the biblical slant of Strawson's thinking, one expects his view of men and women and their place among things to have a biblical character. The expectation is disappointed. The Greek of Strawson's words belies the Hebrew of his thoughts.

Singular Terms

During the 1960s, Strawson was locked in a debate with the philosopher W.V. Quine. Resolved: singular terms (e.g., the proper name "Socrates") can be eliminated from fact-stating language without loss of representational power.[1]

Strawson argues the Negative: the function of identification, which the factual statements that anchor our cognitive dealings with the world must satisfy, requires honest-to-goodness singular terms like "Socrates." These, Strawson concludes, cannot be eliminated in favour of variables, predicates, and quantifiers.

The function, we can agree, must be satisfied. Since there's no reason why perceptual confrontation couldn't do the job, the debate, in its narrowly linguistic form, has limited philosophical interest.

There is however an aspect to the debate that transcends the issue about "Socrates." Quine wears an antecedent commitment on his sleeve, a commitment that many philosophers regard as dogmatic. His concern is to show that a language adequate to *the needs of science* requires no more structure than what propositional logic and quantification theory supply. Although Strawson takes the stage as a defender of ordinary language, he is therefore better understood to be trying to remain faithful to the ordinary life-world.[2]

So far, so good. Strawson's sounds like a move in the direction of the distinction between the world of Genesis 1 and the world of Genesis 2. But as we proceed into his body of work, the clarity is lost.

Strawson is occupied with the categories of particular and general, categories that have linguistic, conceptual, and metaphysical expressions. The dispute over singular terms speaks to that occupation. How disorienting, then, that in the essay titled "Particular and General" he should challenge the idea that the two notions are irreducibly distinct. In a spirit that reflects Quine's treatment of mass terms and count nouns in *Word and Object*, Strawson posits a level of world-representation beneath the level of ascription of properties to objects. The sub-predicative form that typifies that level – "Water here" said from the riverbank; "Water there" said looking through a plane's porthole – Strawson labels "feature-placing." In effect, non-general factual information can be conveyed by directly locating ("placing") a non-singular characteristic ("feature"); conveyed without making use of standard singular terms like "the river" and "Superior." The demonstratives "here" and "there," or their gestural or positional equivalents, are the instruments of direct link to the world.

In saying what he says Strawson in effect agrees that singular terms aren't required for securing the word/world link. A broader point is that feature-placing is tailored to the world of Genesis 1. "Genesis 1 here," so to say. In suggesting that we can reach full-fledged predication from the feature-placing level by a process of addition, Strawson aligns himself with the tradition that Thales inaugurated and of which Plato's metaphysics is the full development. The world consists at base of dispositions in space and time of general (or non-singular) characteristics.[3]

Individuals

Strawson's major work in philosophy is *Individuals*. How do Strawson's individuals connect to the Bible's particulars? The expected answer, that a particular is one type of individual, isn't correct, although it is the nearest Strawsonian approximation. The concept of individuality is (in my technical sense) a metaphysical concept.

An individual is anything with well-defined identity conditions. It's the business of the analyst of being to elicit and/or to spell out the conditions – to supply the wherewithal for answering "Which among the various things is an X?" and "When are two things that are Xs (numerically) the same thing?" Usually, answering requires (1) locating the X in question in a class or type – that is, explaining how Xs differ from Ys – and (2) explaining how an X is set apart from other things of its class or type.

The idea of an individual ranges across type-boundaries. Numbers, for instance, qualify as individuals. General things can be individuals; so can particular things (in the everyday sense and in my specialized one too).[4]

The issue for us has to do with the main concern of *Individuals*: non-general individuals. Strawson's basic point in regard to them is that their identity conditions comprise matters of space and of time.

Is what Strawson offers adequate to Genesis 2's particularity? My claim is that Strawson would like to cross the Jordan but is stuck on the Egyptian side.

A much-discussed chapter is devoted to the creatures of Genesis 2. *Persons*, according to Strawson, are physical things that differ from other physical things in the same sort of way that assorted non-personal physical things differ from one another.[5] They are (non-general) individuals to which distinctive predicates apply – "P-predicates" Strawson dubs them.[6]

In all this, Strawson is sticking to a level of analysis whose contents are generally agreed upon: like tables and chairs, persons are individuals; matters of space and time are central to identifying and reidentifying persons, as they are to identifying and reidentifying tables and chairs; a number of things that are said of persons are said *only* of them. I will now show that Strawson is thinking along a line that, despite its Kantian affinities, keeps him in a friendly relationship to the anti-Kantian Leibniz. The point is like the earlier point about Quine. Strawson somehow cannot maintain the contrasts that he states. In this case, however, the inability is disastrous.

Non-General Individuals and Particulars: Neo-Leibnizeanism

Leibniz's position has at its centre the principle of the identity of indiscernibles (PII). According to PII, if objects O1 and O2 are distinct, some ascription must be true of O1 that is not true of O2. Put the other way round: if O1 and O2 have all the same properties, if (F)(FO1 ↔ FO2), then O1 = O2. Strawson does not accept PII: two things can be identical in the mentioned respect and still be two. As far as non-general things are concerned, the identity conditions make reference not only to properties but also to spatio-temporal matters; location in space and time, for example.

Contrary to what Leibniz maintains, two different things can have the same suite of characteristics.[7] There is however a weaker principle that captures PII's essence. This is (as I call it) the principle of interchangeability of functional identicals (PIFI). If two things are indistinguishable *solo numero*, then a swap makes no (discernible) difference.

PIFI is the principle to which Strawson is committed. If O1 and O2 differ only in spatial location and/or temporal position, a person unaware that O2 has been substituted for O1 would, that fact apart, be at par with a person in the know. This is tantamount to PII. If the (pertinent) property ascriptions true of O1 are the same as those true of O2, it makes no difference which of them one has. We do not care whether the mechanic installs this brake pad or that brake pad, only that the brake pad installed be the right make and model.[8]

Strawson represents himself in *Individuals* as a critic of Leibniz. Like Kant, he rejects PII. But at a deeper level he and Leibniz are indistinguishable. Strawson, because of how he analyses the idea of non-general individuality, cannot avoid PIFI. Kant can. Kant's realm of being includes the region of things-in-themselves that Strawson, in *The Bounds of Sense*, guts from Kant's doctrine of transcendental idealism.

Consider now Strawson's account in *Individuals* of persons. Persons differ thus from (other) material objects: P-predicates apply to them alone. If the category of persons is distinguished by virtue of its sustaining a certain set of ascriptions, persons too are fungibles. That is: Strawson's distinction between persons and (other) material objects doesn't enable him to deny of persons the fungibility that his account ascribes to (other) material objects. An analysis unable to cater for our agreement that persons are not fungibles has some explaining to do. The idea of functional indistinguishability applies in the arena of persons only if we are *thinking* of them as function fillers: Carl as a clerk, Mona as a mechanic, Bob as a bank manager or as a bellhop.[9]

Strawson wants to take a biblical-type position in his opposition to PII. But his toolbox furnishes only (general) predicates and spatio-temporal position. So although the category of non-general individual is available to him, the category of particular is not.

Strawson's position epitomizes the constraining effects of the Athenian style of thinking on a non-Thalean by tendency. Cognitive access to the things that have the properties is through the properties. This is another reason why the debate between Strawson and Quine over singular terms was so unsatisfying. Why should Strawson have insisted on the singular term's irreducibility when, metaphysically, its singularity is not at all singular? It's like insisting on the proper use of a fork when its soup that's being consumed.

On metaphysical grounds, Strawson is committed to PIFI. He is a Neo-Leibnizean. But although his analytic resources aren't biblical, his thinking is. He implicitly distinguishes particulars from among (non-general) individuals. Particulars are (non-general) individuals that PIFI does not govern. Non-particular non-general individuals are accounted for in terms of (a) general, shareable properties, and (b) spatio-temporal positioning.

Persons are particulars. Nothing else of which we are aware in the creation cannot be thought of in wholly functional terms. That is the Bible's view. Only the man created in Genesis 2, and through him other men and women, are inspired with God's kind of existence: particular existence. It's true that we *treat* many other things as particulars. But this, as in the case of pets, is sentimentality of one stripe or another.

Strawson's predicative approach operates on the level of types. It gives classes, not particulars. Any non-general thing is always picked out from a class of things that are distinguishable *solo numero*. Strawson's classificatory word for non-general thing is "individual." But the principle of space and time is only a principle of non-generality. A principle of particularity it is not.[10]

To cater for the particular one must, it appears, start, as the Bible starts in Genesis 2, with one. The resources of Genesis 1 are not a ticket to the world of Genesis 2. To start with the particular is however to accept a principle alien to Athens. Also, in at least one area of existence it is to raise ontology above metaphysics. In Genesis 2, the lump of clay, which is only an individual (God could have started with any handful of the stuff) is made a person by receiving God's breath of life. This again indicates that at the core of the "only one God" position is a thesis of philosophical anthropology. More than a god who is unrivalled, the deity of the Bible is a particular having the character of a person. From a reflective and non-religious viewpoint, monotheism is the anti-philosophical view that persons are particulars. To identify the biblical God with the Platonic principle of being is to confuse Acropolis with Sinai, Academus's Garden with the Garden of Eden.

Persons: Strawson and Plato

The absence of the particular from Strawson's resources is felt at other places in his oeuvre. "Freedom and Resentment" finds Strawson tying the idea of moral agency to (what he calls) *reactive* attitudes. If a person deliberately or through negligence causes harm, the affected party is justified in feeling resentment. It's nonsense, by contrast, to resent an avalanche. In respect of non-persons, one's attitudes are *objective*.

People differ from avalanches. For the reactive attitude to be appropriate, people must *differ more* from avalanches than avalanches do from other natural things. Otherwise, "avalanches differ from people" could have been said in an identical tone of voice. How do people differ more? Each person is a particular. With only individuals to bring to the table, Strawson proceeds to honour the intuition as best he can. He examines our practices and underscores how tight (and wide) a system they comprise. In effect, he winkles out a system whose proponents, apprised of its richness, can hold their own in confrontations with reductionists from the scientific corner. About the key item that anchors the system, the ontological specialness of the men and the women who engage in these practices, he says nothing.

Strawson wants to distinguish people from other (non-general) individuals. His way of distinguishing ("P-predicates apply solely to the former") gives us too weak a contrast. In character, the result differs not at all from the distinction between, say, material objects and numbers ("locational predicates do not apply to numbers"). Two classes or types of individuals are set apart. We can adapt here Judah Halevi's warning against the wisdom of the Greeks, "which has only flowers and produces no fruit." Individuals, in effect, but no particulars.

Let's pay one last visit to Strawson's philosophical logic. Quine is eager to recast a proper name like "Socrates" as a predicate: "Socratize." This is the predicate that applies exclusively to the person who goes by the name. The recasting is fine for Quine. His commitments are fully to science, and his concerns are with its logical structure and hence with features such as economy and elegance. For Strawson, the recasting is not fine. But because he lacks the idea of particularity, his disapproval looks like inertia.

Quine's uniquely applying predicate (the class of objects that fall under it is a singleton) is tailored to his metaphysical position. The only differences among objects all of which are fungibles are in class size. If "Socratize" has only one instance, what need of the proper name? It may seem heartless for Quine to suck the particularity out of his loved ones for the surrogacy of unique membership in a class. If however we are dealing with objects any number of which can in principle satisfy the same predicates, the charge if heartlessness is sentimental. Why not eliminate childish names for adult-bound variables? Strawson, as we know, resists. Unless particulars and individuals are distinguished, the resistance is hard to understand save as dogged fidelity to the vulgate.

When the resistance *is* understood, we appreciate that the issue isn't of logic. Strawson himself commits the very flattening (the assimilation of particulars to non-general individuals) for which he takes Quine to task (the elimination of explicitly singular terms).

No one who understands monotheism correctly would agree that the theological position comes to this, that only one deity Godizes! God's character is not that of a (special) non-general individual. God's oneness cannot be understood in terms of generality and instantiation. God's one-ness is not the *unum* of the transcendentals. The transcendentals – *ens, unum, verum, bonum* – are in fact expressions of the highest kind of generality. God's one-ness is the antithesis. It is an extreme expression of non-generality. Moreover, few things under the sun have it.

In discussing the Bible's moral philosophy, I explained that when the principle of particularity is absent, positions that we feel in our bones to be mistaken can get ratified.[11] Utilitarianism recommends maximizing some quality such as happiness or pleasure. This, again, is like an economist's recommending measures to double net wealth without caring about the continued penury of the vast majority.

In the absence of particulars it makes no sense to attempt to introduce distributive principles (albeit that attempt is made by many utilitarians, in whose bones the feeling is as it is in ours). Utilitarianism is an ecological-type view. It belongs to the conceptual field of Genesis 1. Morality, an *ego*logical-type view, requires the resources of Genesis 2. Kant supplies the latter. To procure them he has however to voyage into the noumenal realm for something more robust than (in effect) individuals. Such obscurities, Kant feels, are essential.

One philosopher of Kant's stature doesn't have these problems. The line that Plato, the arch–system thinker, takes is consistent with the Thalean basis of philosophical thinking, although Plato's (so to speak) ecology is rational rather than natural. Many readers of the *Republic* feel that we have to do here with a Hellenic *1984*. They miss that Plato rejects the principle of particularity. Thus, for Plato, justice is defined as *doing* one's own, not as *having* one's own. The cobbler must cobble, the joiner must join, the ruler, rule. "From each according to what he or she is good at," where "good at" means "good at for the good of the whole." *We* employ the phrase "doing your own thing." It means "doing what you choose to do." *You* are your own thing.

In this telling passage from the *Republic*, Plato is discussing the life of a typical denizen of his ideal city, a carpenter:

> When a carpenter is ill, he asks his doctor to give him an emetic or a purge to expel the trouble, or to rid him of it by cautery or the knife. But if he is advised to take a long course of treatment, to keep his head wrapped up, and all that sort of thing, he soon replies that he has not time to be ill and it is not worth his while to live in that way, thinking of nothing but his illness and neglecting his proper work. And so he bids goodbye to that kind of doctor and goes back to his ordinary way of life. Then he either regains his health and lives to go about his proper business, or, if his body is not equal to the strain, gets rid of all his troubles by dying. (406d–407a)

Substitute a car part for the carpenter, and what is written makes sense. A tire beyond repair gets tossed onto the scrap heap. When it comes to particulars, Plato's claim sounds like it that might have come from Stalin or from Hitler: a person past healing is to be liquidated – reunited with Thales's water. Again, however, Plato does not accept particulars. His being-theoretic analysis involves (the system of) Forms and reflections of Forms in space and time (the Receptacle). It involves no more. Within Plato's framework the disruption of the family, sc. the treatment of "husband" and "wife" as functional terms, makes sense. Our attitudes Plato would dismiss as sentimental.

Aristotle is criticized for defending slavery. In the frame of thinking that has no non-fungibles, slavery can seem less abhorrent. A biblical motif is the need constantly to remind ourselves of the slavery in Egypt lest we ourselves fall unawares into the role of slavers.

The absence of the Jerusalemite principle thus has effects in logic, in ethics, in morals, in politics. And my small set of examples opens the gates into action theory, the area of mind, and other compartments of philosophy.

Both enunciations of the Ten Commandments begin with "I am the Lord your God." In *god is not Great* Christopher Hitchens dismisses the declaration as "throat-clearing"[12] and proceeds to voice the oft-voiced claim that God is a bully. This is wrong-headed. God is the principle of particularity. Without such a principle, moral behaviour doesn't make moral sense. I said that pagan systems can endorse principles of moral-type behaviour: truth-telling; marital fidelity; parental respect. But for these systems, such principles, like rules of the road, enable men and women to get along without too much friction, and hence are not categorical.

Dostoyevsky in Oxford

"Freedom and Resentment" isn't a piece of normative moral philosophy. Like the Bible in advancing the commandments, and like Kant in the *Critique of Practical Reason*, Strawson is exploring the foundations of morality. In the second *Critique*, Kant makes a remark that resonates here. The view that represents freedom as compatible with causal determinacy is, he declares, "a wretched subterfuge."[13]

Dostoyevsky, in *Notes from Underground*, addresses the idea of a world without freedom. Because the innumerable grievances that he feels are denied a legitimate target in such a world, the novella's appropriately nameless protagonist is in a perpetual frenzy. The narration echoes the agitation. "There in its nasty stinking cellar our offended, browbeaten and derided mouse sinks at once into cold, venomous, and above all undying resentment" (21). How unforgettable the Undergroundling's attempt to gain redress for an imagined insult. The preparations extend to the purchase of an imitation fur collar for a threadbare overcoat. Contrary to the man's delusional construction, the officer he thinks had delivered the slight, as he brushes by on the Nevsky Prospekt, notices neither coat nor collar nor (potentially most unnerving to *my* readers) collegiate assessor. What is all this if not a claim about what people are or are taken to be when thought of as (moral) agents? Dostoyevsky, emotionally, like Strawson, intellectually, is resisting the assimilation of men and women to pieces of nature. "People are still people and not piano keys" (38). Augustine was forthright: men and women are like God, for being subjects with real beginnings and real ends. That is the Bible's view too.

Strawson is saying that persons differ in character from other individuals. The difference he draws is however too weak: metaphysical, not ontological.

I spoke about love's affinity for particulars. Strawson speaks similarly of resentment. Committed to PIFI, he lacks the wherewithal for making sense of it all.

In the move from Genesis 1 to Genesis 2, the Bible is trying to take us out of the natural realm: from systems (of mere individuals) to (interacting but autonomous) particulars. That is what Strawson is trying to do too. The system in which men and women are found, men and women as *appropriate* objects of attitudes like resentment, is, he shows, a complex and internally coherent system. But this will not work. It's one system against another. Strawson is still an imitation "free" caller.

Kant uses language midway between Dostoyevsky's hot and Strawson's cool:

> According to [the concept of comparative freedom, that is, freedom on the compatibilist analysis], what is sometimes called "free effect" is that of which the determining natural cause is internal to the acting thing. For example, that which a projectile performs when it is in free motion is called by the name "freedom" because it is not pushed by anything external while it is in flight ... So one might call the actions of man "free" because they are actions caused by ideas we have produced by our own powers ... With this manner of argument many allow themselves to be put off and believe that with a little quibbling they have found the solution to the difficult problem which centuries have sought in vain and which could hardly be expected to be found so completely on the surface.

When the first woman is created, she is acknowledged as the man's equal, "bone of [his] bones" and "flesh of [his] flesh" (23). We have two separate entities, one person and another person.[14] We do not have two members of a larger class, humankind. This isn't a distinction without a difference. With respect to humankind, it matters not which sees the light first, any more than it matters which car part is first off the production line. The Genesis 2 story starts with a specific entity, the man. The Bible is primarily the biography of that man and of his progeny. That man and his progeny have no status in the species that is the subject matter of Darwin & Co.

"Flesh of my flesh." This isn't a vertical subsumption. It's a horizontal movement from a particular to another particular. "Flesh of my flesh" doesn't, that is, amount to "an instance of the same sort of stuff as I am." The man (Adam) isn't saying: "the woman is another one like me." He is saying: "she, like me, is a one."

Petersburg, Dostoyevsky complains, is the most abstract of cities. Peter's burg, Oxford, is also too abstract. It's not P-redicates. It's P-articularity.

Early on, I said that the difference between Athens and Jerusalem can be encapsulated in terms of what the representative wise men of the cultures say. For Thales, water is the principle. For Solomon, God's spirit is the principle. Thales's is the principle of generality; Solomon's, of particularity. In Genesis 1, at the start, we have a verse containing both. Here is my translation of the last part of 1:1.

> And the spirit of God hovered on the face of the water.

This can be seen as a version of the (onto)logical claim that a principle external to the principle of generality governs particularity. The principle of generality does not contain the principle of particularity. God is not the (general) principle of being; God is the principle of particular being.

At the centre of each of the works that the tradition ascribes to Solomon is particularity. The Song of Songs explores love, the paradigm particular-requiring emotion. Proverbs offers cooler advice for men and women – advice that has nothing to do with entities whose behaviour can be predicted. Ecclesiastes focuses with excruciating intensity on what makes us non-systematic: our deaths. It touches on the being of (God-like) entities of this sort who are located within the cycle of nature.

Austin Missing in Action

In *Freedom Evolves*,[15] the latter-day compatibilist Daniel Dennett discusses an anti-determinist claim of J.L. Austin's regarding the modality of possibility. Austin had written, about missing an easy putt, that he might have holed it under the very same conditions. That, on the face of it, is incompatible with compatibilism.[16] On the strength of a possible world analysis, Dennett shows that Austin's claim is unacceptable. True, in circumstances *very like* the circumstances that prevailed, the putt might have been holed. True too, if the golfer had made *slightly more allowance* for the grain of the putting surface, the ball would not have lipped the cup. But Austin doesn't say either of these. His words are: "conditions as they precisely were."

Dennett, whose concern in *Freedom Evolves* is to allay fears that determinism abolishes freedom, is correct about the putt. But what he says about the putter (the golfer, not the club) is incorrect. Under the same conditions, the golfer could have done something else. Attempting to spirit freedom in through quantum indeterminacy (not, I hasten to add, something that Dennett does) is wrongheaded. The difference is in the particularity.

The issue for Dennett comes out differently. Here it is, from the Bible's perspective. The man and the woman disobey. They choose to go against God's instruction. Did they have to do that?

Let's simplify by putting it in Dennett's terms. You are standing on the putting surface. If you hit the ball, you might hole it. Then again, the ball might lip out. Suppose the ball lips out. Could it have dropped under the (exact) same conditions Austin seems to interpret "you might have holed the ball" so that the answer to the question is affirmative. It's this that Dennett is questioning. I have another question. Could you have strode off the green? Could you have struck the ball back towards the tee? Constructed as you are, could you have done any of these things under the (exact) same conditions? Dennett is looking at the wrong thing. He needs not Austin but Augustine, who says that only men and women, particulars, can initiate.

Dennett is looking at factors such as the club head, the green, and the movement of the arms. Austin's terms of discussion take Dennett's eye off the ball, so to speak. Austin says that under those conditions *the ball* might have been holed. The issue is whether, in those circumstances, the *person* could have done something else.

The category of particularity may still seem mysterious. I'll end with a table-turning suggestion of vast generality. The anthropomorphism that is found in the pagan context is, I asserted, superficial. By contrast, the centrality of the particular person in the biblical context goes right to the bottom. Would it not be correct, if so, to take the position that our primary dealings with the world are dealings that reflect Genesis 2, not Genesis 1? We treat everything like a particular. As we mature cognitively, the non-particulars come to be recognized for what they are. It is not the category of the particular that is mysterious. The category of the non-particular, both the non-particular general thing and the non-general individual, precipitates out afterwards. On this way of looking at things, Genesis 2 is an account of the true centre.

Anthropology and Ontology

Pointing out that Descartes sharply distinguishes the human part of the creation from the rest, readers might question the claim that particularity is an "original" biblical notion. Descartes does hold that minds are individuals in a stronger sense than material objects are. But the fact that he takes a somewhat Spinozistic view of the material realm shows that a characterization of the elements of a compartment of being in terms of a principal attribute ("extended thing," "thinking thing") is consistent with the non-particularity of the elements.

For those who endorse, or oppose, claims of distinction of the kind that Descartes makes, it boils down to this. Is being an instance of concept C1 (sc. having the [general] property F1 that C1 expresses, or being an F1-type thing) compatible with being an instance of concept C2 (sc. having the [general] property F2 that C2 expresses, or being an F2-type thing)? The terms of debate here are metaphysical. It's a question of general properties and instantiation.

Charles Taylor argues in "Mind–Body Identity: A Side Issue?" that dualism turns on whether the (sort of) explanatory principles that capture the activity of the rest are not capable of capturing human reality. Structurally, this isn't really distinct from Strawson's position that P-predicates are irreducible to M-predicates, or from Descartes's position that thought and extension are different principal attributes. Having taken, each of them, what he as a philosophical anthropologist believes to be a giant step for mankind, neither Strawson nor Taylor nor Descartes takes the small step of asking *what* the things (individuals) are that are of the distinct kinds that they identify.

10
Suffering and Logic

Job Jobbed

"There was once a man in the land of Uz whose name was Job" (Job 1:1). In life circumstances that would challenge the strongest, Job exhibits the trait for which his name has become a byword. Eventually, Job's defences of patience buckle. Forbearance gone, he enters a grievance for having been, despite a glowing character and a record of God-fearing allegiance, jobbed. If God's practice violates the principles of justice that he enjoins upon us, does God merit our worship?

In this final chapter, I apply the preceding results to the question of the suffering of innocents as dealt with in the Book of Job, a book that is distant from the core of the biblical action. The major distinction drawn in these pages is between the natural story of humankind in Genesis 1 and the non-natural Genesis 2 story of men and women. The power of the distinction to illuminate texts over which interpreters divide is thereby illustrated.

My coverage of the Bible's position on philosophical topics has so far scanted the area of logic. The one reference had to do with the dispute between Strawson and Quine. I return for a closer look at the conflict between Quine's view and the Bible's ontology. Once the distinction mentioned above is translated into a distinction between two ways in which God is present in the world, it emerges that Quine's logic is suited only to the world of Genesis 1.

The suffering of innocents and singular terms? The Book of Job and *Word and Object*? The regimentation of proper names and the regime of divine justice? The reader will do a double-take at the conjunction of books and the jointure of themes. But he or she will also be aware that (to adapt Psalms 121:1) enlightenment not infrequently comes from where one least expects.

The Book of Job begins dramatically. God's intelligence agents have assembled for debriefing. Satan, the one angel named,[1] reports that he has come "[f]rom going to and fro on the earth, and from walking up and down on it" (1:6). Has Satan, God asks (8), observed Job, "a blameless and upright man who fears God and turns away from evil"? Repeated exposure to the words suggests smugness. "To and fro on the earth, you say. Up and down too? Most assiduous, my feathered friend. Even if you were to add in and out and up and down to your protocol, you'd still be wasting shoe leather with Job."

Job is, Satan agrees, dutiful to a fault. Who wouldn't worship so constant a benefactor? "But stretch out your hand now, and touch all that he has, and he will curse you to your face" (11). God rises to the bait. "Very well, all that he has is in your power; only do not stretch out your hand against him!" (12)

Try as I might, I often can't prevent harm from befalling the men and the women for whom *I* wish only good. Like the ill-starred Oedipus I might cause them harm in trying to obviate it. Yet none of this makes me unjust. The issue of God's justice isn't predicated on God's benevolence alone. Too, God's knowledge of the creation and his supremacy count. In a world over which such a deity presides, can bad things happen to good men and women without the president's inviting impeachment?

The dozen lines that open the Book of Job provoke this question. "If God cuts deals with malignant forces, isn't the problem of God's justice, *the theodicy problem*, a pseudo-problem? Doesn't the existence of Satan cast doubt on God's hegemony?" The argument of the Book of Job is that it is compatible with the world's being as – in the final verse of chapter 1 of the Book of Genesis – God himself judges it to be, "very good" (31), that bad things befall the upright and injure the innocent. The writers of the Book of Job are not trying to make the Panglossian case: factor in all the factors, and what seems bad turns out for the best. Mightn't good come of affliction? Regardless, this is no justification. Compassion can be acquired without suffering. Piling on is as likely to brutalize. Like Leibniz and his followers, Job's comforters are loath to accept innocent pain as a baseline datum; God wouldn't in their judgment have tolerated a world containing such a thing. The comforters are, according to the Book of Job, mistaken. Job is as blameless as God says. Satan in the Book of Job does not therefore function as the source of the bad. Satan is the Book of Job's way of securing the datum, innocent suffering, thereby nixing the Leibnizeans and discomfiting the comforters. The question that troubles the reader is whether the tableau, when filled in, won't show a deity complicit in what happens to Job. Does it turn out that the place assigned to Satan either is God's place or else is no place? With an eye on the sequel, let me stress in this regard that Satan, having taken up the charge of testing Job, is said to "[go] out of the presence of the Lord" (12). The words imply that *the harm is inflicted from a place where God is absent*. The implication is of the first importance to the Book of Job's case for divine justice. It will turn out that Job isn't there either.

Job suffers through no fault of his own.[2] How does this square with the world's being good, as it is stated in Genesis 1 to be? If God did not arrange things to prevent what happened to Job, isn't he deficient in one or more of benevolence, power, and knowledge? If God couldn't have arranged things so, wouldn't he draw our sympathy rather than our worship?

The discussion will be devoted to the case for God as set out in the Book of Job. To say that the case is correct would be overambitious. Still, I will correct a mistake that prevents the case from being understood. I hasten to add that in my understanding of it the case is available to deniers of God. At the Book of Job's core is an attempt to demonstrate that the suffering of the protagonist doesn't clash with the world's being good, as per Genesis 1. That good generates no religious commitments to God.

The Perils of Epistemology

Even open-minded readers feel that Job stays his grievance prematurely. The basis of the answer that God delivers to Job at the end seems to be an element central to the two God-defensive positions that are rejected *because* they deny the datum. Elihu, least discomforting of the comforters, claims that in self-ascribing blamelessness Job must be beautifying the evidence. Only God, with his superior knowledge of the hearts of men and women and of the clockwork of the world, is in a position to deliver the last judgment.[3] Leibnizeans say that the basis for bringing down the gavel about good and bad goes beyond the data available to men and women. Only a deficit of knowledge could sustain the verdict of the world's badness.

Here is the beginning of God's response (the lines are from chapter 38; the first line is verse 1; the next two, verses 4 and 5).

> Then the Lord answered Job out of the whirlwind.
>
> Where were you when I laid the foundations of the earth?
> Tell me, if you have understanding.

Isn't God drawing attention to the epistemological deficiency of finite men and women, the deficiency that lies at the intersection of the two rejected positions?

"Where were you?" God asks Job. We are – are we not? – supposed to grant that God was, as verse 5 implies, on the scene when the foundations were laid. "In the beginning, when God created the heavens and the earth" (Genesis 1:1).

Why should God's primordial presence provide for an answer to Job? An eyewitness is more advantageously placed to form beliefs about some activity than is a viewer from afar. "I was on the spot. If you have the temerity to dispute with me, you had better have in hand something that undermines the presumption that I know better." Through the Book of Job, God asserts, hendiadys after hendiadys, that he has the goods and that Job is squinting in through the flyblown window. Here are verses 22 and 25 of the same chapter:

> Have you entered the storehouses of the snow,
> or have you seen the storehouses of the hail …?
> Who has cut a channel [through the firmament] for the torrents of rain,
> and a way for the thunderbolt …?[4]

Isn't the point that because of a deficit of knowledge men and women are in no position to judge? How else are we to construe verse 2? "Who is this that darkens counsel by words without knowledge?" If this *is* the point, disaster for the Book of Job is however in the offing.

God is explicit: Job's position, which is representative of the situation of each one of us – be we arrant sinners or paragons of virtue – is disadvantaged. But the Book of Job is intended to acquit God's world on a charge of constitutional injustice. By the end, do we know what God knows? It would seem not. That being so, Job *is* dropping the ball in dropping the complaint. Since our position at the end is not much better, epistemologically, than it was at the beginning, why moreover should we accept the irredeemable suffering of good men and good women (the Book of Job's premise) as a datum? Perhaps the comforters or the Leibnizeans have it right.

Most of my readers will agree that the words God is described as speaking in the Book of Job are not transcriptions of revelation. That being so, the truth content of what God states is known to men and women – known, then, to Job. What God says is quite intelligible. With regard to the assertion that he cut spillways into the dome, think sprinkler system. As we read, don't we in fact imaginatively transpose ourselves back onto the spot, a few days into the life of the world, when the acetylene torch was applied to perforate the firmament? Since, at the end, it seems that an answer to the main question about God's justice and the suffering of innocents is not in our possession – how are we who never doubted God's power aided by the engineering report? – the implication is that what God knows doesn't suffice for answering. From this it follows that God's case is ultimately an appeal to authority orchestrated by the intimidating roar of the maelstrom.

The epistemological reading strands those of God's party in a dilemma. Suppose that men and women could know what God knows. Since, by the end of the Book of Job, assurances that God has the knowledge are all that they have, Satan's not been answered. *The writers,* one must therefore suspect, are stymied. Suppose that we men and women are excluded from knowing what God knows (maybe human language is inadequate). It follows that a reasoned case will never be available to us for accepting any thesis about God.

The pro-God case associated with the epistemological reading is so question-begging that charity alone would incline the reader to assume that he or she is missing something. Otherwise, doesn't it follow that the pro-God case is a con job? Granted, religious authorities do on occasion, forgivably, propagandize. A sugar coating, fermented à la A.E. Housman, might be just the thing for swallowing the bitter pill. "And malt does more than Milton can to justify God's ways to man." To be sure, no *believer* could accept the con job construction. Believers do not however have privileged access to the intentions of those behind the text. Still, the construction could only get the blue ribbon if it's the only finisher.

There is no sign that the final answer to Job is, in the words of the prolific versifier Anon-or-Trad, "Believe and cease to wonder." Still, it's hard to believe.

In the course of his answer, God asks Job whether he "[c]an ... draw out Leviathan with a fishhook" (41:5). It's high time for *us* to fish.

God's words do contain an answer. The position I take goes beyond saying that the answer has been misunderstood. As I see it, the formulators of the answer are not clear in their own minds, and interpreters have duplicated the confusion. A principle of legal defence asserts: when the case is weak, attack the prosecution. The fact that God resorts to sarcasm solidifies our sense that the writers are thrashing about. "Surely you [Job] know, for you were born then [when I laid the foundations], and the number of your days is [as] great [as mine]!" (21)[5]

In my view, Job is right to accept God's response. But to see that he is we've got to do some reformulating of the original formulations.[6]

At the heart of the misunderstanding on the part of the writers of Job is a widespread error regarding the core of the biblical position. Obviously, the writers of Job are relying on the position in the Pentateuch. The deity of whom the Book of Job speaks is the deity of the Bible, and the world in which Job lives is this deity's handiwork. The reformulation is restorative, then, of the Book of Job's connection with the Pentateuch, especially with the Book of Genesis.

Being There: Two Ways

Consider a sentence from the preceding section.

> We are – are we not? – supposed to grant that God was, as verse 5 implies, on the scene when the foundations were laid. "In the beginning, when God created the heavens and the earth" (Genesis 1:1).

The writers of the Book of Job share the sentiment. *We are supposed to grant this.* Granting it, I submit, causes the difficulty in their case. (Granting it underpins the problematic epistemological reading.) Arguably, however, God was *not* present when the foundations were laid. Recall my claim that Satan, in causing Job's suffering, has gone out of the presence of the Lord. This, read literally, implies God's absence when the bad was done to Job. If so, the point being made isn't the epistemological one.

Here's another excerpt from the preceding section: "God is explicit: Job's position, which is representative of the situation of each one of us – be we arrant sinners or be we paragons of virtue – is disadvantaged." In formulating the sentence, I built in an ambiguity. The reference is automatically taken to be epistemological. "What do we know?" Might I not however be disadvantaged relative to God because of what I am? If a female is sought for a job, I am a non-starter. No epistemology in that.

For the second time in reading the essay (I suppose I should say "at least the second time"), the reader will do a double-take. "You say that God is not present when the foundations are laid. That is downright false. In Genesis 1:1, God is described in so many words as laying the foundations."

I'm fine with the pitch of the hostility. It only serves to increase the impact of the response.

There are two ways of being present. One: Being *on the scene*. A painter is on the scene when the canvas is filled in. Two: Being *in the scene*. Raphael inserts his own likeness into *The School of Athens*. Van Gogh paints a self-portrait.

The *on the scene / in the scene* distinction is a linchpin of the case for God in the Book of Job. If the writers are aware of the distinction, they leave no sign in the text. Equally vital is the fact, of which the writers of the Book of Genesis are aware, that the opening part of the Pentateuch contains two accounts of the world's creation, one in Genesis 1 and one in Genesis 2.

The two ways of being present, and the two stories of creation, make for four combinatorial possibilities for God.

God, I said, is not present when the foundations are laid. The reader who said "downright false" will now appreciate his or her misunderstanding. Also, he or she will appreciate that if the distinction between the two ways of being present turns out to bear on what Scripture is saying, the injustice isn't just to me.

God is not present when the foundation is laid. Is the position that God is not *on the scene*, or is it that God is not *in the scene*? The reader takes me to be denying the former. This I do not deny. I *did* quote Genesis 1:1. My claim is that God is not *in the scene* that the verse depicts. God is not present in the world that is created.

Now that the distinction is etherized, the reader will I imagine come over. But the strains of kumbaya will be short-lived. "What of it if God is not on the scene in Genesis 1? God is *never* present in the creation. He exists apart from the physical world. The distinction therefore distinguishes nothing from nothing in the Bible."

Not so. In Genesis 2, *God is present in both senses*. God is *on* the scene: "In the day that the Lord God made the earth and the heavens" (2:2). And God is *in* the scene – in it as, *mutatis mutandis*, Raphael is in *The School of Athens* and Van Gogh in *Self-Portrait with a Bandaged Ear*: "the Lord God formed [the] man from the dust of the ground, and breathed into his nostrils the [sc. God's] breath of life" (7). God puts something of himself in the world of Genesis 2.

Here is how things are disposed.

	World of Genesis 1	World of Genesis 2
God ON the scene	Yes	Yes
God IN the scene	No	Yes

The key to the Book of Job is the contrast between Genesis 1 and Genesis 2 in the matter of the two modes of being present. God asks Job: "Were you there?" The negative answer, which is expected, is not intended to have the epistemological effect attached to it above. Either the deficit of knowledge is contingent and is not made good in the Book of Job (or elsewhere) although it could in principle be, which means that the case is incomplete, or else the deficit is structural, from which it follows that an effective case for God exceeds human powers to construct. God is saying something else: the world whose creation Genesis 1 describes (this, as I noted in passing, is where the description of the laying of the foundations is found) is not a world that was created for Job or with Job in mind. In fact, it's a world in which Job does not exist. "You were not there then," God is saying, "and you are not there now." This is a point of ontology. It's a claim about what you basically are. The principles of *that* world are not the principles of *your* world.

Genesis 1: It's All Good

God is present *in* the scene in Genesis 2 but not in Genesis 1. To back up the claim that he is present in the Genesis 2 scene, I quoted the chapter's assertion that God breathes life into the first man. "But," the reader will ask, "isn't humankind created in the Genesis 1 story? If God is present in the scene in Genesis 2, and present in respect, specifically, of the human sector of the creation (nothing else gets breathed into), isn't God also present in the scene, and present in the same way, in Genesis 1 (nothing else is created in God's image and likeness)?"

To begin the process of answering, let me quote another line from the preceding discussion.

The argument of the Book of Job is that it is compatible with the world's being "very good" (31) – as in the final verse of Genesis 1 God himself says it to be – that bad things happen to the upright and afflict the blameless.

At the end of the last day on which creativity is exercised, Day 6, God says that the world is "very good." God says this after having said "good" six times on the preceding days. At no point does God voice "bad." Where, now, is this story? It is in chapter 1 of Genesis. "Bad," then, is not at any stage applied to WG1, the world of this story.

Question 1: Why is "bad" not applied in Genesis 1? Question 2: Is this "no bad" condition of WG1 temporary?

Bad is unexemplified in WG1 because WG1 is an integrated whole. There is a place in it for everything and everything is in the place that there is for it. The luminaries are in the skies, the fish are in the seas, the land animals are on the land. Cactuses are in the desert, and palm trees in the tropics.

The fact that everything is in its place does not make WG1 static. An ecosystem such as a forest will do as a model of WG1's dynamic character.

In the forest, the organic material on the floor is food for microorganisms whose digestive processes alter it into a form that seeds can metabolize. Wafted by the winds, seeds that land on the floor germinate and grow into saplings and over time become mature trees whose foliage supplies more nutritive material for the microorganisms. Now and again a tree falls over and, as it decomposes, replenishes the humus. We have a system in rough equilibrium, a system whose parts – microorganisms, plants at various stages of development – are continuously exchanging matter and energy.

God's judgment "good" is to the effect that each thing fulfils its function. The judgment "very good" is to the effect that the end result, the natural world as we know it, is a well-running system.

There is no bad in WG1. The text is explicit, sounding "good" half a dozen times and ending with "very good." The death of an antelope in the jaws of a lion stops a weak member of the cluster from passing on its genes and/or puts an especially adept hunter of the pride in a better position to propagate. Should an antelope survive such an encounter, the outcome accepts the same kind of complex judgment. Varying with the position inside the system that one judges from, the description of lion as serving antelope can be as correct as the description of antelope as serving lion. That's why it's philosophically significant that at the end of Genesis 1, *God* is said to see that the creation is good.

As for the second question: The condition isn't temporary. Bad is never found in the natural system. The system does develop, since it is dynamic, usually remaining in equilibrium for a while, though sometimes – for example, when an ice age descends – shifting from one equilibrium state (torrid/temperate) to another (temperate/frigid). By the end of Genesis 1, WG1 is in existence in a fashion that will not change except in these ways. There is nothing new under the sun.[7]

Although I have used the language naturally, *death* is in a sense absent from WG1 too. Death as the end of existence and death as the termination of a phase need to be distinguished here. We speak of the dying day only poetically, and we do not speak literally of winter killing off autumn. The first line of a lyric by Shmuel haNagid, a Hebrew poet of the Spanish Golden Age, runs thus:

> August is dead, September too, their heat expired. October,
> Mowed down by the scythe, has been joined with them in the crypt.

The example of morning and night or of the seasons is more apposite, conceptually, to what happens in the biological world than the notion of dying that we apply to ourselves and for which, when it occurs to someone close, we don the colour of night and go into mourning. Back to God's question, the one from 38:4, that was formulated sarcastically in verse 21: "Where were you?" The point is that Job and his like are not present in WG1. Like lionkind and spiderkind and treekind, humankind is a biological species. For humankind, too, there is no bad in this world. The death of a human in this world is no more bad than the death of a tree. Not literally death, it is *mutatis mutandis* the same as what happens in the death of August and when the scythe cuts October down. Views like the Hindu one give instruction here. "No one dies," says Krishna to Arjuna in the *Bhagavad-Gita*. God could say the same to a tree. "Your matter is recycled. You go on. The basic unit is the system." It is what is true of WG1. In WG1, everything gets out of life alive, because in WG1 nothing has life apart from the system. Which explains why the issue of mortality isn't broached in Genesis 1.

We are considering the objection that in creating humankind on the afternoon of Day 6, God is also in the scene. This, we now appreciate, isn't what the writers of Genesis intend. No matter the manner in which humankind differs from any other species (and it differs enough to have its emergence delayed until the end of the six days of creation – differs enough that it alone is said to be made "in [God's] image, according to [God's] likeness" [26]), the writers of Genesis 1 intend humankind to be seen as part of the natural system. So if God is not in the scene in respect of the plants and the (non-human) animals, the same goes in respect of humankind.

"Where were you?" The deity who asks is the deity of WG1. From the answer to the first question, it will now be clearer that Job is not in that world. Job has a character that is alien to it. This character is marked, figuratively, in God's breathing life into the first person in WG2. From the answer to the second question, it will be clearer that Job is never in that world. Overall, it will be clear that God is not saying "I was there (in WG1) and you weren't." God is saying: "You are not part of WG1 because I am not present in it." There is no contrast with God's case. God is teaching a lesson in ontology, not boasting that he is smarter.[8]

WG2 and the Potential for Bad

A clear sense exists in which God is not in WG1: the sense in which the painter is not in the picture. The significance of this we will appreciate once we turn to the creation story told in Genesis 2.

Genesis 2 is not focused on the emergence of humankind, the biological species. That's the topic of Genesis 1. In Genesis 2, God creates a particular man, and then a particular woman, and to these two you and I and he and she trace back. Obviously, as the writers of Genesis 1 understand, a unisex species is an impossibility. As it is written, "male and female he created them" (1:27).[9] But in Genesis 2, the man, created first, is present for a time on his own. The solitariness is the Bible's way of making the conceptual point that while the species comprises both sexes essentially, particular men and particular women are wholes in their own right.

In creating the first particular man, God breathes into him the breath of life. Obviously, humankind (in the Genesis 1 story) exists, as treekind and spiderkind exist, without need of artificial respiration. The kind of life of which Genesis 2 speaks in the human case is something "extra." According to the biblical narrative, only we, among the creatures, have it. What is it? It's the kind of life that particulars have, "particular" meaning, roughly, "thing that is not essentially part of a system." That is *God's* kind of life. God, it follows, is present in Genesis 2 in the way that Van Gogh is present in the self-portrait.

All of this can be tied up neatly by returning to the explanation of the absence of bad in WG1. Bad is absent because everything is in its allotted place. So everything does its job. It follows that bad is linked to things not being in their place. This is the story of the transgression in the sequel of Genesis 2. If there are entities that are not just members of the species, then there are in the world things of a sort that can cut across the function lines. This, pretty accurately, is what particular men and women can do – and what they *do* do. The mentioned story is supersaturated with significance. Before it is a story of human depravity, it is a story about what men and women are – better, about what they are not, namely parts of the (WG1) system.

The presence of "good and bad" in WG2 is a function of the status of men and women therein as, each of them, separate. In a system such as a forest, nothing can do bad to anything. An asteroid smashes into the earth: asteroids are part of the solar system; collisions occur. The extinction of the dinosaurs is no different than the extinction of arboreal life through glaciation. But one person can harm another, not only assist and benefit. That is because the world of men and women, in WG2, is a world of separate entities in interaction. More intelligent dinosaurs still would not need legal systems and politicians. But, of course, the bad (and the good) that particular men and particular woman do to one another is not the issue in the Book of Job. Satan would cause Job to have a car accident by flash-flooding the road, not by arranging for a drunk driver.

God is not present in WG1. God's breath of life is absent from WG1. God is by contrast present in WG2. God is present in WG2 in the presence of each particular man and of each particular woman.

The Case for God

We have the elements of the answer to the question of God's justice that the Book of Job offers.

1. The source of bad that the Book of Job considers, the source of innocent suffering, is WG1. God is not present in WG1. Since God's nature is absent from WG1, any coherent story of its creation will do – even a story, like Aristotle's, on which the natural world is uncreated.

2. The source of bad is itself good (i.e., it is not bad). WG1 is, as the Bible puts it, "very good."[10] So there is no faulting God for it.
3. Men and women who suffer (or who *can* suffer) undeserved bad belong to WG2. They are particulars, not parts of the system, and such things are absent from WG1.
4. The suffering that Satan is said to inflict on Job comes from WG1. The sufferers do not exist in WG1. So although there would be no undeserved bad if men and women did not exist, they can hardly complain on that score, either to God or to anyone or anything else.
5. In fact, the existences of particular men and particular women have value. For God is present in them in WG2. In nothing else in the creation is God present.[11]
6. No one who considers the issue of undeserved bad in the Book of Job would say that God would have done better had he not created the innocent men and women who suffer. The claim is that God would have been a more just deity had he created a world in which men and women suffer no undeserved bad. The position is that God could not have done that. Once God created WG1 and WG2, undeserved bad was a possibility.

WG1's effects on WG2 are unavoidable.[12] Bad can come to us although the cause of bad is good, and although those affected have no ground for complaint about how they are made. (If gratitude and ingratitude are in point they should be grateful.) Job and his like come into existence in WG2. That is: the question of God's justice is not asked from the standpoint of the species or of the system that is nature. From nature's standpoint, "good" applies to everything. The creative act that makes the Bible the book that it is is God's breathing life into the first man. WG2, the world in which this occurs, is therefore a world in which there is more than just God-likeness. God is present in the first man, and through him, he is in each one of us. So we can't complain on the score of justice of being in this world.

Job's first utterance when his patience gives out is this curse: "Let the day perish on which I was born" (3:3). If the reference is to WG1's Day 6, Job is confused. Nothing of his sort was conceived and/or came into existence in Genesis 1. For the same reason, no innocent suffering (of a problematic kind) is found in WG1. If Job means WG2, he is flying in the face of the basic conditions for his own (type of, viz. particular) existence.

It confirms the confusion underlying the Book of Job that so loose a grip is had on the distinction here, between a world on (but not in) whose scene God can be said to be, and a world in (as well as on) whose scene God can be said to be. No wonder the end is so unconvincing.

G-Logic and P-Logic

I will now perform a drive-in divorce between Quine's views on the logic of proper names and the Bible's ontological position. Quine's logic is suited to WG1. Since WG2 is the world in which you and I, particulars, exist, Quine's logic is stacked against us.

The point, adjusted to the conceptual environment of the biblical world, is that Quine's logic suits the pagan conception of things. Quine's commitment to science and his logic go hand in hand, for science too is pagan in character. Logic, however, should not be allowed to foreclose on ontology through inattention. The adjustment of Quine's logic to the pagan position, and hence the logic's bias against the biblical position, consist in the restriction of representational resources to general terms and the apparatus of quantification. There are, that is, no singular terms, only general terms and bound variables.

I distinguished particulars from other non-general individuals. Individuality is a matter of clear identification and reidentification conditions. Systems can consist of individuals in this sense. The apparatus of general terms and quantification suits non-particular individuals. It's always "something (in space and time) that satisfies conditions C1, C2, C3." This works for trees, for planets, for anything in WG1. The first particular in the biblical creation, the first person, inhabits WG2. He is inspired with God's breath of life – the breath of life of the uncreated particular. Saying this goes beyond saying that the first person has the God-likeness attributed to humankind in WG1. The latter doesn't suffice for particularity. There is God in the first person. The first person is a particular. Lest the distinction be lost, I'll stress that "God" here must function *not as a general term, but as a name*. For that we need a P-logic, with bona fide names. A G-logic, with general terms and quantificational apparatus, isn't enough. A (unique) Quinizer, the Quinizer, might be found in WG1. Not Quine.

The Bible's principle is God. God is the basic particular. The logical formalization of this must not eliminate the name in favour of predicates and bound variables. Executing the elimination leaves, on the non-general side, only non-particular individuals like trees and planets.

Here's a biblically resonant way of making the point. "In WG1, there are no separate places." To be sure, we refer, colloquially, to the specific place in which a specific tree is found. But for us to understand the tree, we must take it to be part of the ecosystem. The whole of the forest speaks through the tree. There is no "here" in WG1 and there is no "there." There is only "everywhere."

In answer to Moses's question about who he, God, is, God says "I am." This also expresses the point: God is a basic "I." The pronoun is not dispensable. Since God is not in the scene in Genesis 1, there is no "I" in WG1.

This is a motif of the Pentateuch. Several major figures use "הנני," meaning "I am here," and the reader appreciates the force that attaches to the occasions of its use. One can say, to a first approximation, that "hineini" means "I am here, before God." But there is a deeper meaning – of ontology: "Being before God, and sharing God's before-ness of nature, I am not part of the system. I am *mutatis mutandis* what God is: a particular." No pagan who sticks religiously to domestic conceptual resources could say "I am here." Those behind the Bible identify that this is a fundamental deficiency in paganism. The appearance of God to Abraham dramatizes the first reflective appreciation of the deficiency.

The imagery used for God in WG1 and WG2 captures the distinction between individuals and particulars. In Genesis 1, verse 2, God is represented (in the Mechon Mamre translation) as "hover[ing] over the face of the waters." God, that is, is not immersed in the world below. In Genesis 2, verse 8, God is described as "plant[ing] a garden." Only a particular can plant a garden. All other things act in accordance with their underlying principles. God's planting (which goes against the natural processes) is an anticipation of the creation of the first man and of that man's transgression. A garden is separate from the natural system, a transgression against it. If the garden is not tilled and kept, nature will reclaim it. A garden, then, has the (particular) gardener in it, as the lump of clay that is made into the first man has God in it. The life of particulars is a life of transgression.

Quine's ontological slogan is: "To be is to be the value of the variable." This only captures WG1. Berkeley, in formulating his view about existence, added "esse est percipere" to "esse est percipi." Just so, a disjunctive slogan is needed to eke out Quine's atomic one. "To be is to be the value of a variable, sc. a (non-particular) individual, or it is to be a particular." Since, in the Bible, particulars are the things that have value, we can rephrase this in a more resonant form: "To be is to the value of a variable or it is to be a valuable."

Finishing the job

1. Why is "the prosecuting angel" (for "Satan") appropriate? Satan is operating in WG1, where there are no particulars. So Satan's functioning is like that of the constituents of WG1. Some instance of "watery precipitation" inundates some instance of "field." The field being Job's, its crops are drowned and he goes begging. Some instance of "smallpox virus" infects some instances of "animal body." It infects the bodies of Job's family members, killing them and leaving him bereft.
2. Why is the goodness of WG1 separate from God-ness? WG1 is missing something that makes bad possible. The claim that it is "all good" is really the claim that WG1 is beneath good and bad.
3. How else can verse 2 of chapter 38 of Job be construed? "Who is this that darkens counsel by words without knowledge?" The problem could be the attribution of bad to WG1. Job doesn't appreciate that God is not present in WG1. The attribution doesn't apply.

Conclusion
Does Western Religion Rest on a Mistake?

In philosophy as constituted in Greece, metaphysics dominates ontology. Free of that Greek influence, the Bible's philosophy recognizes as basic a distinctive principle on the non-general side. Metaphysics, for the Bible, is appropriate only to Genesis 1. Water, water, everywhere. We have general things: water. We have times (the beginning, and then, and then, etc.) and places (under, above, in the middle, etc.). That's it. Abraham, in his inaugural lecture, calls out the name of God to the world, a world that knows only metaphysics. He offers ontology. God, whose name is the irreducibly particular "I AM," is the Bible's principle. Abraham calls out that principle. He calls it out to a world that does not know God – on the intellectual side, the world of the Greek philosophers. This makes clear how to take the Bible's opening image of God. It's not that biblical thought levitates above philosophical bedrock, concerning itself with the contingent and the variable. Rather, the Bible introduces, in theological form, a principle of being unavailable within (Western) philosophy.

The principle, we've seen, is stated at the centre of the Bible. Let's take one last look.

"I am the Lord your God … you shall have no other gods before me." This, the overarching commandment, insists that *you*, a person, must pay heed. A casual reader might reason as follows. "Since there is nothing other than you (or than me, or than her, or than him) to which the commandment could be addressed, an emphatic impersonal formulation – *"God is the only deity!"* – does the same job.

The casual reader could be forgiven for equating the two. Not so commentators and interpreters. Not only is the commandment incumbent *on you*; also, it is *of you*. It's with regard to what you are (and to what he is, and to what she is, and to what I am) that the Lord is the deity. The Lord God is *your* deity. If, *per impossibile*, an *it* – a non-human creature – were amenable to instruction, refusal on its part would draw no sanction. *Its* deities, the principles of *its* kind of existence, are those other gods. The principle of particularity, which is stated in God's self-revelatory 'I AM WHO I AM," bears only on men and women. Men and women are particulars. To do justice to their character, a proprietary principle is needed. God personifies that principle. And this, again, penetrates through to the ontological meaning of monotheism.

There is water, the general; and there is God, the particular. The spirit of God hovers over the surface of the deep.

Abraham is trying to right the philosophical ship; to prevent it from being liquidated, like the Egyptians in the Red Sea. As Abraham sees it, the pagans, despite all that they know, do not know themselves. Their particularity they do not understand. It's no wonder that Abraham the philosopher comes forward in/with God's name as a reformer of human conduct, interpersonal and communal.[1]

I referred on several occasions to Platonic philosophy and to Kantian philosophy, expressing my objective thus: to show that Jewish philosophy, the philosophy propounded in the Bible, is as much philosophy as are these exemplars. The philosophies referred to bear on the objective more than as illustrations. The philosophy of the Bible involves elements characteristic of each of the two. Genesis 1 is like Plato's philosophy, although biblical thinking about the natural world is committed to necessity of the nomological grade; and the development of the moral/ political dimension in the story of the Tower matches the Platonic position (while criticizing it in the name of ontology). The position is that Plato's constructions are unacceptable because they falsify the nature of men and women. Genesis 2 has marked similarities to Kant's view. Only, the Bible does not as sharply differentiate the level of appearances and the level of things-in-themselves. The sharpness of the differentiation has always been felt as a problem in Kant; so much so that Strawson, for instance, simply does away with the duplexing.

Philosophically, all of this is up for grabs. Let us grant that the principle of particularity isn't among the nuts and bolts of the metaphysical *analysans* of non-general individuality. Is Abraham's great notion essentially religious? Does it have defensible theological content? The Bible represents Abraham as receiving this notion from God and as acting (in) God's name. That does not by itself sustain an affirmative answer.

The question that titles this conclusion is therefore being taken in one of the two ways in which it *can* be taken. Assuming that the Bible's principle *is* irreducible, is an attitude of worship towards reality indicated? I should make at least a mildly conciliatory remark about the other way of taking the question.

If the Bible's teachings are false, if its principle is not a basic one, then the ground is undercut for accepting that "God" refers to an otherwise unavailable something. That is obvious. Still, those who are inclined to assert the antecedent should look before they leap the leap of unfaith. Rejecting the biblical way does not come free of charge. One cost may be the deep sense that we have of what we are – a sense that we have apart from Greek philosophy and modern science.

Abraham's departure from his father's house is a philosophical departure. The irony in this regard is that as a belief-system, paganism, from which Abraham is departing, is only marginally religious in character. At core, it's a response to nature in which worship, often in the register of fear, is the practical form that wonder takes. Change wonder to curiosity, and substitute Bunsen burner for sacrificial fire, and you have the essence of science. This is ironic because Judaism takes Abraham's response itself to be religious when, considered dialectically, it's hard to see why it should be that.

In my presentation, paganism is the position of Genesis 1. It does not surprise me that the first account of the creation has clear correlates in Greek cosmogony and in early Greek philosophy. This adds force to the question whether the biblical position is essentially a religious position. From this perspective, the position of the Bible looks like a philosophical critique of an apologetic attitude towards science.

The Bible is the charter of the emerging Israelites. It is a philosophical work. Shouldn't it, as a philosophical work, be for all?

I offered explanations of the Bible's sectarian character. One explanation appealed to the fact that the Bible's truths are ethnically inflected. A second did not have this reconciliatory slant. In discussing the doctrine of Israelite exceptionalism, I argued that in this aspect the Bible *is* sectarian – objectionably so from the standpoint of the philosophy. So unless the national element is a stopgap, adopted because of the resistance of pagans to Abraham's message, there's a dual agenda: Bibleism + Nationalism. I've shown that the origin of the Bible's belief system, in the annals of Abraham, is on the former side. No one would agree that God's call to Abraham is first and foremost national. Once it is appreciated that whatever else he is, Abraham is a philosopher, reconciling the two becomes a tortuous exercise. Think here of the encounter between Elijah and the Baalites on the Carmel. The episode makes the point while duplicating the difficulty. Elijah's challenge is presented to waverers *within* the Israelite community. "Who among the waverers," the story is saying, "wouldn't want in the end to be on the E-team?" Obviously, you cannot present a person as wavering unless he or she has some sense of the alternatives. That, however, is only a situational point. Why should the challenge not be generalized to all by instructing them in the side that, initially, they have no sense of?

The question remains. If the Bible is a work of philosophy, does Western religion rest on a mistake?

The Bible looks religious. The presence of a transcendent God is not mere trimming. But although it seems so both to atheists who repudiate the Bible as well as to true believers who embrace it for dear life, God's role is not to be taken at face value. "[M]y face shall not be seen" (Exodus 33:23).

What is needed in context, situationally, is not necessarily indispensable for theoretical or conceptual reasons. It could be for reasons of public relations that in representing its position as not only new but also improved, the Bible represents the position as anchored in God. At any rate, the idea of worshipping a principle of particularity is an odd idea.

It's an odd idea. But its oddity only emerges under analysis. Accordingly, I have to take a wavering line on a question that readers will press. Is the position that one can interpret the Bible as promoting the ontological notion of particularity, without accepting any of its assertions concerning God as a being, or is it that the thinkers behind the Bible do not literally intend any of the religious statements that the text contains?

My main question, a more basic question, has however been whether there is a Jewish philosophy, and I'll end with a word about that.

Is there a Jewish philosophy? "No" asserts the first professor of philosophy in modern Israel. Recovering the views of the first professor of philosophy in Israel, and of the most articulate holder of the chair, I argue "Yes." Is the Bible, which sets out this philosophy, a religious document? "Yes," Roth answers. From this I dissent. The philosophical position of Abraham and of Moses requires nothing transcendent. What it requires – what the philosophers argue for – is something non-natural. The theological ism called "monotheism" is the vehicle used to get that requirement across.

Western religion rests on a mistake. Granted, Western religion is more than the Bible, a lot more. Judaism ≠ Bibleism. Nevertheless, maintaining that adherents to the associated religious world view(s) can take in stride the jettisoning of the scriptural basis goes beyond wishful thinking. "What about *adding* a transcendent element?" The fact that the Bible itself is consistently (mis)read as teaching transcendence makes this a question that only a person committed to religiosity anyway would ask.

Considerable conceptual space separates paganism from full-fledged Bible-based religiosity; separates, say, Olympian religion from Christianity. This is the space of immanent non-naturalism. Even granting the "Yes" to the concluding question, it doesn't follow that atheists are entitled to what they believe. Unless they are prepared to relinquish a lot that is near and dear to the shared thinking and the shared conduct of all of us, they may still be able to intone the Shema – intone it, even, with the very meaning that the formulators intended.

"If the lamp of philosophy is kindled, the lamp of religion goes out." So said Abraham ibn Daud, quoting the fear of philosophy that gripped many Jewish thinkers.[2] The fear, which Ibn Daud tries to quell, as does Maimonides, is based on a misunderstanding of the Bible. Beneath his tamarisk tree in Beer-Sheba Abraham lit the philosophical lamp. Given the views that Ibn Daud and Maimonides endorse about God and the creation, conscripting Aristotle for the purpose, it's the patriarch's philosophy that they need to fear. That philosophy does dim, if not snuff out, the lamp of religion. To be a follower of the original Abraham is to endorse, with a specific ethnic inflection, the human enterprise. It is not, in the religious way, to be a follower of God.

If he were among us today, Abraham would call out those who call out God's name.

Notes

Introduction

1 "Bible" refers throughout to the Hebrew Scriptures. Unless otherwise indicated, I quote the New Revised Standard Version translation, the NRSV. The bibliography supplies, under "Bible," the full reference for the source from which I quote the NRSV, as well as bibliographical data for all sources/editions/translations referred to or quoted.

2 Roughly and readily, a particular is an entity that is not essentially a part or an aspect of a wider whole made up of entities of the same kind. The deity of the Bible fills the bill. No pagan deity does.

3 Whatever historical reality the depiction has, it rationalizes the belief system's inward turn. But it can hardly be a merit of the Bible-based position that it never developed a Paul.

4 *The Raven, the Dove, and the Owl of Minerva*, ix.

5 www.halakhah.com/pdf/kodoshim/Menachoth.pdf, 113.

6 "Messianic Texts," in Levinas, *Difficult Freedom*, 89.

7 "Bible" (= "The Book") is a splendid title for the written expression of the enterprise. But if a descriptive name is wanted, "Critique of Pure Paganism" would therefore be a good choice.

8 To what degree is Judaism synchronized with Bibleism? The short answer is: incompletely. As for Christianity, it, I would say, is completely unsynchronized with the Bible's philosophy. The sharp contrast gives sense to the case that, during the Church's formative period, Marcion made for excluding the Hebrew Scriptures from the Christian canon.

9 Kant's philosophy is not self-certifying, nor is Plato's. The same goes for Abraham's. If Bibleism's critique of pagan thinking is flawed, there will still be a significant gain. Those who regard Abraham's philosophy as

the way and the life will understand that a non–God-based defence of its teachings is required; or, more radically, that commitment to the truth points to a different Promised Land.

Chapter 1

1 Wilfrid Sellars, "Philosophy and the Scientific Image of Man," 1.
2 The translation is from the New American Standard Bible.
3 xlix. Next quotation: ibid.
4 *To be a Jew*, 18.
5 A pantheon that happens to have exactly one member differs from a pantheon that *must* have exactly one. The Olympian pantheon better not be disqualified for not being of the latter sort, since, as we'll see, the biblical pantheon isn't of that sort either! To understand the various positions here, "one and no more" said of *the membership* of a class, and "one" said of *a member*, have to be set apart.
6 For short: the Shema. (The Shema is the first of the two assertions set off near the start of this section.) "Shema Yisrael" means "Hear O Israel."
7 The essay lends its name to a collection of papers on matters Jewish. *Is there a Jewish Philosophy?* All quotations/references specify pagination in this edition.
8 Guttmann, 3.
9 "Is there a Jewish Philosophy?," 5. Quotation following: ibid., 6.
10 Compare Alexander Altmann, "Jewish Philosophy," the *Encyclopedia Britannica*, 1962, vol. 13, 37: "The term 'Jewish philosophy' denotes the attempts made by Jews, at various periods in their history, to harmonize the tenets of their religious faith with prevailing trends in the philosophy of their environment. Attempts of this kind arose … from apologetical motives." Wikipedia advances a similar claim, although the focus is more like Roth's. "Jewish philosophy, until modern Enlightenment and Emancipation, was pre-occupied with attempts to reconcile coherent new ideas into the tradition of Rabbinic Judaism; thus organizing emergent ideas that are not necessarily Jewish into a uniquely Jewish … framework and world-view. With their acceptance into modern society, Jews with secular educations embraced or developed entirely new philosophies to meet the demands of a world in which they now found themselves."
11 "Is there a Jewish Philosophy?," 2–3. Quotations following: ibid., 5, 8.
12 A work might turn out to be parochial, despite that a philosophical intention lies behind it. According to Roth, the Bible's culture-specificity is in keeping with its motivation.

13 Maimonides, *Guide for the Perplexed*, vol. 1, ch. 71; vol. 3, chs. 27 and 28.

14 While confessing that he had asserted such a view in *De Doctrina Christiana*, Augustine, acknowledging that the dates render the claim impossible of truth, here takes the line that biblical ideas might have filtered down through someone who knew the language.

15 In *Guide for the Perplexed*, vol. 1, ch. 63, Maimonides interprets God's "I am who I am" in Aristotelian terms: "[God is] a Being of absolute existence, that has never been and never will be without existence." If God's mode of existence differs from the mode – contingent – of men and women, how can men and women, despite being enlivened by God's breath of life, be God-like? Many things other than men and women exist contingently. Maimonides's reading makes nothing of the personal pronoun, a particle that, among creatures, only men and women use, and (for reasons given below) not because they alone have language.

16 "Is there a Jewish Philosophy?," 7.

17 "Is there a Jewish Philosophy?," 7.

18 Williams, "Plato: The Invention of Philosophy," 148. Quotation two paragraphs hence: ibid.

19 Despite what seems an ontological focus, Aristotle doesn't break with the pattern. In the convoluted effort in *Metaphysics* Zeta (esp. $1028^{b}30$ff.) to locate the substance of a thing, the thing's essential nature, the thing's what-it-is-to-be, Aristotle tries to do the job in metaphysical terms: the material basis; the formal component; the compound of these. But why, I ask, must what is essential be hidden? Why couldn't the thing itself in some cases be the substance? Aristotle's language shows his bias. Like the Latin "substance," the Greek "hypokeimenon" means "underlying thing." Williams employs the same loaded language. In an early essay of mine, "Prime Matter, Predication, and the Semantics of Feature-Placing," I argue that individualization in the non-general sphere is required in Aristotle's metaphysics not by ontology but by logic.

20 The rabbinical tradition (Genesis Rabbah) tells of young Abraham smashing the idols in his father's idol shop!

21 Zeus is an inchoate expression of Greek philosophy; God, by contrast, is a clear expression of the Bible's philosophy. But the Greek side did have *its* Moses, here being identified as Plato.

22 It does not have to do with the anthropomorphism. "Anthropomorphism" is in any case a misnomer.

23 In cases of the latter kind, the unity is achieved through interlinkage of the principles. The same interlinkage features the first chapter of Genesis.

24 Barnes, *Early Greek Philosophy*, 16. Next quotation: ibid., 56.

25 In saying "invent," Barnes is only apparently at odds with himself. His credit to the Greeks wouldn't have to be revoked because science and philosophy are rooted in something – something else – in Greek culture, especially as Mesopotamian culture and Egyptian culture had that something yet developed neither.

26 In the Introduction to the Anchor Bible Genesis, Speiser makes the same mistake. "[C]aprice ... is the norm of the [pagan] cosmos" (xlix).

27 The corresponding part of the *Enuma Elish*, echoes of which are audible in Genesis, is appreciably the same. Here, from *The Seven Tablets of Creation*, is tablet 1, ll. 1–9.

When in the height heaven was not named,
And the earth beneath did not yet bear a name,
And the primeval Apsu, who begat them,
And chaos, Tiamut, the mother of them both
Their waters were mingled together,
And no field was formed, no marsh was to be seen;
When of the gods none had been called into being,
And none bore a name, and no destinies were ordained;
Then were created the gods in the midst of heaven

28 Kreisel, "Moses Maimonides," 246: "In the eyes of staunch Jewish traditionalists, Aristotelian philosophy is synonymous with heresy. How ... could a person so totally at home in the world of rabbinics engage in the study of such thought, let alone openly embrace it ...? Many Jewish rationalists viewed Jewish legal studies as at best secondary to the philosophic pursuit, upon which depended one's true felicity." What aside from misunderstanding of Scripture could explain an attitude towards the Jewish way of the sort that one has towards a preference for this or that pastime? It's almost inconceivable that the stakes should be that low.

29 The essay is in the collection listed in the bibliography: 29–73. The quotation is from 50.

30 Recall Roth's words: "pervasive factors the removal or alteration of which would change the nature of things." The deepest findings of science, the laws of nature, are invariant with respect to the physical world. The invariance of philosophical truths is closer to the invariance of the truths of logic.

31 The implicit reference is to the first man and the first woman in Genesis 2. On what grounds does the Bible not take the two to belong to one of the three spheres? That's a basic question for us.

32 Aristotle, *Metaphysics* 982^b10–15.

33 Zeus, being the sky god, could no more be alone than heavens could be earthless. A single Olympian deity is possible, though – by agglomeration. Think blobs of mercury.
34 Sommer, 148. Next quotation: ibid., 14.
35 Another example: in *The Origins of Biblical Monotheism*, Smith, simply by counting the deities that the Israelites worshipped (God, El, Asherah, etc.), denies that monotheism is a rupture.
36 1 Corinthians 13:12 (New International Version): "Now I know in part; then I shall know fully, even as I am fully known."
37 It's often said that Christian philosophical thought has a greater affinity for Plato than for Aristotle. My thesis that Greek-based philosophy subsumes ontology under metaphysics, which applies both to Plato and to Aristotle, implies that the differential affinity isn't an ultimate difference. This philosophical chestnut comes to mind. *All aspiring philosophers had to choose: Aristotle or Plato? Aristotle chose Plato.*
38 The contrast between cognitive routes to God is reflected on the plane of practice. It's no accident that in the Christian frame, asceticism is a standing option, not to say an ideal whose non-enactment can stimulate a sense of personal failing. From the Christian perspective, the attitude for a finite being is openness to saturation from above. Just as water, when heated, can take on more solute, the self, through denials and penances, is made receptive to God's salvific force. In the Jewish frame, hair shirts, vows of silence or of chastity, and the like, are discouraged. The defence of the particularity that marks the (capital "g") Godliness of men and women guides and informs practice.

Chapter 2

1 A similar claim appears at 13:4. This is the first instance in which the covenantal name "Abraham" is used. See note 7.
2 Although the NRSV's rendering is close to the first option, as it stands it verges on incoherence. I can call on you, that is, ask you, to coach the team. I can call on you, that is, visit your home, for a chat. What could it mean to call on your name? As we'll soon see, a lot hangs on getting the verse right.
3 Not that it would be inconsistent with biblical teachings for Abraham, in Genesis 12, to have encountered a number of deities. The problem is that his condition would look like the condition of a Mesopotamian pagan.
4 Roth's main reason has to do with morals. This, we'll see, is too flimsy a reason.

5 Abram's insight, to put it less figuratively, has to do with his nature as a person. In speaking God's name, he is speaking of his nature, as he began to understand it back in Mesopotamia.
6 Why "whom we know as 'Adam'"? The first person created is denominated "the man." In Hebrew, "man" is "adam." "The man" appends to the common noun the definite article, which, transliterated, is "h"! After proper names like "Cain" and "Abel" are up and running, "adam" begins to function as one. The first instance is at 4:25. Unaccountably, the Authorized Version renders "the man" as "Adam" in Genesis 2's verse 19. Only the definite description figures in the chapter.
7 Only in chapter 17 does the name "Abram" that the parents chose give way to the God-given "Abraham." The chapters prior to 17 anticipate the change.
8 Even supposing that some historical tradition had a proto-Abraham settling in a desert region, the fashioners of the text could have made figurative use of the locale. See Jeremiah 2:2. Could it be that the inauspiciousness seeds the ground for the message's subsequent propagation exclusively among Abraham's kin? By the time we reach Moses, the dice have come up snake eyes. The biblical strain of Israelite exceptionalism ("the chosen people") is a *fait accompli*. It's Us and Them.
9 Early in the Bible, doesn't God appear unmediated to all of humanity? Since the population consists at the time only of two, this is not a theoretical concession.
10 After exploring the issue of God's role in Genesis 1, we'll understand why Genesis 2's creation story begins so differently.
11 God, in the story, does seem to have a national agenda. This raises the vexed issue of Israelite exceptionalism, that is, chosenness.
12 In one sense, Abraham's truth (assuming that it is one) is literally a freeing: from (extra-human) nature. Mesopotamia is not nature. But Mesopotamian thought might be restricted to the natural. The story of the Exodus, liberation from bondage in Egypt, confirms this.
13 Hesiod: "Chaos was born first." Born from what? Here's a plausible answer. The condition expressive of the first-born's nature is *no stable form. Formlessness*, the absence of form, is the Hesiodic equivalent of (god-less) nothingness. An illustrative model of the birth of chaos would be a homogeneously white TV screen that pixilates, with the pixels in helter-skelter motion. Describing a snowstorm, Thomas Mann (*The Magic Mountain*, 463) reverses the film: "Gusts that would suffocate you drove flurries in wild, driving, sidelong blasts, pulled snow up from the valley floor in great eddies, set it whirling in a mad dance – it was no longer snowfall, it was

a chaos of white darkness." This idea of an existent nothingness supplies what is needed to make sense, without appealing to God, of the idea that the world is created *ex nihilo*, an idea that otherwise would require an (extra-natural) creator. Hesiodic nothingness is not the "nihilo" of the Latin phrase in its usual theological use. It's a kind of pre-physical condition. (Mann's phrase "chaos of white darkness" does not seem right. The mad dance is chaos. The white darkness is formless.) The wherewithal is thus in hand systematically to reformulate the Genesis 1 story in pagan terms. The NRSV rendering of verse 2 with "formless void" is potentially misleading. "Tohu va'vohu" purports instability (and hence indiscernibility) of form, not its absence. The psychological verbs underlying the Hebrew conjunction suggest a drunkard's lurching about. The very phrase "formless void" attests to conceptual confusion. A void is empty; it doesn't lack form. Robert Alter's "welter and waste" (*Genesis: Translation and Commentary*) is in this regard preferable.

14 Two other grounds are often adduced for denying that God's role in Genesis 1 can be disposed of in this way. (1) Doesn't Genesis 1 alone describe creation as being *ex nihilo*? Although the Authorized Version supports the affirmative, Genesis 1:1 is more accurately read as saying that God acts upon a pre-existent chaos. In adding the adverb, the NRSV's rendering of 1:1 cleaves to the Hebrew: "when God created the heavens and the earth, the earth was a formless void." (2) The creation has a pattern or design that implicates intelligence. I tackle this ground in the next chapter.

15 Dropping the initial preposition, the verb of Genesis 2:4 that corresponds to "created" in 1:1 is "הבראם," an anagram of (Hebrew) "Abraham." Is Abraham signing his name to the part of the text that counts?

Chapter 3

1 Genesis 1's sequel is also relevant. But it comes a good deal later, in the Genesis 11 story of the Tower of Babel.

2 Visit www.bible-researcher.com/rashi.html. Rabbi Isaac is seeking a verse that sounds like Genesis 1:1. Why not God's first appearance to the patriarch of the children of Israel? The beginning of Genesis 2 is structurally like that of Genesis 1. So it fills the bill. Obviously, though, Exodus 12:2, for resembling Genesis 1:1 in content too, is better.

3 Genesis 6:19–20, 7:15: Noah loads a pair of each species onto the ark. 7:2–3: Noah loads seven pairs of clean (sc. edible) animals and a single pair of unclean ones. Here is a unitary reading compatible with granting that 6:19–20 and 7:15 come from one earlier source, 7:2–3 from another. "One

pair" responds to the idea that all species survive the flood. "Seven pairs &c." responds also to the idea that the people on board have to eat, and might during the ordeal run out of fruits and vegetables. A difficulty here is that 7:8, though originating according to DH in the same source as 7:2–3, has "two and two." But 7:8 can be read as saying not that two of each species enter the ark but that the animals board in pairs.

4 Day 7 is first mentioned in verse 2 of Genesis 2. I discuss this placing below.

5 The emergence of vegetation in the afternoon of Day 3 only *appears* to deviate from the pattern. The Bible treats plants more like scenery.

6 God calls the dome "Sky" (8). It's a happy coincidence from the standpoint of English that the dome is, functionally, a dam. Some older translations use "firmament"; some have "vault." The Hebrew word is cognate with "ductile." The dome/dam/vault/firmament is like a (convex) sheet beaten from an ingot. "Can you [Job], like God, spread out the skies, hard as a molten mirror?" (Job 37:18)

7 God's creation of the man prior to the creation of the woman isn't equally problematic. The first man is the first person. Persons can be alone. The Hesiodic need for more than one is biological. The Bible's concerns in Genesis 2 aren't biological. The gendering in the text is an artefact both of the language and of the fact that the narrative is moving towards a couple who can bear children.

8 A Jackson Pollock is a non-designed artefact. No significant generality will be lost here if we take it as true that all artefacts are designed.

9 The implicit explanandum is a barren field – a "waste and void" that breeds grasses, then shrubs, then trees. Those behind the narrative know that such a field does not of itself bring forth the greenery. The operative point is only the point of everyday experience that the natural world will on its own develop along these lines.

10 Without some such appeal, God's "good" and "very good" in Genesis 1 are hard to make sense of. But observe that "bad" does not appear until Genesis 2. This implies that "good" in Genesis 1 doesn't mean what we initially take it to mean.

11 Hebrew for "heavens" is "shamayim." "Sham" means "there." "Mayim" means "water." So: "[up] there is where the water is." Since there are clear days and overcast days, we can assume a similar separation above the dome as below; a separation into dry and wet areas; and we can assume that the separation above is understood by the writers to occur naturally. After all, we observe it happening constantly.

12 Had the thinkers known about evaporation and condensation, they would happily have eliminated the dam from the story.

13 An English variant of "Caleb" would be "Doug." (I'm informed that "Caleb" isn't cognate with [Hebrew] "dog," but means "whole-hearted.")
14 Not every Jackson Pollock splatter is a Jackson Pollock spatter. But nothing is lost if we assume that all artefacts are integrated.
15 It may seem odd that they do not use the model of sexual reproduction. Here, we get an organized entity (a newborn), where the creators (the parents) do not proceed by planning and implementing.
16 Hume is speaking of living things. The point extends to the inorganic.
17 One glaring difference: the pagan stories typically describe cosmogenesis in sexual terms. This is in part why, especially in Genesis 2, the emergence of the man and of the woman is portrayed in terms that depart from that. They are, in effect, artefacts.
18 A moment ago I said that a special relationship between the creation and the creator is described in verse 26. In fact, verse 22, which has to do with fish, does the same. This might have alerted interpreters to the mistake I am imputing here.
19 Such connections can always be asserted. But their intelligibility depends on one's capacity (which I assume to be non-existent) to truth-evaluate irrevocable counterfactuals. "For prime numbers to have been like horses, they would have had to consume hay."
20 This often gets formulated as the claim that men and women have souls. The formulation belongs more to the conceptual field of Genesis 2.
21 God's non-physicality is a fairly secure implication of the fact that God creates the physical world. I say "fairly secure" because of the difficult issues as to whether God creates *ex nihilo*.
22 Sacks, "The Lion and the Ass," 43.
23 If Sacks were right, religious folk would be in difficulty. Although it's not my purpose here to make a case for these folk, when we come to Genesis 2 we will see that an actual similarity does hold between men and women and (as the Bible conceives God) God.
24 If A has no proprietary niche, it is likely, *qua* ubiquitous, to affect the proprietary niche of B in unaccountable ways, some negative. But nature, as the Book of Job stresses, can devastate men and women too.
25 The word translated "dominion" figures in verse 28 as it does in verse 26. As to the fact that in verse 28 "dominion" is coupled with a word, rendered "subdue," whose root is the basis of the verb "to conquer": half the usages of the latter that the definitive Even–Shoshan Dictionary lists have mild associations. Think of "subdued tones." The phrases "smooth over" and "smooth out" approximate the operative sense. Hebrew "highway" is a revealing cognate. A paved road moderates otherwise abrupt transitions

and is often *eo ipso* a route through otherwise impassable and between otherwise mutually inaccessible domains.

26 The Genesis 2 story does have God giving men and women something of himself in a sense that cake A does not in this illustration give of itself to cake B.

27 See Weinberg, *The First Three Minutes*, 83–4, on thermal equilibrium. The following quote is from 89–90:

> [I]n a glass of water at room temperature, there are continual reactions in which a water molecule breaks up into a hydrogen ion … and a hydroxyl ion … or in which hydrogen and hydroxyl ions rejoin to form water molecules. Note that in each such reaction the disappearance of a water molecule is accompanied by the appearance of a hydrogen ion, and vice versa, while hydrogen ions and hydroxyl ions appear or disappear together. Thus, the conserved quantities are the total number of water molecules *plus* the number of hydrogen ions, and the number of hydrogen ions *minus* the number of hydroxyl ions.

28 In chapters 5 and 10, I will interpret "very good" more simply. On the simpler interpretation, the point about the gesture towards Genesis 2 in Genesis 1 has to be sustained in some other way.

29 "God created a man in order that the world should contain beginnings." Augustine, *The City of God*, XII:20. It follows, if so, that the creation of the natural world isn't a real beginning. I'll look closely at the Shema in the following chapter. We can see here why it is appropriate that the Shema be declaimed, as traditional Jewish practice enjoins, by a dying person.

Chapter 4

1 Kirk and Raven, *The Presocratic Philosophers*, 35–6.

2 Greek thinking is *stalled* at the level of Genesis 1. That's the implication. Speaking for philosophy, Kirk and Raven prefer Genesis 1 to Genesis 2. Roth, it seems, sees Genesis 1 from the standpoint of Genesis 2. He may see it that way because he is so close to Judaism, to which Genesis 2 is crucial. This would explain, in biographical terms, why he unfairly reproaches the Bible about science. Ironically, Genesis 1 gives us something like the anathematized Spinoza's *natura naturans*.

3 Akhenaten ruled for seventeen years and died circa 1335 BCE. Rabbinic Judaism gives Moses's dates as 1391–1271 BCE. Roughly at the time of Hammurabi, hence at a time appropriate to the story of Abraham, Marduk gets elevated over the other Mesopotamian deities. But Marduk's elevation is like Zeus's, to a position of first among equals.

4 Allen *et al.*, "The Natural Philosophy of Akhenaten," 89. The dearth of evidence of enslavement in Egypt is often remarked. Indirect Egyptian influences on Israelite worship are possible even if the Bible doesn't tell it like it was. Assmann himself endorses such a view.

5 "Elohim" has a singular form. See Psalm 114:7.

6 I draw upon www.biblegateway.com. Sacks's translation is found in the commentary mentioned in chapter 3. Alter's translation is from *Genesis: Translation and Commentary*.

7 It confirms what I say here that half the translations render as "breath of life" different Hebrew formulations in Genesis 1:30 and Genesis 2:7. 1:30 is only referring to living things, in the biological sense. Not until Genesis 2 is the special kind of being that each person has introduced. The data are gathered at the end of this chapter.

8 A footnote in the Jewish Publication Society rendering states that the original of the key word in 2:7 is "adam." In fact it is "ha-adam."

9 The text of 2:7 could easily have been, on the lines of 1:26, "no man was present to till, and the Lord God created man." It in fact is "no man was present to till, and the Lord God created the man."

10 The verb form is the same in English for the first and second person singular and for the three plurals. "Them" captures the difference.

11 The third person singular pronoun appears in 1:27. "It" is in apposition to, effectively, "humankind," which is grammatically singular. Type term + plural, found in English ("Lion are dangerous"), is unavailable in biblical Hebrew. Commenting on verse 27, Robert Sacks writes ("The Lion and the Ass," 46):

> The Hebrew word for God is plural from a morphological point of view even though it is normally accompanied by a verb in the singular. [In verse 26], however, the author chose to use a plural verb. A similar difficulty arises in the case of His image in the present verse. The object of His creation is first described as him and then as them. These two difficulties are ultimately identical. The image of God appears in two different forms – a male and a female – though both are said to be in the image of God. And yet, from the first part of Verse 27, it appears as though God created only one thing. Both difficulties would be solved if there were a certain limited kind of duality in God Himself, at least sufficient duality to allow for the possibility of two separate images. What does this mean?

Here is a clarifying translation of verse 27 that removes Sacks's one thing/two things difficulty. "So God created the human [sc. the type] in his image, in his image he created it [not: him], male and female he created them." The uses of the singular "it" is, again, grammar-based. True, "them" could have been avoided by writing, as Sacks himself nearly suggests, "he created it [the type] to have both male and female forms." Just so, whoever created the natural number [not: the natural numbers] created it [not: them] in both odd and even forms. Since the Hebrew singular in verse 27 refers to a type, it's just as well that the plural "them" is employed also. This works against the thought that the subject-matter consists of particular persons like the first man and the first woman of Genesis 2. Observe also that the verse does not say that God creates males and females. Sacks's "a male and a female" is an error.

12 In Genesis 1, God creates "male and female" (27), not "man and woman." You cannot have heavens without earth. Just so, male and female are made for each other. The language is that of the system. Remarkably, some translations – for example, the Knox Bible – put "man and woman." A reader might think that in saying "male and female [God] created them," the Bible is *distinguishing* human from non-human reality. On the contrary. The point of the phrase is *to prevent* the two stories of emergence in Genesis 1 from being distinguished. Of animals we naturally think in species terms, and shift to individual terms only in special cases, for example, of pets. In inserting "male and female," the Bible is underscoring that the treatment of the human sector in Genesis 1 doesn't differ.

13 Let me distinguish, verbally at this stage, between *particulars* and *individuals*. Collections are made up of particulars. Systems are made up of, at most, individuals.

14 The earlier argument that the unity is fictional had to do with the presence of purpose in Genesis 1, not with Genesis 1 itself. Genesis 1 is to all intents and purposes the pagan creation story.

15 Observe the double parallel between God's enlivening the first man and God's communing with the lawgiver. God "breathe[s] into [the first man's] nostrils the breath of life." With Moses, God converses "mouth to mouth" (Numbers 12:8). Both phrases – "ויפח באפיו" and "פה אל פה" – are alliterative with respect to the same vowel. The anatomical facts match too: two facial orifices that function in respiration. In the one case, God gives his special knowledge to mankind; in the other, his special sort of life.

16 The miracle of Hanukkah reflects the bush. The oil salvaged from the Temple, sufficient for a single day, burned for eight.

17 At the start of Genesis 2, the man and the woman are figured as domestic animals. In return for their tilling and keeping, they are looked after. Provided that there are but a few around, domestic animals constitute a middle term between the type and the particular. We project onto pets the particularity that we have.

18 This is, *mutatis mutandis*, the point that I made about the number of God-like deities.

19 "[A]nd the dust returns to the earth as it was, and the breath returns to God who gave it" (Ecclesiastes 12:7). The NRSV comments: "the *breath* of life is God's breath (not the 'soul'), which sustains all living things." Psalm 104 is cited in amplification/support. Creatures "return to their dust" when God "take[s] away their breath" (29). The word translated as "breath" in the two verses ("רוח") is rendered in many translations as "spirit." It is the word used in Genesis 1:2 ("wind" in the NRSV), not the one that appears in Genesis 2:7. (Shouldn't the NRSV's Ecclesiastes 12:7 have "wind," not "breath"?) Since the NRSV's handling of the verbal difference between the creations of Genesis 1 and of Genesis 2 displays a certain fastidiousness, the elision regarding "man" and "the man" asks for treatment of the sort that I supplied earlier. More to the present point: there is, we see, a biblical distinction between X's returning to dust (= X's death) and X's returning to its dust (X's dissolution). The second alone is reversion to what X was previously. God's spirit, in Genesis 1, is the (anti-entropic) principle of organization. When it is weak, disorder is in the ascendant; when it is absent, chaos rules. Thus the cosmogenesis of Genesis 1. In Genesis 2, God's breath is the underlying principle of particular existence. Thus the (distinctive) anthropogenesis.

20 Throughout, I substitute "bad" for the NRSV's "evil." The Bible has in mind something that it regards as unavoidable in the human world and that at the end of the day it does not want the world to be clear of.

21 The text doesn't say that the tree is of eternal life. Maybe they have to eat of it each day to stay alive. Maybe they have to remain in the Garden to be immortal. Outside the Garden, trees are sometimes bare.

22 Although philosophy, the Greek creation, allows the category of non-necessary truth, it's not surprising that the category is subject to reductive and/or eliminative pressures. If, according to John Locke, we had the cognitive wherewithal, the (apparently contingent) relations between changes and their causes would appear to us like the (necessary) relations between twice two and four.

23 All the French translations use *seul* ("only") for *one*. French thus appears by itself to deconstruct the Shema.

24 "The meaning of the divine name YHWH," 38. Quotation following: 39. I've replaced the quotation marks that, as the article's title shows, Gianotti suppresses from the mention of God's name.

25 See Zimmerli, *Old Testament Theology in Outline*, 20.

26 The tension between Esau ("a man of the field" [Genesis 25:27]) and Jacob ("a quiet man, living in tents" [ibid.]) over the birthright is on one level the tension between the pagan or natural conception of things and the God-based one.

27 In chapter 10, we'll see that the contrast here underlies a latter-day dispute between P.F. Strawson and W.V. Quine over predicates and names.

28 Albright, *From the Stone Age to Christianity*, 259: "Yahweh can only be derived from the verbal stem HWY, but cannot be the ordinary imperfect (qal) of the verb, but must be causative [hiphil]."

29 The Septuagint renders "I am who I am" thus: "ἐγώ εἐμι ἐ ἐν." Back-translated, this becomes "I am the one." It is only under the heavy influence of Greek thought that the latter could yield most of the readings that Gianotti lists.

Chapter 5

1 The commandments are enunciated at Exodus 20:2–17 and at Deuteronomy 5:6–21.

2 Why only the majority? Agreeing that morality requires a transcendent anchorage, an outsider could repudiate moral practices as groundless.

3 Some commandments as usually identified straddle several verses. While preserving the order, one could therefore cut more or less finely.

4 See Exodus 34:29, Deuteronomy 4:13. See also Deuteronomy 10:1, 3.

5 It's a simplification to talk of an exclusive and exhaustive division of the Decalogue. OS stands slightly apart from 1G, NIW, and NV. The last of the first quintet in the usual arrangement is even more an outlier. HFM has an affinity that its predecessors lack for the commandments that follow, since interpersonal conduct is at issue.

6 Both "Yul is bald" and "Yul is not bald" lack truth-values (true or false) unless "Yul exists" is true. Their having truth-values *presupposes* Yul's existence.

7 The uneven spacing of rows 3 and 4 will be explained.

8 It's not just that the creature C has a cognitive grasp of God's doings (C's writing the story of the beginning shows that C has such a grasp). C can so far repudiate God's actions. The additional premise is that C is like God: made in God's image and likeness; inspired with God's breath.

9 "Parents bring children into the world. Where in 1G is God's function as maker mentioned?" The answer, which I'll give in the next section, strengthens the claims of the last arrangement of the columns and the rows.

10 The slight that such making delivers to God's dignity follows from the violation. On the pagan side, Ouranos's coming after Gaia is not felt as *lèse majesté*. Similarly, in the real world encounter of different pagan religions, the blending of the pantheons is an option. Observe how amicably deities

from different pantheons portion out our days of the week. Thursday is Thor's day – the day of the Norse Mars. Saturday honours Roman Saturn. God's inability to accept other gods is like the inability of a square to take on a fifth side.

11 Parity and disparity between 1Ga and HFM are about equal. Like us, our parents are creatures. Though "before" us, their children, our parents are not extra-natural. The disparity explains why HFM is a hinge between the Pentalogues.

12 I am speaking here of Genesis 2, not of Genesis 1.

13 In speaking biologically/causally of human affairs, "parents bring children into existence" is misleading. An entity with a certain genetic constitution forms as the result of a churning of the matter/energy in a region of the world. The twenty-three-chromosomed entities that have interacted sexually are just factors in the process. Parents in the proper (non-biological) sense play the role vis-à-vis offspring that God does in regard to the world.

14 Although, colloquially, Rover and Lassie are readily enough described as Spot's father and mother, in the same discursive environment their description as Spot's parents has the feel of a trope. Just so, "sire" and "dam" are available for our kind (jokes aside) only in the frame of an institution like slavery.

15 The relationship of oak to acorn better typifies the non-human "parental" relationship than the relationship of father and mother to child. Thinking of non-human animals as fathers and mothers is anthropomorphic, just as is thinking of a (bird) nest or a (beaver) lodge as real estate.

16 The existence of the extra-human world has to be accepted, and so too must the implications of its existence. Here, problems for the Bible can arise. These problems (as we shall see) would be problems for morality too, which confirms the second of my theses.

17 Hesiod, *Theogony*, ll. 132–3.

18 Not that there was any informed doubt that in the human sphere parent transfers God-likeness to child. I distinguished Genesis 1's "image and likeness" from Genesis 2's "breath of life." Those behind the final document, I also said, relate Genesis 1 and Genesis 2 more closely than the underlying conceptual content justifies. The "breath of life" idiom doesn't in any case lend itself easily to describing human procreation. The Bible uses "know" here. No male non-human "knows" a female non-human.

19 Although theistic deities, not being physical, cannot have sensations, the full gamut of emotions can be part of their make-up.

20 1Gb, "have no other gods before me," means "have no pagan-type gods before me."

21 All four combinations are possible: monopaganism; polypaganism; monotheism; polytheism. Here's another illustration of the disarray in scholarly forums. "[T]he underlying faith of Israel that there exists one, indivisible, God ... [is] a radical departure from polytheism and idolatry" (Donin, *To Be a Jew*, 18). If God alone among deities is one and indivisible, how is that, and how is it significant? It's no answer to say that it's significant *because* only God is one and indivisible.

22 If the extra-natural realm in which God "dwells" is not spatio-temporal, the idea of multiplicity gets no easy foothold. It would also be true that if a multiplicity of God-like gods existed, none would be "before" any other. In speaking of other deities, the Bible always uses the plural.

23 Corporate emblems or logos often are non-resembling images.

24 Maimonides, *Guide for the Perplexed*, vol. 3, ch. 32. The episode of the Golden Calf showed that the Israelites needed something of the kind. Since the perpetrators were punished, a lesson was learned. Be the historical reality of the Exodus story as it may, the underlying idea seems valid. God evinces his dim view of sacrifice in requiring (Exodus 20:24) altars "only ... of earth." Compare Isaiah 1:11: "What to me is the multitude of your sacrifices?"

25 Men and women are made in God's image and likeness; they alone are inspired by God's breath. The interest on the part of, say, Jacob, to determine God's nature – "Please tell me your name" (Genesis 32:29) – is an interest in self-knowledge.

26 In Elijah's theophany (1 Kings 19), God is said not to be in the wind, not in fire, not in the quaking earth.

27 Compare the way that Samuel brings the rain – 1 Samuel 12:18 – and Elijah's way – 1 Kings 18:42–5. The Bible is telegraphing that rain is a natural phenomenon. The wise prophet won't predict rain in the desert.

28 God, outside the web of physical causation, is never too far away to hear us. So the idea that men and women in different places should talk to God at the same time does not skate over an obvious difficulty.

29 The traditional dates for Abraham are 1812–1637 BCE. The Code of Hammurabi is dated 1772 BCE. Providentially, if providence speaks English, "Hammurabi" is a near anagram of "Abraham," the patriarch's God-given name.

30 Since Plato's view of what counts as good conduct (notably in the theory of justice in the *Republic*) is at odds with what we regard as morality, philosophical critics who use the *Euthyphro* against the Bible have some explaining to do.

31 Ellis, "Humanism and Morality," 138.

32 Greek progenitors don't seem to be distressed in the way that we are by this kind of thing. Jocasta and Laius send infant Oedipus to be exposed. The non-biblical thing that is going on here appears in Numbers 20. God instructs Moses to command the rock by way of extracting water. Moses disobeys; he strikes the rock with his staff. One strike? That might have been forgiven. But two strikes and he's out. God gives the reason for denying him entry to the Promised Land: "you did not trust in me, to show my holiness" (12). Behaving towards nature as does Agamemnon, Moses smudges the biblical distinction between people and things. Modern moral philosophy is becoming more and more Greek. The commitment to science further and further attenuates the idea of agency.

33 I responded to "God … rested on the seventh day from all the work that he had done" (2:2) in the next-to-last paragraph of chapter 2.

34 Alter, *Genesis: Translation and Commentary*, 7.

35 Quotations following: "Jewish Thought as a Factor in Civilization," 56. Next quotation: ibid.

36 Although Roth is committed to saying that a person who accepts that there is only one deity qualifies as a monotheist, he wants at the same time to avoid equating Plato's theological position with the Bible's. So we have *a monotheism* in the Bible, and *a monotheism* (a different one) in Plato.

37 Our emotions in the case of Ishmael go against God. How is the child to blame? We can feel that in representing Hagar as mocking the childless Sarah, the Bible is trying to redirect our natural feelings. As to Cain and Abel: in a sense, God does accept Cain's "killing" of Abel. The case is not however of the same kind as that of David and of Ahab. Cain and Abel are types, FARMER and SHEPHERD. Farming requires fencing off land against grazing animals. "Cain" is cognate with "(real) property." Shepherds move freely over the terrain, like breath exhaled into the air – which indeed is the physical meaning of the Hebrew word "abel." (The word "abel" is familiar to English readers as the word "vanity" that begins the Book of Ecclesiastes. Its sense is of insubstantiality and evanescence.) Cain's "killing" of Abel is the supplanting of shepherding, mobile cultivation, by (stay-at-home) farming. In a world with a growing population, the shift was bound to occur. But although shepherding has vanished, the men and the women who made their living as herders haven't. Cain is criticized because of "am I my brother's keeper?' (4:9)

38 The question isn't rhetorical. At this anthropological stage, too many unknowns exist about the agricultural way. But should Cain's way prove viable, God will accept him. Observe the parallel between God and Cain. Cain puts an end to the livelihood of Abel; God does the same to the

livelihood of the Eden dwellers. (If Cain is presented as the first internal dealer of death, God qualifies as the first *external* one.) Just as Cain denies responsibility for Abel, God, in expelling them from the Garden, does the same to the man and the woman. The wandering of Cain, to find an acceptable way to live, is an emblem of God's wandering after the Eden-phase.

39 "And the Lord went his way, when he had finished speaking to Abraham; and Abraham returned to his place" (18:33). Emphasis on "his" can be sensed. Although bound by a covenant, God and Abraham are not quite on the same page. It would be another matter if the Bible criticized Abraham for marching out of step with God. If Abraham's dealings with God dramatize an inner struggle, the conclusion is the same.

40 Roth, "Jewish Thought as a Factor in Civilization," 50.

41 Ibid., 38. Next quotation: ibid.

42 Ibid., 54.

43 Roshwald, "Leon Roth," 345. Roth was the first professor of philosophy in modern Israel. In 1928 he accepted the Ahad Ha'am Chair in Philosophy at the recently founded Hebrew University of Jerusalem.

44 Guttmann, *Philosophies of Judaism*, 11.

45 The slogan over Auschwitz's gates is Platonic, not biblical. The philosopher-rulers of Plato's *kallipolis* also advise "Do your job," advice that might equally have read: "Abandon hope." Hope is foreign to a world that is rationally engineered. Dostoyevsky, with unintended irony given his history of gambling, puts it well (*Notes from Underground*, 34): "what's the point of wishing by numbers?"

46 Levi, *Survival in Auschwitz*, 40. The quotations following are from 40–1.

47 Ibid., 86.

48 "Action" is without meaning for a person who believes that whatever he or she does is as likely to lead downwards as upwards. Someone who starts up the car will, under normal circumstances, intelligibly say "I am buying a newspaper" even if an accident *en route* upsets the purchase. A person who, flipping a coin, says "I am flipping a head" is talking nonsense.

49 Levi is at pains to point out that during *his* period in Auschwitz, killings for no discernible reason ceased to be the norm. This makes it (more) possible intelligibly to compare conditions inside and outside. Levi says that he was in this regard fortunate to have arrived at the camp in 1944. It was alchemical too, so to speak, that he had a profession that the Nazis sought.

50 Levi, *Survival in Auschwitz*, 90.

51 Ibid., 88.

52 Ibid., 90.

53 Ibid., 95–6. Next quotation: 97.

54 Compare the protagonist's suicide in Sophocles's *Antigone*. Antigone is conveying through this action that her life is her own. The suicide is an affirmation of the life. Steinlauf's washing in Auschwitz is like Antigone's hanging herself in the bricked-up vault.

55 Levi, *Survival in Auschwitz*, 87.

56 See the discussion of "hineini" in chapter 10. Since Zeus is nothing without Poseidon, he also cannot say "I am here."

57 Levinas, *Of God Who Comes to Mind*, 91. Quotation following: 90.

58 The American/Israeli educator Walter I. Ackerman, who was among the first GIs to reach Belsen, described to me his experience. After the initial shock, he was frantic to help. He was (in this Levinas-sounding phrase) beside himself. Compare Levinas (*Difficult Freedom: Essays on Judaism*, xiv): "The Other's hunger – be it of the flesh or of bread – is sacred; only the hunger of [yet another] limits its rights."

59 One hates for a reason. So one can be reasoned into and out of it. As to love, here, for extraterrestrials, is Thomas Mann's description (*The Magic Mountain*, 225–6): "[an] experience [that] can paralyze and suspend a man's ability to form opinions, even rob him of the right to form them, or better, induce him to waive that right."

60 All quotations are from 5 and 6 of (the ironically titled) "Ethics and Spirit," in Levinas, *Difficult Freedom*.

Chapter 6

1 Babylonian Talmud, Tractate Shabbat, Folio 31a. See www.come-and-hear.com/shabbath/shabbath_31.html. The ruler, we see, goes way back as a pedagogical tool for making students measure up!

2 Quotations following: 100, 114, 58–9, 59.

3 White, "The Historical Roots of our Ecologic Crisis."

4 The first sentence quoted is from 4; the second, from 3.

5 The text here is Soloveitchik, *The Lonely Man of Faith*. The quotation below is from 35.

6 See also the final sentences of the section headed "SIGN 3" in the discussion of the sabbath.

7 It is for this reason, again, that the editors of the NRSV are mistaken to assert that men and women are pre-eminent in Genesis 1. Their coming later than all else – at least than all else mammalian – is a truth for Darwin too.

8 The claim is part of the Genesis 2 story's sequel. Observe, though, that verse 1 of chapter 9 echoes verse 28 of Genesis 1. This intermixing of the

two strains is as it should be, since the world is starting up again after the flood.

9 "The Unnatural Jew," 361.

10 All change in Genesis 1 is recycling. Schwarzschild's gibe at the environmentalists that "nature is a fickle mother … she kills many of her own children" (356) is conceptually obtuse.

11 Stravinsky's "The Rite of Spring" is subtitled "Pictures of Pagan Russia in Two Parts."

12 A position can't be anthropocentric if in principle there is nothing other than the *anthropos* that could centre it. Since the world contains non-*anthropoi*, the centre cannot be people as we ordinarily think of them. For Kant, it's the transcendental subject, spinning the unity of the whole out of the unity of apperception.

13 We will discuss these matters more fully in chapter 8.

14 Schwarzschild, "The Unnatural Jew," 351.

15 Schwarzschild, "The Unnatural Jew," 355, rejects the criticism that the Bible's man is alienated from nature. The quotation from Job (as well as the discussion of Genesis 1) indicates that the biblical scholar and the scholars of Frankfurt are at sea. Theodor Adorno is reported (357–8) to have recommended that men and women "try to live such that you can believe that you were a good animal." How would we go about giving up niche-freedom? What would we be if, *per impossibile*, we forswore particularity?

16 God's exploitation of nature in the Bible is part of the Genesis 2 account that places men and women in a *cultivated* place. Failure to appreciate this affects Jeanne Kay's "Concepts of Nature in the Hebrew Bible." According to Kay (309), "the Hebrew Bible's principal environmental theme is of nature's assistance in divine retribution." This is not an environmental theme.

17 "Individual" functions here in P.F. Strawson's sense: individuals are items with clear identification and reidentification conditions. The category includes properties such as redness and things such as trees. Particulars (each man and each woman, perhaps nothing else) are non-general individuals that elude Strawson's terms of metaphysical analysis: general properties and spatio-temporal position. The Bible's God is the epitome of a particular. That explains why the man of Genesis 2 is said to come into being when inspired with God's breath of life. Strawson's metaphysics is a philosophical version of paganism.

Chapter 7

1 "Bab-ilu" in Akkadian, the early Semitic language of Assyria and Mesopotamia. Hebrew "Babel" is thus close to the original.

2 The reference is to the Babel of the biblical narrative. Relations to the real-world Babylon must emerge from interpretation, not guide it. Thus my choice of "Babelite."
3 Shinar = Sumer. Consumers of the text, the first as eyewitnesses even, will have known that Babylon is near sea level. See note 11 below.
4 "Small numbers" means "numbers comprising only individuals connected by bonds of a family sort, along with the core group's servants, camp-followers, etc."
5 Water, in the Bible, is the primary agent of dissolution. In Genesis 2, a process of irrigation unfreezes a world in which life is locked down. But the flood is too much water. Germs for life's revival have to be kept dry in the ark.
6 Proponents of DH ignore the genuine possibility that the redactors left a lot out. Isn't it reasonable to assume that what was omitted was omitted *because* it could not be fitted into the jigsaw?
7 A sign is that Hebrew "flood" is in spelling and sound similar to the verb "to confuse" that can be seen in "Babel."
8 Items on the same level divided by vertical lines are linked explanatorily, whether via efficient causality or via final causality. That is: according to an interpreter, the Bible's narrative links them in one of these ways.
9 Genesis 2:10–14 locates the Garden relative to four rivers. The two real ones signal that the story isn't just a good read. The imaginary ones warn against mounting an expedition.
10 Speiser, 75.
11 When the Bible is put together, a story in which God undermines a Babylonian tower has uplift for the weepers by Babylon's waters. The Bible in its more historical-looking parts can be read for clues about the past. But the *biblical* significance of the historical materials lies in the contribution that they make in the new settings.
12 Speiser, xlviii.
13 Ibid., xlix. Quotation immediately following: ibid.
14 A clear parallel exists between the story as Speiser reads it and the content of Genesis 1. Order is in both cases introduced into a chaotic state.
15 A system comprising a multiplicity of deities must have the characteristic of discord. Functionally, a group of gods in full agreement on all matters would be indistinguishable from a single, unschizophrenic god.
16 Clarity is the issue, not potency. "Monotheism, on the other hand, is predicated on the concept of a God who has no rivals. A principled obstacle to delivering a univocal message therefore falls away." That's what Speiser should have written.
17 Speiser always treats "city and tower" as a unit. That, I believe, is why he cannot acknowledge the "patent" problem.

18 The contrast between God's calling to Abraham and the city builders' conceiving the plan on their own is a datum, no more. Once we figure out why *Abraham's* project gets the nod, it will remain for us to judge the differential approval.

19 It is of course the Bible writers' idea to make the builders' activity as like God's activity in Genesis 1 as possible.

20 In fact, one singular form is present. Hers's my translation of verse 3. "And each person said to his fellow." The NRSV renders the words as follows. "And they said to one another." The verse continues: "Come, let us make bricks." So the NRSV's deviation from the letter of the text isn't in the least misleading.

21 Observe the deep conceptual linkage between this claim and the exclusive use of "good" in Genesis 1. The man is not part of the system.

22 "Could God have accorded particularity to a non-human animal?" It's a foolish question. The Presocratic philosopher Xenophanes's mockery of human religious belief – he claims that cows, if they had religion, would represent their deities as horned – does not extend to the Bible's views.

23 What the NRSV translates as "the same" is, in Hebrew, the plural of "one." The King James rendering of "the same words" as "one speech" is thematically superior.

24 The standard DH view is that Genesis 1 is a P-text, Genesis 11 a J-text. If so, what I say here attests DH's neutrality on the Bible's interpretability.

25 Imagine Plato's *Republic* being injected into the Greek philosophical environment immediately after Thales, Anaximander, and the other Presocratics, had advanced their views about the world!

26 Cain could not have built Enochville single-handed. The point is that he built it along with other "he's" and "she's," each of whom agreed to lend a hand.

27 The sense of the Hebrew is that they will show no restraint. Not that they will run wild. Rather, the usual judgments of good and bad won't apply. Good for a collective differs from good for the elements. Indeed, with respect to collectives, judgments about what is good for the elements can't even be made.

28 *Zoar* means "narrow" or "small."

29 It isn't quite quit of him. King David, as close to God as anyone, is in the line of Moab, the issue of Lot's incestuous coupling with the older of his two daughters in the cave. See 8n17.

30 I mentioned the chain of events from Cain's fratricide to his founding of a city. The city is the locale for judicial institutions, where competing claims (like those of Abel and Cain) are adjudicated. It's an exact parallel that in

Sophocles's *Oedipus at Colonus*, Thebes is departed for Athens, where the first court of law, the Areopagus, is founded.

31 Gordis, "The Tower of Babel and the Birth of Nationhood," opening paragraph.

32 Abomination? Homosexuality is naturally thought of as disruptive of family. This suggests a non-homophobic reading of this part of the Bible; to which reading might be added as support that Abraham is an adoptive father to Lot!

33 It's hard to know what to make of this; but it's left unclear whether Lot has sons-in-law. See verse 14.

34 After Sodom is razed, God reluctantly permits Lot, whose *modus vivendi* is urban, to settle in Zoar, "a little [city]" (19:20). Keenly appreciating that he did not "do well" in Sodom (I quote God's words from Cain's story), Lot, starting afresh, will presumably make a better go of it. As we've seen, Lot doesn't have the stuff to persevere.

35 The prevarication can't be said to be a half-truth, rather than a lie, on the grounds that Sarah is Abraham's half-sister. If it were a half-truth, Isaac would have represented Rebekah as a cousin.

36 Lot, whose wife is absent when the angels come calling, might be seen as a procurer. The episodes are pre-plays of the descent of the children of Israel into Egypt. Jacob is made to confront a similar challenge. The story of Shechem the Hivite confirms that the text wants us to think of Abraham as pimping. Having murderously prevented Shechem from taking (Jacob's daughter) Dinah as a wife, Simeon and Levi ask (Genesis 34:31): "Should our sister be treated like a whore?" D[i]NA[h] is not to be shared.

37 In observing that the cooperation of the tower builders is rare in human affairs, I remarked that the line of narrative beginning with the man and the woman sees cooperation fraying from the outset. A further reason is present here for suspecting a fox in the henhouse. To Sarah, Abraham is a devoted husband, and to Lot (the closest to a brother), he is a dutiful keeper.

38 The story of the Israelites and the Moabites, in Numbers 25, is a grislier replay of the grisly story of the Hivites, with Aaron's grandson Phinehas in the role of Simeon and Levi. Some interpreters (usually, interpreters on the religious flank) cite Moses's wedding a Cushite as a reason additional to the one mentioned at Numbers 20:12 for God's excluding him from the Promised Land.

39 Talmud, Tractate Avoth 5:19: "Whenever love depends upon something and it passes, then the love passes away too. But if love does not depend upon some ulterior interest then the love will never pass away." Although

Shakespeare is right that "Love is not love / Which alters, when it alteration finds," the heart, contrary to Avoth's "never pass away," goes where it goes.

Chapter 8

1 "Im Anfang war die Tat." Another English rendering: "In the beginning was the deed."
2 The echo is louder in the original: "Die welt is die Gesamtheit der Tatsachen." Tractatus 1:1 draws out what according to Wittgenstein is implicit in Tractatus 1: "The world is everything that is the case."
3 " … nicht der Dinge."
4 Wittgenstein, an expert sculler in that flow, knew Goethe's "In the beginning." See Rowe, "Goethe and Wittgenstein." In John's Gospel, God is said never to rest. If the omega in the *Tractatus*, a call to silence and a fade to black, is an echo of God's rest on the seventh day, Wittgenstein is in for a surprise.
5 While the noun "deed" is linked to the verb "to do," even sophisticated users of English are unlikely to see "deed" and "fact" as synonymous. English contains the noun-facient suffix "facient."
6 Tractatus 1.2: "Die Welt zerfällt in Tatsachen." That is: "The world divides into facts."
7 In quoting from the *Critique of Pure Reason*, I supply the standard *Akademie* edition A/B page numbering.
8 Arguably, the empiricism/rationalism typology derives from Kant, whose architectonic mode of thinking enforces Teutonic precision. Also, Kant is writing the history according to the slogan *pre-Kant ergo propter Kant*.
9 An internal reason exists why the Bible does not keep the two separate. Nonetheless, the permeability of the line leads interpreters astray.
10 Early and late, Kant lectured on anthropological matters. See Schmidt, "Kant's Transcendental, Empirical, Pragmatic, and Moral Anthropology."
11 I use "im-mediate" (and related forms) and "given-ness" to keep alive the technical Kantian senses. For the same reason, "intuitional" is used in preference to "intuitive," which has a connotation external to Kant's intent.
12 The idea of an active intellect features Descartes's thinking throughout. In the early *Rules for the Direction of the Mind*, Rule Twelve, Descartes writes: "in so far as our external senses are all parts of the body, sense-perception, strictly speaking, is merely passive" (vol. 1, 40). In the mature *Principles of Philosophy*: "all sense-perception involves being acted upon" (1.23, vol. 1,

201). From this he infers (ibid.): "it cannot in any way be supposed that God perceives by means of the senses."

13 When you give yourself a gift, you are in part passive, as when you scratch your nose. *Qua* actively intellectual, God is in no wise tickled.

14 In this connection, the claims that the pioneering analytic interpreters of Kant make are revealing. Bennett: "A non-sensible intuition would presumably be a capacity for acting informatively, whatever that may mean" (*Kant's Analytic*, 55–6). Elsewhere (*Kant's Dialectic*, 19), Bennett calls the idea "a full-scale catastrophe." Strawson characterizes active intuition thus: "a mode of awareness in which the faculty of awareness was not affected by the object because it created its own object" (*The Bounds of Sense*, 254). "Kant," he proceeds, "frequently remarks that we are unable to comprehend [the] possibility [of intellectual intuition]"; to which he adds: "an important reservation." The interpreters agree that the idea of an active intellect in the frame of transcendental idealism is important to Kant; both find the notion gibberish; and both are unsympathetic to transcendental idealism. The anthropological reading throws out the active intellect without *ipso facto* disposing of transcendental idealism.

15 The question on the side of X is "What is it to be a bat?," not "What is it like to be a bat?" One cannot properly address the phenomenological question without also addressing the being-theoretic one. Being a bat, for all we know, may be the same as being a stone.

16 The first three questions are posed in the *Critique of Pure Reason*. See A804–805/B832–833. The claim that the three reduce to the fourth is in the Jäsche Logic. All quotations here are from Kant, *Logic*, 29.

17 Incest isn't a non-human taboo. That Lot's line is continued through an act of incest (and while he is drunk) provides a positive basis for the narrative's placing him in a cave. It's a way of extenuating without condoning.

18 The point here goes against the thinking of those who subscribe to the usual reading. In chapter 3, I criticized this reading.

19 In its present form, the claim resembles a factual generalization. It will be reconstituted below as conceptual.

20 The same constellation is instanced in the core philosophical canon. Although Descartes characterizes men and women as "something intermediate between God and nothingness" (*Meditations*, pt 4 [vol. 2, 38]), he argues for the distinction – we have minds, other creatures don't – without essential appeal to God's nature.

21 Shakespeare, *The Tempest*, 2.2.59. One can imagine a scripture – an ecological one – saying that to minimize the difference we should comport

ourselves thus-and-so. Such a scripture too would begin with the sense of difference. It's not that animals will not comply with our requests for a change. It's that they do not have to change.

22 Readers not co-opted by philosophy will note that *God's* control is not total.

23 The primeval part comprising the creation stories is usually regarded as the most straightforwardly committed to the extra-human.

24 The reaction "good" in each phase of creation would otherwise be the chuff of a big cat.

25 Why isn't God a suitable companion? God, in the Bible, is a personified principle, not a full-fledged thing. It is true, though, that a companion will have to exemplify the principle.

26 The idea of a "partner" (2:18) is a fuller idea. A partner's character is shared, not just comprehended. In the woman, the man finally finds such a one. The man's reaction has philosophical content. "[T]his one," he says of her (23), "shall be called Woman." This *one*; this *particular* being. She, he says of her (ibid.), is "bone of my bone and flesh of my flesh." The evident delight enfolds an ontologist's remark. "I am a particular; she too is one." God could have repeated the words, *mutatis mutandis*, when he breathed into the creation: "I am one. He, the man, shares *my* one-ness."

27 The NRSV, like the Authorized Version, translates as "cattle" a word meaning "large land mammal." "Cattle" is conceptually misleading, especially regarding Genesis 1:24, since in common parlance the word connotes domestication.

28 The collision would not naturally be described as catastrophic for the comet, any more than the eradication of smallpox would for the virus. The asymmetry indicates that the description is not of the happening "in itself."

29 This is perfectly Darwinian: the reduction of the weak and the increase of the strong benefit the whole.

30 The arithmetic does not apply in the case of species. The survival of 70 per cent of the bison as a result of the cull is success. A 30 per cent infant mortality rate is dismal failure, whatever benefit accrues to the 70 per cent who survive.

31 "Isn't a brake pad a particular?" A brake pad is a functional entity. As such, it isn't a full particular. We do not care which replacement pad we buy.

32 Or helping them. Due to the tidal wave, the beaches might return to a pristine state, increasing economic prosperity.

33 This is the message of the Book of Job. "Where were you," God thunders at Job (38:4), "when I laid the foundations of the world?" In effect: "The world of Genesis 1 contains no particular men or particular women. So particular persons like Job, if harm comes to them from interaction with

that world, have no grievance. The design of that world involves no flaw for being compatible with such harm to the men and the women whose coming into being is described in Genesis 2. In the world of Genesis 1, humanity is never harmed."

34 A striking element of Kant's position is the doctrine that space and time aren't features of the world as it is in itself. Consider here the representation of things "[i]n the day that the Lord God made the earth and the heavens" (Genesis 2:4) as changeless: "no plant of the field was yet in the earth and no herb of the field had yet sprung up – for the Lord God had not caused it to rain upon the earth, and there was no one to till the ground" (5). The story is man-centred. Thus the reversal of "the heavens and the earth" of Genesis 1:1. Thus the stress on the lack of a tiller to work the ground. The whole is represented as frozen, timeless, until the tiller, who processes the ground with *his* needs in view, arrives. The water mentioned here, the agent that gets things going, is not natural water. It's related to the water that Abraham finds in Genesis 21. (Prior, the biblical principle had been unavailable.) Change in the world of Genesis 1 is of a different variety than change in the world of Genesis 2. Time, as we know it, belongs to Genesis 2.

35 Kant's use of the plural, "things-in-themselves," needs to be justified. For a more text-based line of argumentation that the census of facts in the *Tractatus* is monistic, see Glouberman, "*Tractatus*: Monism or Pluralism?"

36 *The Crossing*, 46.

37 *The Crossing*, 45: "What you have in the trap is teeth and fur, nothing more. The wolf itself is unknowable. Both the wolf and what the wolf knows. To ask to know the wolf is like asking to know what the stones know."

38 Genesis 2 cannot deal with the issue as does Job. In the world of Genesis 2, nature is relativized to men and women.

39 Numbers 21:4–9. Hebrew "copper" puns on "snake." The story suggests vaccination: an antivenin made of venom.

Chapter 9

1 Quine's position is set out in *Word and Object*. Strawson's position is exposed in a number of papers; see "Singular Terms and Predication."

2 Strawson's position has an undeveloped *phenomenological* character. A main point in "On Referring" is that language-users, using linguistic expressions, do the referring.

3 See the penultimate paragraph of the section in chapter 5 headed "Holy Ground."

4 The idea has normative content. Anything lacking identity and identification conditions is suspect.
5 Compare Aristotle: men and women are just distinctive sorts of animals – rational ones.
6 At the centre of the class of P-predicates are predicates that express properties or states or characteristics having to do with consciousness.
7 On Leibniz's metaphysical position, space and time are basic and distinctive determinations of non-basic things. Space and time Leibniz calls *phenomena bene fundata*.
8 The reader will now understand why love doesn't apply to fungibles.
9 Observe that taking "husband" or "wife" as functional terms is felt to be a mistake. When Eve introduces Adam as her husband, this effectively means: "the particular man with whom I compose a married couple." "Parent" is a *biblical* P-noun, as is "partner."
10 Strawson's preparedness directly to locate some general thing – "Red[ness] is here" – confirms that deep in his thinking is the idea that space and time are only principles of non-generality.
11 We saw this in dealing with Roth. "[L]ogical arguments have little effect on the emotions. The Jewish contribution is not a theory of morals but its practice, and practice depends on feeling." Almost uniquely among feelings, love has philosophical significance.
12 *god is Not Great*, 99.
13 Kant, *Critique of Practical Reason*, 99. Extended quotation below: ibid. So Kant would reject the label "compatibilism."
14 "[T]his one," the first man says of the first woman (ibid.), "shall be called Woman." Emphasis is needed on both parts of "this one"? It's *this* one, as opposed to the animals that God tried earlier. And it's this *one* because this, as opposed to an animal, is a one.
15 See "Austin's Putt," in Dennett, *Freedom Evolves*, 75–7.
16 The compatibilist position tries to make sense of "John could have done otherwise" or "It was possible for John to do otherwise" consistently with accepting that the laws governing physical things are deterministic.

Chapter 10

1 The NRSV's "Satan" is not in Hebrew a proper name. A more accurate rendering is "the satanic one." The root of the phrase's adjectival part is a verb whose English infinitive is "to prosecute." What appears as "Satan" is therefore, roughly, "the prosecuting angel."

2 No more than the Crown Prosecutor in the British system does the prosecuting angel in his standard role do evil. In having God deliver Job into Satan's power, the Book of Job is taking a liberty with the standard role.

3 The writers put the answer into God's mouth. If one reads the answer in this way, one would have to doubt their capacity to say more.

4 These lines refer back to Genesis 1:6–8. Most of the Book of Job's imagery comes from or is cognate with that of Genesis 1.

5 Without denying that God is speaking sarcastically, I will in the sequel give these words a reading that is theoretically significant.

6 It could be that the case for God wobbles because those who propound the case see, or think they see, a difficulty in it. In the next section, my preference is supported.

7 Ecclesiastes (from which this last is a quotation) observes the distinction between WG1 and WG2. People come and go; the system abides. *Pace* Ecclesiastes, in whom the content of this observation causes Sartre-type nausea, the whole can be regarded, *qua* system, as being of lesser value because there is no beginning and no ending. "Remember your creator in the days of your youth, before the days of trouble come, and the years draw near when you will say 'I have no pleasure in them'" (12:1). True, if you were part of the system, you wouldn't grow old. Neither would you be you, however. Moreover, you have value. It's appropriate, then, that, according to tradition, a dying person is supposed to declaim the Shema.

8 Elihu propounds an (epistemological) argument that sounds like God's in chapter 38. "[N]o one can look on the light, when it is bright in the skies" (37:21). Marvin H. Pope, in the Introduction to the Anchor Bible installment on Job, xxii, repeats himself in glossing Elihu's remarks in chapter 37 and God's answer in chapters 38 to 41. So either God's answer is the same, and the criticism reapplies, or else something is being missed.

9 Recall: the pronouns in Genesis 1 are, with the one explicable exception, all plural; in Genesis 2, all singular.

10 Why isn't Satan's active role in Job that of an evil-doer? When he inflicts the harms, Satan isn't in the presence of the Lord. *How could he be? God is not present in this world.* Satan is cancer attacking an individual, or a tree in the woods crushing a walker. To be sure, if poor eating habits make us more susceptible to cancer, or if silviculture undermines the stability of trees, Satan is not entirely to blame.

11 This does not establish that men and women have value. We do however feel that being possessed of life imparts value. Our disgust at the careless or wanton destruction of non-human life backs up the intuition. So the

differential self-valuing of men and women is not arbitrary, since they differ from all other living things in not being parts of the whole.

12 The reverse is true too. There may be no bad in WG1. But men and women of WG2 can pollute, despoil, etc. This, however, is not Job's issue.

Conclusion

1 Plato, by contrast, is drawing the implications for the pagan thinking of his culture that less consequent thinkers failed to draw.

2 The quotation is from *Ha-Emunah ha-Ramah* [= *The Exalted Faith*]. Ibn Daud (c. 1110–1180) made the first attempt to integrate Aristotelian philosophy into Jewish thought.

Bibliography

Allen, James P. "The Natural Philosophy of Akhenaten." In *Religion and Philosophy in Ancient Egypt*, ed. James P. Allen et al. Yale Egyptological Studies 3, William Kelly Simpson, ed. New Haven: Yale University Press, 1989: 89–101.

Albright, W.F. *From the Stone Age to Christianity*. Garden City: Doubleday, 1957.

Alter, Robert. *Genesis: Translation and Commentary*. New York: W.W. Norton, 1996.

Aristotle. *Metaphysics*, trans. W.D. Ross. Oxford: Clarendon Press, 1924.

Augustine. *City of God*, trans. Henry Bettenson. Harmondsworth: Penguin, 1984.

Barnes, Jonathan. *Early Greek Philosophy*. Harmondsworth: Penguin, 1987.

Bennett, Jonathan. *Kant's Analytic*. Cambridge: Cambridge University Press, 1966.

– *Kant's Dialectic*. Cambridge: Cambridge University Press, 1974.

Bible. *New Oxford Annotated Bible*, ed. Bruce M. Metzger and Roland E. Murphy. New York: Oxford University Press, 1991.

Dennett, Daniel. *Freedom Evolves*. London: Penguin, 2004.

Descartes, René. *The Philosophical Writings of Descartes*, trans. Robert Stoothoff and Dugald Murdoch. 3 vols. Volume 1: Cambridge: Cambridge University Press, 1985. Volume 2: Cambridge: Cambridge University Press, 1984.

Donin, Rabbi Hayim Halevy. *To be a Jew*. New York: Basic Books, 1972.

Dostoyevsky, Fyodor. *The Possessed*, trans. Constance Garnett. New York: Barnes and Noble Classics, 2004.

– *Notes from Underground*, trans. Jesse Coulson. Harmondsworth: Penguin, 1972.

Ellis, Brian. "Humanism and Morality." *Sophia* 50 (2011): 135–9.

Frayn. Michael. "A previously unpublished fragment from Wittgenstein's *Philosophical Investigations*." *The Observer Weekend*, 26 January 1964. http://www.stevepetersen.net/wittgenstein-fog.html.

Gianotti, Charles R. "The meaning of the divine name YHWH," *Biblioteca Sacra* 142 (1985): 38–51.

Glouberman, Mark. "Prime Matter, Predication, and the Semantics of Feature-Placing." In *Language in Focus*, ed. A. Kasher. 75–104. Dordrecht-Holland: D. Reidel, 1976.

– *The Raven, the Dove, and the Owl of Minerva: The Creation of Humankind in Athens and Jerusalem*. Toronto: University of Toronto Press, 2012.

– "*Tractatus*: Monism or Pluralism?" *Mind* 89 (1980): 17–36.

Gordis, Daniel. "The Tower of Babel and the Birth of Nationhood." http://azure.org.il/include/print.php?id=536.

Guttmann, Julius. *Philosophies of Judaism: The History of Jewish Philosophy from Biblical times to Franz Rosenzweig*. London: Routledge and Kegan Paul, 1964.

Hazony, Yoram. *The Philosophy of Hebrew Scripture*. Cambridge: Cambridge University Press, 2012.

Hesiod. *Theogony, Works and Days, Shield*, trans. Apostolos N. Athanassakis. 2nd ed. Baltimore: Johns Hopkins University Press, 2004.

Hitchens, Christopher. *god Is Not Great*. New York: Emblem Editions, 2007.

Homer. *Iliad*, trans. Robert Fagles. Harmondsworth: Penguin, 1990.

"Jewish Philosophy." [Alexander Altmann]. *Encyclopædia Britannica*, 1962.

Kant, Immanuel. *Critique of Practical Reason*, trans. Lewis White Beck. Indianapolis: Bobbs-Merrill, 1956.

– *Critique of Pure Reason*, trans. Norman Kemp Smith. London: Macmillan, 1933.

– *Logic*, trans. Robert Hartman and Wolfgang Schwarz. Indianapolis: Bobbs-Merrill, 1974.

– *Prolegomena*, trans. James W. Ellington. Indianapolis: Hackett, 1977.

Kay, Jeanne. "Concepts of Nature in the Hebrew Bible." *Environmental Ethics* 4 (1988): 309–27.

King, Leonard William. "Enuma Elish." In *The Seven Tablets of Creation*. London: Luzac, 1902.

Kirk, G.S., and J.E. Raven. *The Presocratic Philosophers*. Cambridge: Cambridge University Press, 1957.

Kreisel, Howard. "Moses Maimonides." In *History of Jewish Philosophy*, ed. Daniel H. Frank and Oliver Leaman. London and New York: Routledge, 1997.

Levi, Primo. *Survival in Auschwitz*, trans. Stuart Woolf. Toronto: Maxwell Macmillan International, 1993.

Levinas, Emmanuel. *Difficult Freedom: Essays on Judaism*, trans. Seán Hand. Baltimore: Johns Hopkins University Press, 1990.
– *Of God Who Comes to Mind*, trans. Bettina Bergo. Stanford: Stanford University Press, 1998.
Maimonides. *Guide for the Perplexed*, trans. M. Friedländer. London: Routledge and Kegan Paul, 1904.
Mann, Thomas. *The Magic Mountain*, trans. John E. Woods. New York: Vintage, 1996.
McCarthy, Cormac. *The Crossing*. New York: Vintage, 1995.
Pascal, Blaise. *Pensées*. New York: E.P. Dutton, 1958.
Plato. *Republic*, trans. F.M. Cornford. New York: Oxford University Press, 1960.
Pope, Marvin H. Anchor Bible [Job]. Garden City: Doubleday, 1965.
Quine, W.V. *Word and Object*. Cambridge, MA: MIT Press, 1960.
Roshwald, Mordecai. "Leon Roth: A Philosopher–Teacher," *Modern Age* 48 (2006): 337–46.
Roth, Leon. *Is There a Jewish Philosophy? Rethinking Fundamentals*. London: Littman, 1999.
Rowe, M.W. "Goethe and Wittgenstein." *Philosophy* 66 (1991): 283–303.
Sacks, Robert M. "The Lion and the Ass: A Commentary on the Book of Genesis." Installment I, chs. 1–10. *Interpretation* 8 (1980): 29–101.
Schmidt, Claudia M. "Kant's Transcendental, Empirical, Pragmatic, and Moral Anthropology." *Kant-Studien* 98 (2007): 158–82.
Schwarzschild, Steven S. "The Unnatural Jew." *Environmental Ethics* 6 (1984): 347–62.
Sellars, Wilfrid. "Philosophy and the Scientific Image of Man." In *Science, Perception and Reality*. 1–40. London: Routledge, 1963.
Smith. Mark S. *The Origins of Biblical Monotheism: Israel's Polytheistic Background and the Ugaritic Texts*. Oxford: Oxford University Press, 2001.
Soloveitchik, J.B. *The Lonely Man of Faith*. New York: Doubleday, 2006.
Sommer, Benjamin. *The Bodies of God and the World of Ancient Israel*. Cambridge: Cambridge University Press, 2009.
Speiser, E.A. Anchor Bible [Genesis]. Garden City: Doubleday, 1964.
Strawson, P.F. "Freedom and Resentment." In *Freedom and Resentment and Other Essays*. London: Methuen, 1974. First appeared in Proceedings of the British Academy, 48: 1–25.
– *Individuals*. London: Methuen, 1959.
– "Particular and General." In *Logico-Linguistic Papers*. London: Methuen, 1971. First appeared in *Proceedings of the Aristotelian Society* 59 (1953–4): 233–60.
– "Singular Terms and Predication." In *Logico-Linguistic Papers*. London: Methuen, 1971. First appeared in *The Journal of Philosophy* 58 (1961): 393–412.

– The *Bounds of Sense*. London: Methuen, 1966.

Taylor, Charles. "Mind–Body Identity: A Side Issue?" *The Philosophical Review* 76 (1967): 201–13.

Weinberg, Steven. *The First Three Minutes*. Updated ed. New York: Basic Books, 1988.

White, Lynn, Jr. "The Historical Roots of Our Ecologic Crisis." *Science* 155 (1967): 1203–7.

Williams, Bernard. "Plato: The Invention of Philosophy." In *The Sense of the Past*. Princeton: Princeton University Press, 2006: 148–86.

Wittgenstein, Ludwig. *Tractatus Logico-Philosophicus*, trans. C.K. Ogden. London: Routledge, 1922.

Zimmerli, Walther. *Old Testament Theology in Outline*. Edinburgh: T. & T. Clark, 1978.

Index

Material in endnotes is indexed by chapter and note number. "5n29" refers to chapter 5, note 29.

Abbreviations
PP: principle of particularity
Ten Commandments. See pp. 77–8.
G1: Genesis chapter 1
G2: Genesis chapter 2

www.ingramcontent.com/pod-product-compliance
Lightning Source LLC
LaVergne TN
LVHW090156080826
844660LV00013B/828/J

* 9 7 8 1 4 8 7 5 0 3 4 0 6 *